AQA Mathematics

Book 1

Foundation (Linear)

GCSE

Series Editor

Paul Metcalf

Series Advisor

Andy Darbourne

Lead Authors

Sandra Burns

Shaun Procter-Green

Margaret Thornton

Authors

Tony Fisher

June Haighton

Anne Haworth

Gill Hewlett

Steve Lomax

Jan Lucas

Andrew Manning

Ginette McManus

Howard Prior

David Pritchard

Dave Ridgway

Kathryn Scott

Paul Winters

Nelson Thornes

This edition published in 2013 by:
Nelson Thornes Ltd
Delta Place
27 Bath Road
CHELTENHAM
GL53 7TH
United Kingdom

13 14 15 16 / 10 9 8 7 6 5 4 3 2

A catalogue record for this book is available from the British Library

ISBN 978 1 4085 2146 5

Cover photograph: Steve Debenport/Getty Images

Illustrations by Rupert Besley, Roger Penwill, Angela Knowles and Tech-Set Limited

Page make-up by Tech-Set Limited, Gateshead

Printed in China by 1010 Printing International Ltd

Photo acknowledgements
Alamy: p162
Fotolia: p7, p26, p62, p77, p149, p152, p179, p204, p215, p225, p235, p260
Getty Images: p48, p101, p104
iStockphoto: p23, p46, p87, p109, p125, p141, p166, p185, p187, p191, p275
NASA: p186

Contents

Introduction

Nelson Thornes has developed these resources to ensure that the book and the accompanying online resources offer you the best support for your GCSE course.

All resources have been reviewed by subject experts so you can feel assured that they closely match the specification for this subject.

The print and online resources together unlock blended learning; this means that the links between the activities in the book and the activities online blend together to maximise your understanding of a topic and help you achieve your potential.

These online resources are available on 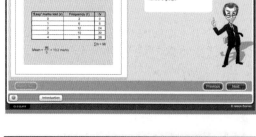 which can be accessed via the internet at **www.kerboodle.com/live**, anytime, anywhere.

If your school or college subscribes to kerboodle you will be provided with your own personal login details. Once logged in, access your course and locate the required activity.

For more information and help on how to use kerboodle visit **www.kerboodle.com**.

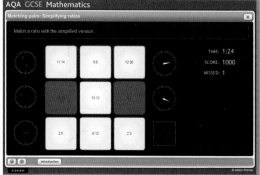

How to use this book

To help you unlock blended learning, we have referenced the activities in this book that have additional online coverage in Kerboodle by using this icon:

The icons in this book show you the online resources available from the start of the new specification and will always be relevant.

In addition, to keep the blend up-to-date and engaging, we review customer feedback and may add new content onto Kerboodle after publication!

Welcome to GCSE Mathematics

This book has been written by teachers who not only want you to get the best grade you can in your GCSE exam, but also to enjoy maths. Together with Book 2 it covers all the material you will need to know for AQA GCSE Mathematics Foundation (Linear). Look out for calculator or non-calculator symbols (shown below) which tell you whether to use a calculator or not.

In the exam, you will be tested on the Assessment Objectives (AOs) below. Ask your teacher if you need help to understand what these mean.

AO1 recall and use your knowledge of the prescribed content

AO2 select and apply mathematical methods in a range of contexts

AO3 interpret and analyse problems and generate strategies to solve them.

Each chapter is made up of the following features:

Objectives

The objectives at the start of the chapter give you an idea of what you need to do to get each grade. Remember that the examiners expect you to do well at the lower grade questions on the exam paper in order to get the higher grades. So, even if you are aiming for a Grade C you will still need to do well on the Grade G questions on the exam paper.

On the first page of every chapter, there are also words that you will need to know or understand, called Key Terms. The box called 'You should already know' describes the maths that you will have learned before studying this chapter. There is also an interesting fact at the beginning of each chapter which tells you about maths in real life.

 Learn...

The Learn sections give you the key information and examples to show how to do each topic. There are several Learn sections in each chapter.

Practise...

Questions that allow you to practise what you have just learned.

E The bars that run alongside questions in the exercises show you what grade the question is aimed at. This will give you an idea of what grade you're working at. Don't forget, even if you are aiming at a Grade C, you will still need to do well on the Grades G–D questions.

These questions are Functional Maths type questions, which show how maths can be used in real life.

These questions are problem solving questions, which will require you to think carefully about how best to answer.

These questions are harder questions.

These questions should be attempted **with** a calculator.

These questions should be attempted **without** using a calculator.

Assess

End of chapter questions test your skills. Some chapters feature additional questions taken from real past papers to further your understanding.

Hint

These are tips for you to remember whilst learning the maths or answering questions.

Study tip

Hints to help you with your study and exam preparation.

1 Angles

Objectives

Examiners would normally expect students who get these grades to be able to:

G

recognise acute, obtuse and right angles

understand the terms 'perpendicular' and 'parallel'

identify scalene, isosceles, equilateral and right-angled triangles

F

recognise reflex angles

estimate angles and measure them accurately

use properties of angles at a point and on a straight line

E

use angle properties of triangles including the sum to 180°

show that the exterior angle of a triangle is equal to the sum of the interior opposite angles

D

recognise corresponding, alternate and interior angles in parallel lines

understand and use three-figure bearings.

Did you know?

Angles in snooker

If you want to play snooker well, it is important to understand how the balls rebound from the cushions around the edge of the table. World class snooker players improve their game by spending many hours practising how to make the balls rebound at the correct angles. Use of angles is particularly good for making sure you are not 'snookered'!

Key terms

acute angle
right angle
obtuse angle
straight angle
reflex angle
vertically opposite angles
perpendicular
parallel
transversal
alternate angles

corresponding angles
interior
bearing
triangle
equilateral triangle
isosceles triangle
scalene triangle
right-angled triangle
exterior angle

You should already know:

✔ how to recognise and use simple fractions

✔ how to use a protractor

✔ compass directions: north, south, east, west

✔ the meaning of clockwise and anticlockwise.

Learn... 1.1 Angles

An angle is an amount of turn. It is usually measured in degrees.

One full turn, or complete circle, measures 360°.

One half turn measures 180°.

An angle between 0° and 90° is an **acute angle**.

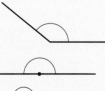

An angle of exactly 90° is a **right angle**.

It is always marked with a small square.

An angle of between 90° and 180° is an **obtuse angle**.

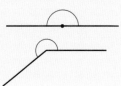

An angle of exactly 180° is called a **straight angle**.

An angle between 180° and 360° is a **reflex angle**.

Example: State whether each of the following angles is acute, obtuse or reflex.

     a 256°   **b** 79°   **c** 112°   **d** 91°

Solution: **a** 256° is between 180° and 360° so it is a reflex angle.

     b 79° is between 0° and 90° so it is an acute angle.

     c 112° is between 90° and 180° so it is an obtuse angle.

     d 91° is between 90° and 180° so it is an obtuse angle.

Practise... 1.1 Angles

G F E D C

G

1 How many degrees are there in:

     a a quarter turn

     b one-third of a turn

     c one-sixth of a turn?

2 What fraction of a full turn is:

     a 30°   **b** 45°   **c** 270°   **d** 180°?

3 The diagram shows the four main compass directions: north, south, east and west.

     a Clare faces north and makes a half turn. Which way is she facing now?

     b Jane faces east and makes a quarter turn clockwise. Which way is she facing now?

     c Leroy faces west and makes a quarter turn anticlockwise. Which way is he facing now?

     d Gemma has made a half turn and is now facing west. Where was she facing before she turned?

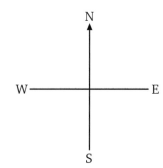

4 State whether each of the following angles is acute, obtuse or reflex.
Give a reason for each answer.

a	125°	**e**	157°	**i**	148°	**m**	300°
b	62°	**f**	46°	**j**	206°	**n**	25°
c	89°	**g**	195°	**k**	100°	**o**	98°
d	312°	**h**	10°	**l**	200°		

5 For each marked angle:

i write down whether it is an acute angle, an obtuse angle or a reflex angle

ii **estimate** the size of the angle

iii use a protractor to **measure** the size of the angle.

Check that your answers agree with your answers to part **ii**.

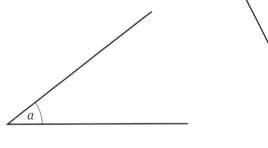

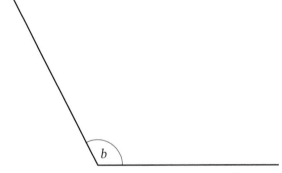

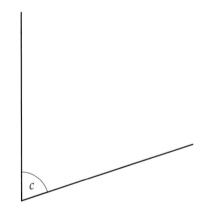

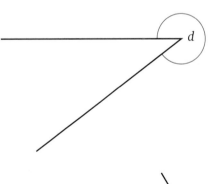

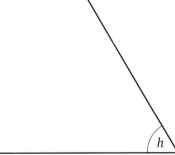

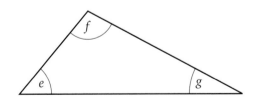

> **Hint**
>
> You can draw in 90° lines on a copy of
> the angle or divide 90° in two to help
> you estimate the size of the angle.

Learn... 1.2 Angles and lines

Angles meeting at a point form a complete turn or circle.
So angles at a point add up to 360°.

Angles at a point

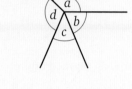

Angles on a straight line form a half turn.
So angles on a straight line add up to 180°.

Angles on a straight line

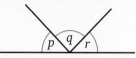

$$p + q + r = 180°$$

$$a + b + c + d = 360°$$

Where two lines cross, the **vertically opposite angles** are equal.

Two lines crossing or meeting at right angles are called **perpendicular** lines.

Example: Work out the size of the marked angles.

a

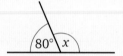

Not drawn accurately

b

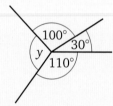

c

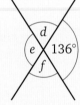

Solution:

a   Angles on a straight line add up to 180°.
$$80° + x = 180°$$
So $$x = 180° - 80° = 100°$$

b   Angles at a point add up to 360°.
So $$y = 360° - (110° + 30° + 100°)$$
$$= 360° - 240°$$
$$y = 120°$$

c $$d = 180° - 136° = 44°$$ (angles on a straight line)
$$e = 136°$$ (vertically opposite angles)
$$f = 44°$$ (vertically opposite to d)

Practise... 1.2 Angles and lines

G F E D C

F

1   Calculate the size of the angles marked with letters.

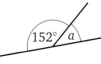

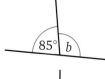

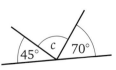

Not drawn accurately

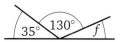

2   Calculate the size of the angles marked with letters.

Not drawn accurately

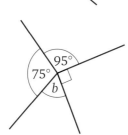

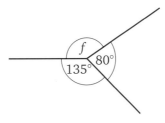

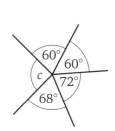

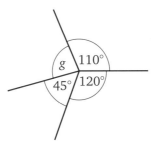

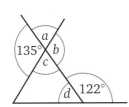

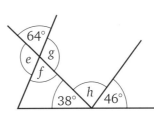

3   Calculate the size of the angles marked with letters *a*–*h*.

Not drawn accurately

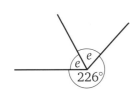

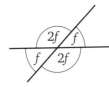

4   Work out the size of each of the angles marked with letters.

Not drawn accurately

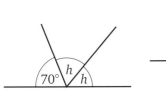

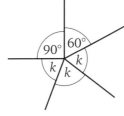

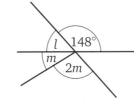

5   Two angles on a straight line are in the ratio 3 : 2

Work out the two angles.

6   Three angles meet at a point. The smallest is 10° smaller than the middle-sized angle.
The largest is 10° larger than the middle-sized angle.

Work out the three angles.

Learn...   1.3 Angles and parallel lines

Two lines which stay the same perpendicular distance apart are called **parallel** lines.

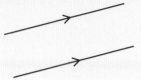

The arrows show that the lines are parallel.

A line through the two parallel lines is called a **transversal**.

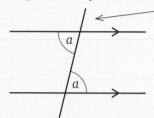

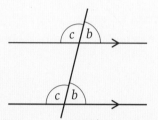

Several pairs of equal angles are formed between the parallel lines and the transversal.

The angles marked *a* are **alternate angles.**
They are equal.

The angles are on opposite sides of the transversal.

The angles marked *b* are **corresponding angles.**
They are equal.

The angles are in similar positions on the same side of the transversal.

The angles marked *c* are another pair of corresponding angles.

Angles *d* and *e* are **interior** or **allied angles.**

They always add up to 180°.

So $d + e = 180°$.

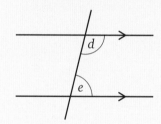

Example: Work out the value of the marked angles. Give reasons for your answers.

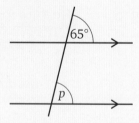

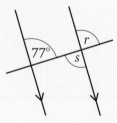

Solution: $p = 65°$ (corresponding angles)

$q = 38°$ (alternate angles)

$r = 77°$ (corresponding angles)

$s = 77°$ (alternate angles or vertically opposite angles)

Notice that it is often possible to find angles by more than one method (as for angle *s*).

Study tip

Always give the correct term, such as corresponding angles, when you are asked to give the reasons for your answers.

Practise...   1.3 Angles and parallel lines

D

In this exercise the diagrams are not drawn accurately.

1   Work out the values of angles x, y and z.

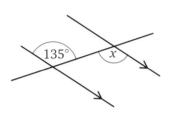 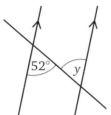 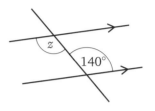

2   Work out the values of the angles marked with letters.
Give reasons for your answers.

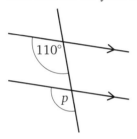 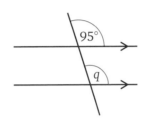 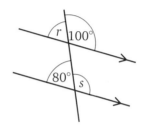

3   Work out the values of angles x, y and z.
Give reasons for your answers.

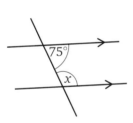 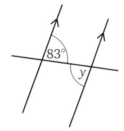 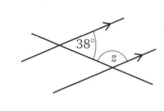

4   Work out the values of the angles marked with letters.
Give reasons for your answers.

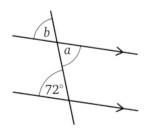 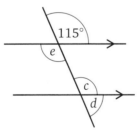 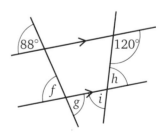

5   **a**   Are lines AB and CD parallel?
Give a reason for your answer.

  b   Are lines EF and GH parallel?
Give a reason for your answer.

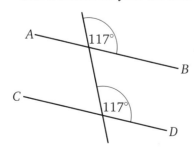 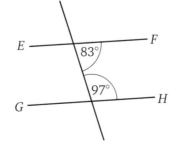

> **Hint**
>
> Remember you can use facts about angles at a point or on a line as well as angle properties of parallel lines.

D

! 6   Calculate the size of the angles marked with letters.

a

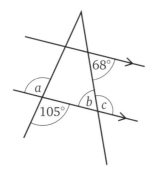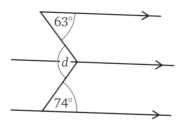

c

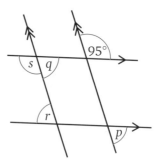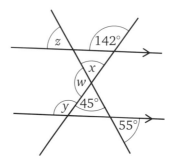

b

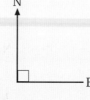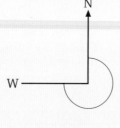

d

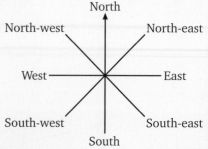

Learn...   1.4 Bearings

Directions can be described using the points of the compass such as south, north, west and so on.

Directions can also be described using three-figure **bearings.**

A three-figure bearing gives the angle measured in a clockwise direction from the **north** line.

Angles of less than 100° need a zero placed in front to make them three figures.
For example, a bearing of 80° is written as 080°.

So **south** has a bearing of 180°, **east** has a bearing of 090° and **west** has a bearing of 270°.

Other directions can all be described using bearings.

Example: Write down the bearings of the following compass directions.

    a   north-east   **b**   south-west

Solution: **a**   North-east is halfway between north and east
               so the bearing is halfway between 0° and 090°.
               So north-east is on a bearing of 045°.

     b   South-west is halfway between south and west.
               Halfway between 180° and 270° is 225°,
               so south-west is on a bearing of 225°.

Example: What are the three-figure bearings of directions A, B and C from the point O?

a 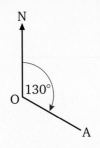   **b**    **c**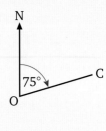

Solution: **a**   Bearing of 130°   **b**   Bearing of 325°   **c**   Bearing of 075°

Bearings from one place to another can be found by measurement or by calculation.

Example: What are the three-figure bearings of directions A from B, P from Q, and D from E?

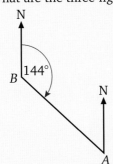   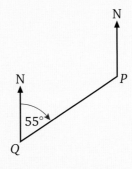   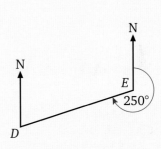

Solution: The bearing of *A* **from** *B*   The bearing of *P* **from** *Q*   The bearing of *D* **from** *E*
              is 144°   is 055°   is 250°

Example: Branton is on a bearing of 105° from Averby.

              Work out the bearing of Averby from Branton.

Solution: Draw a sketch.

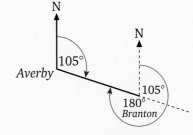

              If you walk from Averby to Branton you are walking
              on a bearing of 105°.

              To return to Averby from Branton you have to turn
              round to face the opposite direction (half a turn
              or 180°).

              So in total you are now on a bearing of 105° + 180°
              from north.

              So facing towards Averby **from** Branton, the angle measured clockwise from north is
              105° + 180° = 285°.

              So the bearing from Averby **from** Branton is 285°.

> **Hint**
>
> Remember to put the north line at the place you are working
> the bearing out '**from**'.
>
> E.g. in this example the bearing is 'from Branton' so the
> north line is drawn at Branton then the angle is measured
> clockwise from north around to the line joining Branton to
> Averby (as shown by the arrow on the angle arc).

Practise... 1.4 Bearings

D

1 For each diagram, write down the three-figure bearing of *D* from *E*.

a N
E 115°
D

c N
D ——————— E

e N
132° E
D

b N
D
29°
E

d N
D
74°
E

f N
D
9°
E

2 Use a protractor to draw accurate diagrams to represent these bearings.

a 140° **c** 210° **e** 085° **g** 163°

b 045° **d** 320° **f** 108° **h** 258°

3 Thatham is on a bearing of 078° from Benton.

Work out the bearing of Benton from Thatham.

Use a sketch to help you.

4 Newby is on a bearing of 250° from Reddington.

Work out the bearing of Reddington from Newby.

5 Here is a map of an island.

P is a port, T is a town and B is a beach. H_1 and H_2 are hotels.

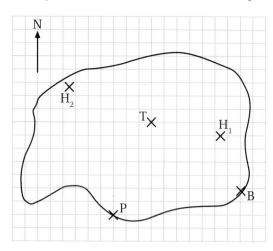

a Which hotel is on a bearing of 055° from the port?

b Measure and write down the bearing of the beach from the port.

c Measure and write down the bearing of the port from the town.

 **Learn...**   **1.5 Angles and triangles**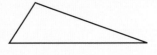

There are three main types of **triangle**:

| **Equilateral triangle** | **Isosceles triangle** | **Scalene triangle** |

- Three equal sides
- Three equal angles
- Each angle $= \dfrac{180°}{3} = 60°$

- Two equal sides
- Two equal angles
- The equal angles are opposite the equal sides and are called the base angles even when the triangle is on its side.

- No equal sides
- No equal angles

The same number of dashes on the sides show equal sides and the same number of arcs on angles show equal angles.

Any triangle with a right angle is called a **right-angled triangle**. A right-angled triangle can be scalene or isosceles.

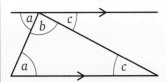

right-angled scalene triangle   right-angled isosceles triangle

The sum of the three angles in any triangle is always 180°. You can prove this as follows.

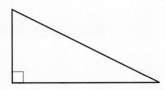

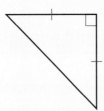

The alternate angles are equal. Therefore $a + b + c = 180°$

If a side of the triangle is extended an **exterior angle** is formed.

The exterior angle of a triangle is always equal to the sum of the two interior opposite angles.

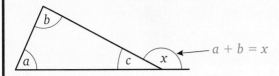

$a + b = x$

This can be shown to be true using angle properties you have learnt previously.

If the third angle inside the triangle is c,

then $a + b + c = 180°$ (angle sum of a triangle)

and $c + x = 180°$ (angles on a straight line)

So $a + b = x$

Example:

In a triangle *ABC*, angle *BAC* = 50° and angle *BCA* = 70°

Draw a sketch of the triangle.

Work out the size of angle *ABC*.

Solution: Angle *BAC* is the angle between sides *BA* and *AC*, that is the angle inside the triangle at *A*.

Angle *BCA* is the angle between sides *BC* and *CA*, that is the angle inside the triangle at *C*.

Angle *ABC* is the angle inside the triangle at *B*.

Angle *ABC* = 180° − (50° + 70°) = 60°

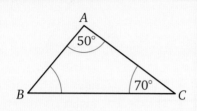

Example: Work out the size of angle *y*.

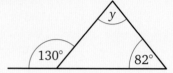

Solution: *y* + 82° = 130°

So *y* = 130° − 82° = 48°

Practise... 1.5 Angles and triangles k

  G F E D C

1 From the triangles below write down the letters of all triangles that are:

a equilateral

c scalene

b isosceles

d right-angled.

   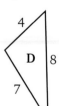

Not drawn accurately

> **Study tip**
>
> If an exam question contains diagrams that are not drawn accurately then you must not try to measure angles with a protractor.

2 Work out the size of the angles marked by letters.

a

c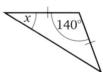

e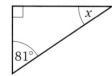

Not drawn accurately

b

d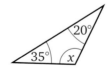

f

3 An isosceles triangle has a base angle of 56°.

Work out the size of the two other angles in the triangle.

E

4 Work out the angles marked by letters.

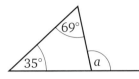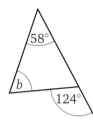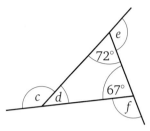

Not drawn accurately

5 Work out the angles marked with letters. Give a reason for each answer.

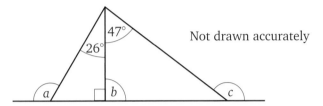

Not drawn accurately

6 Calculate the angles marked with letters. Give a reason for each answer.

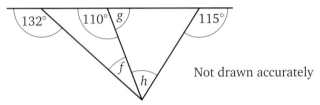

Not drawn accurately

7 The diagram shows a side view of a roof truss.

Work out the angles the beams form with the floor (angles *x* and *y*).

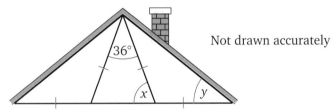

Not drawn accurately

8 Ben is working on a ladder as shown.

The angle between the ladder and the wall is 35°.

For Ben to use the ladder safely, the angle between the ladder and the ground must be between 70° and 80°.

Is Ben using the ladder safely?

Show working to justify your answer.

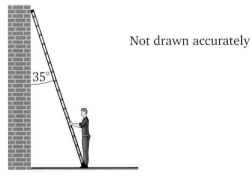

Not drawn accurately

1 Assess k

G

1 What fraction of a full turn is:

a   90°   b   135°   c   60°?

2 Here is a list of angles.

122°   17°   39°   242°   97°   305°   196°   82°

From this list, write down:

a   two acute angles   b   two obtuse angles   c   two reflex angles.

F

3 Work out the size of each of the marked angles.

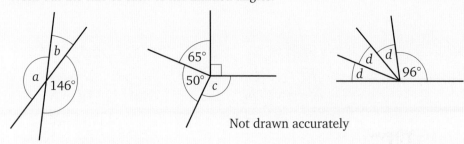

Not drawn accurately

4 Is *ABC* a straight line?

Show how you would decide

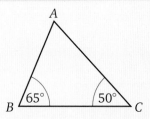

F
E

5 Work out the angle marked by each letter and state what type of angle it is.

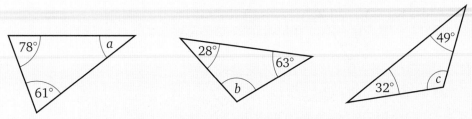

Not drawn accurately

E

6 Three angles form a straight line. The angles are *x*, 2*x* and 60°.

Work out the value of *x*.

7 Show that *ABC* is an isosceles triangle.

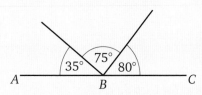

D

8 Triangle *ABC* has a right angle at *A* and angle *B* is 12° more than angle *C*.

Work out the sizes of angles *B* and *C*.

9 Work out the size of each of the marked angles.

Give a reason for each answer.

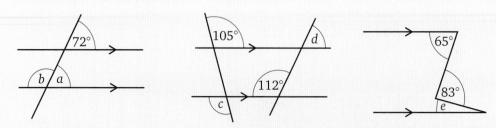

Not drawn accurately

10 For each diagram write down the three-figure bearing of *P* from *Q*.

a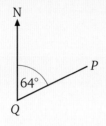

b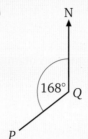

c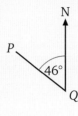

Not drawn accurately

11 The diagram shows the positions of three buoys *A*, *B* and *C*.

B is due east of A and C is due north of A.

The bearing of *B* from *C* is 129°.

Work out angle *x*.

What is the bearing of *C* from *B*?

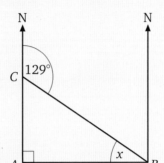

Not drawn accurately

12 Show that the line *XA* is parallel to *BC*.

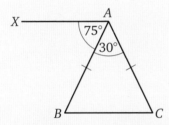

Not drawn accurately

13 For each of the diagrams in Question 10, write down the bearing of *Q* from *P*.

Practice questions 🅺

1 Two sides of this triangle are equal in length.

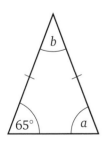

Not drawn accurately

a What special name is given to this type of triangle? *(1 mark)*

b **i** Write down the value of *a*. *(1 mark)*

ii Work out the value of *b*. *(2 marks)*

AQA 2008

2 **a** The diagram shows three angles on a straight line.

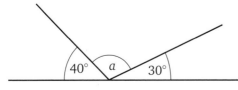

Not drawn accurately

Work out the value of *a*. *(1 mark)*

b The diagram shows two intersecting straight lines.

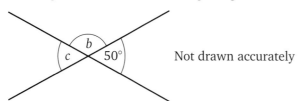

Not drawn accurately

    i Work out the value of b. *(1 mark)*
    ii Work out the value of c. *(1 mark)*

c The diagram shows a right-angled triangle.

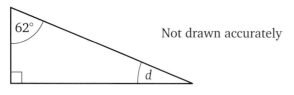

Not drawn accurately

    Work out the value of d. *(2 marks)*

AQA 2008

3 In the diagram AB is parallel to CD.

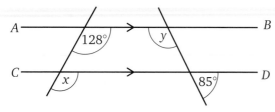

Not drawn accurately

    a Write down the value of x. Give a reason for your answer. *(2 marks)*
    b Work out the value of y. *(2 marks)*

AQA 2008

4 Rebecca has three rectangular sheets of paper.
She cuts each sheet into two pieces.
She now has six pieces, A to F, shown below.

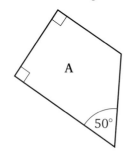
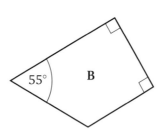

Not drawn
accurately

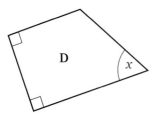
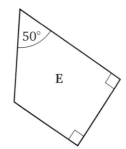
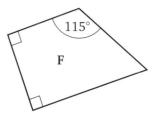

    a Which piece is part of the same rectangle as A? *(1 mark)*
    b Which piece is part of the same rectangle as B? *(1 mark)*
    c Calculate the size of angle x on piece D. *(2 marks)*

AQA 2006

2 Types of numbers

Objectives

Examiners would normally expect students who get these grades to be able to:

G

understand place value in large numbers

add and subtract large numbers (up to three digits)

multiply and divide large numbers (up to three digits by two digits)

understand positive and negative integers

find the factors of a number

F

multiply and divide whole numbers by 10, 100, 1000, ...

multiply large numbers (two digits by two digits)

add and subtract negative numbers

use inverse operations to check answers

use hierarchy of operations to carry out calculations (BIDMAS)

add and subtract positive and negative numbers

E

multiply and divide positive and negative numbers

recognise prime numbers

C

find the Least Common Multiple (LCM) of two numbers

find the Highest Common Factor (HCF) of two numbers

write a number as a product of prime factors.

Did you know?

Padlocked

Buying on the internet uses **prime numbers**. They keep credit card numbers safe. The product of two very large prime numbers is used as a code. The prime numbers themselves are the key to unlock the code.

The **product** is the result when you multiply numbers together.

Key terms

prime number	positive number
product	negative number
place value	quotient
inverse operation	factor
sum	common factor
difference	highest common factor (HCF)
BIDMAS	multiple
directed number	least common multiple (LCM)
integer	index

You should already know:

✔ how to add, subtract, multiply and divide simple numbers

✔ place value for hundreds, tens and units.

Learn... 2.1 Place value

The value of each digit in a number like 6 349 157 depends on its position:

Six million, three hundred and forty-nine thousand, one hundred and fifty-seven

Thousands					
M	H	T	U	H	T	U
6	3	4	9	1	5	7

6	Millions	6 000 000
3	Hundred Thousands	300 000
4	Ten Thousands	40 000
9	Thousands	9 000
1	Hundreds	100
5	Tens	50
7	Units	7
		6 349 157

Leave spaces (not commas) between groups of three digits.

When writing a number like **sixteen thousand and forty-nine**, take care not to miss out any zeros.

Thousands					
H	T	U	H	T	U
	1	6	0	4	9

Study tip

Take care not to miss out zeros like this one – it shows there are no hundreds.

When you **multiply a number by 10**, all the digits **move one place to the left**.

When you **divide a number by 10**, all the digits **move one place to the right**.

For example:

$5790 \times 10 =$

Thousands					
H	T	U	H	T	U
		5	7	9	0
5	7	9	0	0

$5790 \div 10 =$

Thousands					
H	T	U	H	T	U
		5	7	9	0
			5	7	9

The value of each digit is multiplied by 10.

For example,

$90 \times 10 = 900$

An extra zero is needed at the end.

The value of each digit is divided by 10.

For example,

$90 \div 10 = 9$

The zero disappears.

When you **multiply by 100**, the digits **move two places to the left** (to the right when you divide).

When you **multiply by 1000**, the digits **move three places to the left** (to the right when you divide).

Example: Which is smaller: 50 million or 13 500 000?

Solution:

Millions			Thousands					
H	T	U	H	T	U	H	T	U
	5	0	0	0	0	0	0	0
	1	3	5	0	0	0	0	0

Compare the most significant digit at the front (on the left-hand side).

Writing 50 million in full and comparing it with 13 500 000 shows that:

13 500 000 is smaller.

In words this is thirteen million, five hundred thousand.

It is also equal to thirteen and a half million or 13.5 million.

Practise... 2.1 Place value

G F E D C

1   **a**   Write down the value of the digit 3 in:

     i   5327   **ii**   9034   **iii**   13 278

  b   Write down the value of the digit 7 in:

     i   74 689   **ii**   735 180   **iii**   17 140 094

2   Write these numbers in words:

  a   2746   **f**   90 503

  b   9058   **g**   135 418

  c   9805   **h**   602 700

  d   12 346   **i**   2 045 000

  e   73 060   **j**   35 000 000

3   Write these in figures:

  a   eight million

  b   eighty thousand

  c   eighteen thousand

  d   five thousand, four hundred and twenty-nine

  e   two thousand and sixty-seven

  f   fifteen thousand, nine hundred and seven

  g   three hundred and forty-five thousand

  h   one hundred and thirty thousand, five hundred

  i   six million, seventy-four thousand, nine hundred and five

  j   twenty million, four hundred thousand.

> **Hint**
>
> Take care not to miss out any zeros.

4   Write these numbers in figures in order of size. Start with the smallest:

7 million   one hundred and seventy thousand

seventeen million   782 000

5   A maths teacher asks her class to write two thousand and forty-seven in figures.

  a   Upama writes 247. Write this number in words.

  b   Jack writes 200 047. Write this number in words.

  c   Write two thousand and forty-seven correctly in figures.

6   **a**   **i**   Find all the three-figure numbers that can be made using each of the digits 2, 5 and 8 once.

     ii   Write the numbers from part **a i** in order of size. Start with the largest.

  b   **i**   Find all the four-figure numbers that can be made using each of the digits 3, 7, 1 and 6 once.

     ii   Write the numbers from part **b i** in order of size. Start with the smallest.

7   **a**   The number 7320 is multiplied by 10.
In the new number, what does the digit 3 represent?

  b   The number 7320 is divided by 10.
In the new number, what does the digit 3 represent?

G

F

F
E

8 The table gives the heights of some mountains in Europe.

Mountain	Height (m)
Dom	4545
Matterhorn	4479
Mont Blanc	4807
Monte Rosa	4634

a Write the mountains in order of height, starting with the tallest.

b Write the height of the tallest mountain in words.

9 Here are five number cards:

8 4 9 5 1

a Use all five cards to make the largest possible even number.

b Use all five cards to make the smallest possible odd number.

c Use all five cards to make the number that is nearest to fifty thousand.

d Use all five cards to make the number that is nearest to fifteen thousand.

> **Hint**
> **Even** numbers end in 0, 2, 4, 6 or 8.
> **Odd** numbers end in 1, 3, 5, 7 or 9.

10 a Write these in figures:

  i 425 million

  ii half a million

  iii quarter of a million

  iv 1.5 million

  v 35.6 million

  vi 7 billion

> **Hint**
> 1 billion = 1 000 000 000

b Divide each number in part **a** by 10.

c Multiply each number in part **a** by 10.

11 a Copy the table. Using the information given, fill in the table using figures.

The population of London is about seven and a half million.

About a quarter of a million people live in Newcastle.

About three quarters of a million people live in Leeds.

The population of Portsmouth is about two hundred thousand.

City	Population
London	
Newcastle	
Leeds	
Portsmouth	

b About one tenth of the UK's population is left-handed. About how many people in each city are left-handed?

> **Hint**
> To find one-tenth, divide by 10.

Learn...   **2.2 Working with whole numbers**

There are sometimes quick ways to add, subtract, multiply or divide whole numbers.

But if you can't see a quick way, you should use one of the standard methods shown below.

They work for any numbers. Start adding, subtracting and multiplying with the units (on the right). Start dividing with the most significant digit (on the left).

You can check each answer by using the **inverse** (the opposite).
Addition and subtraction are inverses.

Multiplication and division are inverses.

Example: **a** $468 + 137$ **b** $563 - 148$

Solution: **a**   4 6 8   **b** $5\,^5\!6\,^1\!3$
            + 1 3 7   − 1 4 8   You cannot take 8 from 3.
            6 0 5   4 1 5   Use one of the 6 tens to help.
            1 1

$6 + 3 + 1 = 10$ tens $8 + 7 = 15$
carry 1 hundred   carry 1 ten

> **Study tip**
> Line up the digits to add or subtract digits with the same place value.

> **Study tip**
> When subtracting, remember to put the larger number on top.

To check the answer to part **a**, subtract.   To check the answer to part **b**, add.

   $^5\!6\,^1\!0\,^9\!5$ 4 1 5
  − 1 3 7   + 1 4 8
   4 6 8   5 6 3
                                1

You should get back to the number you started with.

Example: **c** 68×9 **d** $93 \div 4$
                                           There is 1 left over –

Solution: **c**   6 8   **d**   **2 3 r1**   this means 'remainder 1'.
          ×   9 $4\overline{)9\,^1\!3}$
         6 1 2
         6 7 $2 \times 4 = 8$
                  $8 \times 9 = 72$ There is 1 ten left over –
$6 \times 9 = 54$ carry 7 tens   add this to the units.
$+ 7 = 61$

To check the answer to part **c**, divide.   To check the answer to part **d** multiply.

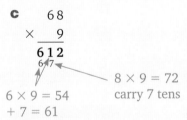

     6 8   You should get back to the   2 3   92 + the remainder, 1,
$9\overline{)6\,1\,^7\!2}$ number you started with.   ×   4   gets back to 93
                                           9 2

$6 \times 9 = 54$ $2 \times 4 = 8$ $3 \times 4 = 12$
$61 - 54 = 7$ tens left   then $+ 1 = 9$ carry 1 ten

You may need to multiply more difficult numbers.

Two multiplication methods are shown in the next example below. Most students find the first method easier. It works by splitting both numbers into tens and units.

The second method is a more traditional method. You can use this method if you prefer it.

Example: **e** 36×24

Solution: **e**

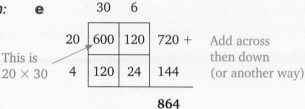

	30	6	
20	600	120	720 +
4	120	24	144

This is 20 × 30

864

Add across
then down
(or another way)

$$\begin{array}{r} 36 \\ \times\ 24 \\ \hline 144\ + \\ 720 \\ \hline 864 \end{array}$$

Multiply 36 by 4 then by 20.

To multiply by 20, put zero here (this multiples it by 10), then multiply by 2.

If you know both methods, you can use one to work out the answer and the second to check. You can also check this multiplication by dividing as shown below.

$$24\overline{)8\ 6^{14}4} \quad \mathbf{3\ 6} \longleftarrow 6 \times 24 = 144$$

$3 \times 24 = 72$
There are 14 tens left over.
Add them to the units.

Build up a table of the values you need:
$1 \times 24 = 24$
$2 \times 24 = 48$
$3 \times 24 = 72$
$4 \times 24 = 96$
$5 \times 24 = 120$
$6 \times 24 = 144$

You may spot quicker ways. 144 is twice as big as 72, so there are six 24s in 144.

$864 \div 24 = 36$ (the number you started with), so the multiplication is correct.

Practise...   2.2 Working with whole numbers Ⓚ   Ⓖ Ⓕ Ⓔ Ⓓ Ⓒ

1   Work out:

a	$35 + 46$	**c**	$846 + 73$	**e**	$356 + 249$	**g**	$4587 + 2139$
b	$89 + 67$	**d**	$68 + 374$	**f**	$374 + 486$	**h**	$314 + 59 + 48$

Use the inverse operation to check each answer.

Hint

The inverse of + is − .

2   Work out:

a	$73 - 46$	**c**	$139 - 83$	**e**	$862 - 576$	**g**	$7511 - 4392$
b	$82 - 64$	**d**	$271 - 149$	**f**	$700 - 148$	**h**	$6805 - 2679$

Use the inverse operation to check each answer.

Hint

The inverse of − is + .

3   Here is a list of numbers: 27   54   63   86   34   46

   a   Write down two numbers from the list which add up to 100.

   b   Write down two numbers from the list which have a difference of 40.

   c   What is the largest total you can make by adding three different numbers from the list?

4   **a**   Write down six different pairs of numbers which have a sum of 100.

   b   Write down six different pairs of numbers which have a difference of 25.

Hint

The **sum** is what you get if you add. The **difference** is what you get if you **subtract**.

5   Work out:

a	16×5	**f**	136×9	**k**	$135 \div 5$	**p**	$710 \div 9$
b	54×6	**g**	289×4	**l**	$584 \div 2$	**q**	$300 \div 12$
c	35×8	**h**	628×7	**m**	$352 \div 3$	**r**	$775 \div 25$
d	18×7	**i**	$56 \div 4$	**n**	$752 \div 8$	**s**	$810 \div 18$
e	245×3	**j**	$96 \div 6$	**o**	$831 \div 7$	**t**	$578 \div 34$

Use the inverse operation to check your answers.

6   Work out:

a	26×45	**c**	32×83	**e**	52×39	**g**	93×65
b	54×17	**d**	78×41	**f**	86×47	**h**	86×79

Do your answers look reasonable?

7   Given that $8 \times 4 = 32$ and $4 \times 8 = 32$

a   write down **two** other multiplications which give the answer 32

b   write down the values of   **i** 8×400 **ii** 80×400 **iii** $320 \div 4$

8   Here is a list of numbers: 5   7   8   11   13   36   45

a   What is the largest number you can make by multiplying two different numbers on the list?

b   What is the smallest number you can make by multiplying three different numbers on the list?

9   **a**   Write down six different multiplications that have an answer of 120.

b   Write down six different divisions that have an answer of 12.

10   Carol says $806 - 349$ is 543.
Imran says it is 467.
They are both wrong.

a   Explain the mistakes they have made.

b   What is the correct answer?

Carol	Imran
806	$^78^10^16$
$-\ 349$	$-\ 349$
$\mathbf{543}$	$\mathbf{467}$

11   Sally says 89×7 is 956.
Mike says it is 119.
They are both wrong.

a   Find each mistake in their working.

b   What is the correct answer?

Sally
89
$\times\quad 7$
$\mathbf{956}$
$9\ 3$

Mike

	80	9	
7	56	63	**119**

12   Tina thinks $735 \div 7 = 15$

a   What mistake has she made?

b   Work out the correct answer.

13   You can use these four number cards to make a lot of different four-figure numbers.

7	4	8	3

a   Find the **sum** of the largest possible number and the smallest possible number.

b   Find the **difference** between the largest possible number and the smallest possible number.

14 Find the missing numbers in these calculations:

a $75 + \square = 102$ c $\square - 94 = 428$ e $\square \div 3 = 29$

b $87 - \square = 19$ d $\square \times 4 = 348$ f $96 \div \square = 8$

15 a The table shows some information about a farm.

i What is the total number of animals?

ii How many more sheep than cows are there?

iii How many more sheep than pigs are there?

Animals on the farm	
Cows	32
Pigs	26
Sheep	83

b The farmer wants to put a fence around a field.
He plans to leave a gap of 2 metres for a gate.
The farmer has budgeted £5500 for the fence.
The fencing costs £50 for 3 m.
Can the farmer afford the fence he needs?

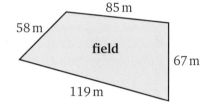

16 The chart below gives the distances in miles between some cities.
For example, the distance between Derby and York is 88 miles.

Distance chart

Distance in miles

Bristol			
127	Derby		
196	70	Leeds	
217	88	25	York

A salesman lives in Leeds. One day he has to go to Bristol, Derby and York.

a Find the route with the shortest distance. It must start and end in Leeds.

b The next day, the salesman has to travel from Leeds to Bristol.
On the way back he has to take a detour.
He checks his mileage for the day.

How many extra miles did his detour add to the journey?

Start	86 952
Finish	87 360

Learn... 2.3 Order of operations

Some calculations have more than one operation.
The word **BIDMAS** can help you remember the correct order to do them:

B	I	D	M	A	S
Brackets	**Indices**	**Divide**	**Multiply**	**Add**	**Subtract**

These go together.
When they are both in a calculation,
work from left to right.

These go together.
When they are both in a calculation,
work from left to right.

You will meet indices in Chapter 9. For now, be careful to do the other operations in the right order.
The most important thing to remember is to add and subtract last unless they are in a bracket.

For example, in $1 + 2 \times 5$, **multiply** before **adding**. The answer is 11, not 15.

When a calculation is a mixture of adding and subtracting only, you must work from left to right.
This also works when the calculation is a mixture of multiplying and dividing only.

For example, $35 - 8 + 25 = 27 + 25 = 52$ and $28 \div 7 \times 5 = 4 \times 5 = 20$

Example: **a** $9 + 8 \div 4$

   $= 9 + 2$ Divide before
   $= 11$ adding.

   c $3 \times 4 - 8 \div 2$

   $= 12 - 4$ Multiply and divide
   $= 8$ before subtracting.

b $10 \div (2 + 3)$

   $= 10 \div 5$ Brackets
   $= 2$ first.

d $\dfrac{20 - 2 \times 4}{3} = \dfrac{(20 - 2 \times 4)}{3}$ Do the top first –
   as if it had a

   $= \dfrac{(20 - 8)}{3}$ bracket.

   $= \dfrac{12}{3}$

   $= 4$

Practise... 2.3 Order of operations

G F E D C

1 Work out:

a $(7 - 3) \times 6$ **e** $5 + 3 \times 4$ **i** $15 - 6 \div (2 + 1)$

b $8 + 4 \div 2$ **f** $18 \div 2 + 1$ **j** $7 \times 2 + 3 \times 5$

c $6 \times 5 - 2$ **g** $7 - (4 + 3)$ **k** $12 \div (4 - 2)$

d $9 - (4 + 3)$ **h** $(2 + 3) \times 5 - 4$ **l** $8 + 6 \div 2 - 1$

2 Say whether each is **true** or **false**. For those that are false, give the correct answer.

a $2 + 4 \times 7 = 42$ **d** $(9 - 2) \times 4 = 1$ **g** $8 - 4 \div 2 + 1 = 3$

b $18 - 4 \div 2 = 16$ **e** $9 - (5 - 3) = 1$ **h** $6 \times 4 - 2 \times 5 = 14$

c $14 \div (4 + 3) = 2$ **f** $6 \div (2 + 1) = 4$

3 Work out:

a $\dfrac{8 + 6 \times 2}{5}$ **b** $\dfrac{4 \times (8 - 5)}{6}$ **c** $\dfrac{20}{4 + 2 \times 3}$ **d** $\dfrac{9 \times 4 - 6}{18 - (2 + 1)}$

4 Bob says that $8 - (3 - 2)$ has the same answer as $8 - 3 - 2$.
Is he correct? Explain your answer.

5 Insert brackets to make these correct.

a $2 + 3 \times 4 = 20$ **c** $12 - 9 - 2 = 5$ **e** $15 + 7 - 2 \div 5 = 16$

b $15 \div 3 + 2 = 3$ **d** $15 + 7 - 2 \div 5 = 4$ **f** $8 - 3 \times 6 - 2 = 20$

6 Copy these. Fill in the missing numbers to make them correct.

a $4 \times 3 + \underline{\ } = 20$ **c** $(12 - 6) \div \underline{\ } = 2$ **e** $(12 + 8) \div 4 - \underline{\ } = 3$

b $4 \times (3 + \underline{\ }) = 32$ **d** $12 - 6 \div \underline{\ } = 9$ **f** $12 + 8 \div 4 - \underline{\ } = 3$

⚠ 7 Work out:

a $35 \times (52 - 49)$ **b** $60 + 95 \div 5$ **c** $(28 + 6) \times 9$ **d** $\dfrac{9 + 18 \times 7}{15}$

⚠ 8 Insert brackets to make these correct.

a $70 - 25 + 15 = 30$ **c** $32 + 16 \div 4 = 12$ **e** $72 \div 8 \div 2 = 18$

b $16 \times 5 - 3 = 32$ **d** $29 + 37 - 12 \div 6 = 9$ **f** $20 - 2 \times 9 + 2 = 198$

F
E

E

9

a Work out $(2 + 7) \times 3$

b Use all of the following to write a single calculation whose answer is as large as possible:
  - each of the numbers 4, 5 and 6 (once only)
  - each of the operations $+$ and $\times$ (once only)
  - one pair of brackets.

10

a Work out $4 + 4 + \frac{4}{4}$

b Can you make each of the numbers 1 to 20 using up to four 4s and mathematical symbols?

11

Use $+ - \times \div$ to make these statements true.

a $2 \_ 3 \_ 4 = 9$

b $2 \_ 3 \_ 4 = 14$

c $2 \_ 3 \_ 4 = 1$

d $2 \_ 3 \_ 4 = 24$

e $2 \_ 3 \_ 4 = 3$

f $2 \_ 3 \_ 4 = 1\frac{1}{2}$

Learn... 2.4 Positive and negative integers

A **directed number** has a positive or negative sign to show whether it is above or below zero.

An **integer** is any positive or negative *whole* number or zero, for example, $-2, -1, 0, +1, +2 \ldots$

Note in **positive numbers** the $+$ signs are often missed out.

You can use a number line to put integers in order.

A number line is like a thermometer standing on its side with ordinary numbers instead of temperatures.

Example: Put these numbers in order of size, smallest first.
$9 \quad -13 \quad -37 \quad 36 \quad -25 \quad -4 \quad 18$

Solution: These numbers are shown on the number line.

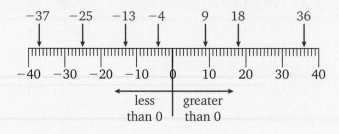

To write them in order, start on the left.

In order the numbers are: $-37 \quad -25 \quad -13 \quad -4 \quad 9 \quad 18 \quad 36$

Practise... 2.4 Positive and negative integers G F E D C

G

Use a thermometer or number line to help.

1 Put these temperatures in order. Start with the warmest.

a $-1\,°C$ $2\,°C$ $-2\,°C$ $1\,°C$ $0\,°C$

b $8\,°C$ $-7\,°C$ $6\,°C$ $0\,°C$ $-9\,°C$ $3\,°C$

c $14\,°C$ $-8\,°C$ $5\,°C$ $-10\,°C$ $26\,°C$ $-15\,°C$ $23\,°C$

2 Here are some temperatures.

$9\,°C$ $-4\,°C$ $17\,°C$ $20\,°C$ $-23\,°C$ $-5\,°C$ $-12\,°C$

Write down the temperatures that are

a   higher than $15\,°C$

b   lower than $0\,°C$

c   lower than $-10\,°C$

d   higher than $-5\,°C$.

3 Put these numbers in order, smallest first.

a $+6$ -8 $+5$ $+1$ $+9$ -4 -3

b -16 18 -10 -27 11 0 -19

c 134 -98 47 -103 260 -145 84

4 Here is a list of numbers.

$+2$ -8 $+5$ -1 $+9$ -4 -3

Which numbers are

a   greater than 4

b   less than 0

c   less than -5

d   greater than -3?

5 Judy says that -16 is more than 15. Is she correct?
Explain your answer.

6 Put the correct sign, $<$, $>$ or $=$, between these numbers:

a -5 __ -8

b -4 __ -3

c -5 __ 2

d 7 __ -7

e -9 __ 9

> **Hint**
> $<$ means **less than**. $>$ means **greater than**.

⚠ 7 a   Write down all the integers that lie between -3 and $+6$ (not including -3 and $+6$).

b   How many integers lie between -87 and -98 (not including -87 and -98)?

2.5 Adding and subtracting positive and negative integers

There are two uses for + and − signs: + means **add**
+4 means the positive number 4

− means **subtract**
−4 means the **negative number** −4

You can use a number line to add or subtract positive and negative numbers.

To add numbers – this gives the **sum** of the numbers:
- Find the first number on the number line.
- Go **up (or right)** to add a positive number or **down (or left)** to add a negative number.
- The answer is the number you end on.

To subtract numbers – this gives the **difference** between the numbers:
- Find the first number on the number line.
- Go **down (or left)** to subtract a positive number and **up (or right)** to subtract a negative number. Note that this is the opposite direction to when you are adding.
- The answer is the number you end on.

Examples: Adding   Subtracting

a $30 + -10 = 20$

b $-5 + 15 = 10$

c $-10 + -20 = -30$

d $10 - 20 = -10$

e $-10 - 20 = -30$

f $-10 - -30 = 20$

The rules are:

Adding a positive number	$+\,+$	does the same as	$+$
Adding a negative number	$+\,-$	does the same as	$-$
Subtracting a positive number	$-\,+$	does the same as	$-$
Subtracting a negative number	$-\,-$	does the same as	$+$

So, for example, $30 + -10 = 30 - 10 = 20$ and $-10 - -30 = -10 + 30 = 20$

2.5 Adding and subtracting positive and negative integers

Practise...

Use a thermometer or a number line to help.

F

1 **a** The temperature is −3°C. It rises by 4°C. What is the new temperature?

b The temperature is −7°C. It rises by 2°C. What is the new temperature?

c The temperature is 1°C. It falls by 4°C. What is the new temperature?

d The temperature is −2°C. It falls by 3°C. What is the new temperature?

2 Find the value of **a** $-3 + 6$ **c** $-5 + -3$

b $2 + -5$ **d** $-6 + +1$

3 Find the difference between the temperature at midnight and the temperature at midday on each day.

Temperature in a greenhouse		
Day	**Midnight**	**Midday**
Monday	3 °C	12 °C
Tuesday	0 °C	10 °C
Wednesday	−1 °C	7 °C
Thursday	−2 °C	4 °C
Friday	−4 °C	0 °C
Saturday	−6 °C	−1 °C
Sunday	−9 °C	−3 °C

4 Find the value of **a** $2 - 6$ **c** $-3 - -5$

b $-1 - 5$ **d** $-7 - +4$

5 Work out these additions and subtractions. Look at the patterns you get.

a **i** $4 + 3$ **iii** $4 + 1$ **v** $4 + -1$ **vii** $4 + -3$

ii $4 + 2$ **iv** $4 + 0$ **vi** $4 + -2$

b **i** $4 - 3$ **iii** $4 - 1$ **v** $4 - -1$ **vii** $4 - -3$

ii $4 - 2$ **iv** $4 - 0$ **vi** $4 - -2$

6 Find the missing number in each of the following:

a $-4 + \_\_ = -1$ **e** $1 - \_\_ = -4$

b $-5 + \_\_ = 0$ **f** $2 - \_\_ = 3$

c $2 + \_\_ = -3$ **g** $-4 - \_\_ = 0$

d $-1 + \_\_ = -4$ **h** $-1 - \_\_ = -6$

7 Sam says that $-1 + -5$ has the same answer as $-1 - +5$.
Is he correct? Explain your answer.

8 Find the next three numbers in each pattern:

a 6 4 2 0 ....

b -11 -8 -5 -2 ....

9 What must be added to:

a -2 to make 6 **b** 3 to make -3 **c** 12 to make 7?

10 Work out:

a $12 - 23$ **e** $-53 - 24$

b $-15 - 19$ **f** $29 - -46$

c $28 - -35$ **g** $72 - 98$

d $-21 - -34$ **h** $-45 - -37$

11 Some cities and their temperatures at midnight are shown on the map.

a Which city is the warmest?

b Which city is the coldest?

c Find the difference in temperature between:

    i London and Vienna

    ii London and Rome

    iii Brussels and Oslo

    iv Madrid and Moscow.

Midnight temperatures

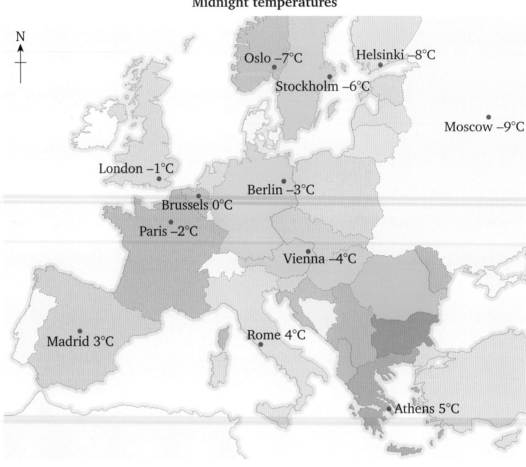

d In London, the temperature rises 3 °C by 6 am.
What is the temperature at 6 am?

e In Stockholm the temperature falls 2 °C by 6 am.
What is the temperature at 6 am?

12

ENGLISH HILLS AND LAKES			
Heights of hills		**Depths of lakes**	
Catstycam	+889 m	Coniston	−56 m
Great Dodd	+857 m	Grasmere	−25 m
Helvellyn	+951 m	Ullswater	−60 m
Scafell Pike	+978 m	Wastwater	−79 m

a How much higher is Catstycam than Great Dodd?

b How much deeper is Coniston than Grasmere?

c Find the difference in height between:

    i the top of Helvellyn and the bottom of Ullswater

    ii the bottom of Wastwater and the top of Scafell Pike.

13   Each number in a magic square is different.

The sum of each row, each column and each diagonal is the same.

a   Copy this magic square and fill in the missing numbers.

b   If you add or subtract the same number to each box you get another magic square. Explain why.

c   Make another magic square.

d   Check that it works, then give a copy to a friend to solve.

0		4
	1	−3
−2		

14   Three whole numbers have a sum of 10.

a   One of the numbers is 14. Give an example of what the other two numbers might be.

b   One of the numbers is 16 and the other two numbers are equal. What are they?

2.6 Multiplying and dividing positive and negative integers

You can write multiplications as additions. For example, 5×2 is the same as adding 5 lots of 2.

a $+5 \times +2 = +2 + +2 + +2 + +2 + 2 = +10$ and $+5 \times +2 = +5 + +5 = +10$

b $+5 \times -2 = -2 + -2 + -2 + -2 - 2 = -10$ and $-2 \times -5 = -5 + -5 = -10$

    5 lots of −2   2 lots of −5

These show that multiplying one positive by one negative number gives a negative answer.

a and **b** show that changing the sign of one of the numbers changes the sign of the answer.

Starting with $+5 \times -2 = -10$ and changing $+5$ to -5,

the result will be $-5 \times -2 = +10$

This shows that multiplying two negative numbers together gives a positive answer.

The results for muliplication are also true for division. So when **multiplying or dividing**, remember:

When signs are the **same**	$+ \times +$ or $- \times -$ $+ \div +$ or $- \div -$	the answer is positive $+$
When signs are **different**	$+ \times -$ or $- \times +$ $+ \div -$ or $- \div +$	the answer is negative $-$

Example: **a** $+2 \times +5 = +10$ This is the same as 2×5 Decide on the sign of the answer, then multiply the numbers.

b $+4 \times -3 = -12$

c $-7 \times +5 = -35$ Signs different gives negative

d $-3 \times -2 = +6$ Signs same gives positive

e $+12 \div +3 = +4$ This is the same as $12 \div 3$

f $+15 \div -5 = -3$ Signs different gives negative

g $-20 \div +4 = -5$

h $-18 \div -2 = +9$ Signs same gives positive

Study tip

Take care! Multiplying and dividing follow these rules, but adding and subtracting don't.
For example, $-3 + 5 = 2$ NOT -2.
Remember to use a number line for adding and subtracting.

The answer when you multiply numbers is called the **product**.

The answer when you divide numbers is called the **quotient**.

Practise...

2.6 Multiplying and dividing positive and negative integers

(k)

G F E D C

1 Work out:

a $+3 \times +5$

b $+2 \times -6$

c $-8 \times +5$

d -7×-2

e $+5 \times +7$

f $+4 \times -8$

g $-6 \times +7$

h -9×-8

2 Work out:

a $+12 \div +3$

b $+16 \div -2$

c $-30 \div +5$

d $-32 \div -4$

e $+42 \div +6$

f $+63 \div -7$

g $-64 \div +8$

h $-36 \div -9$

3 Which of these are correct? If the answer is wrong, write down the correct answer.

a $+3 \times +4 = +12$

b $+2 \times -8 = +16$

c $-4 \times +5 = -20$

d $-6 \times -2 = -12$

e $4 \times 7 = -28$

f $4 \times -6 = -24$

g $-9 \times 7 = 63$

h $-7 \times -8 = 56$

i $+9 \div +3 = -27$

j $+8 \div -2 = -4$

k $-15 \div +5 = +3$

l $-20 \div -4 = -5$

m $36 \div 6 = -6$

n $-56 \div 7 = -8$

o $-48 \div 8 = -6$

p $-54 \div -9 = 6$

4 Find the missing number in each of the following.

a $5 \times \underline{\quad} = -25$

b $-2 \times \underline{\quad} = 14$

c $-4 \times \underline{\quad} = 0$

d $-3 \times \underline{\quad} = -24$

e $-16 \div \underline{\quad} = -2$

f $27 \div \underline{\quad} = -3$

g $-7 \div \underline{\quad} = 7$

h $24 \div \underline{\quad} = -6$

5 Ian says that $+7 \times -5$ has the same answer as $-7 \times +5$.
Is he correct? Explain your answer.

6 a Find all the pairs of integers that have a product of -16.

b Find all the pairs of integers that have a product of 20.

7 Find the values of these:

a $\dfrac{-5 \times +4}{+2}$ b $\dfrac{+6 \times -4}{-2}$ c $\dfrac{-2 \times -9}{+3}$ d $\dfrac{-8 \times -3}{-4}$

8 Work out:

a -25×4

b 6×-47

c -32×-80

d 26×-15

e $-94 \div 2$

f $-72 \div -3$

g $275 \div -5$

h $-432 \div -9$

9   A quiz has 12 questions.
Contestants get two points for a correct answer.
One point is taken off for each wrong answer.

a   Find the missing points (*) in this table of results.

Contestant	Questions correct	wrong	Points
Rory	6		*
Ann	8		*
Neil	4		*
Kath		10	*
Peter		3	*
Moira		5	*

b   Find   **i**   the highest possible number of points
ii   the lowest possible number of points.

c   How many correct answers give
i   3 points   **ii**   −9 points   **iii**   18 points   **iv**   −3 points?

10   **a**   Find two integers whose sum is −8 and whose product is 12.

b   Find two integers whose sum is −7 and whose product is –18.

c   Find two **negative** integers whose difference is 5 and whose product is 24.

Make up integer descriptions of your own. Ask a friend to find the integers.

Learn...   2.7 Factors and multiples

A **factor** is a positive whole number that divides exactly into another number.
For example, the factors of 16 are   1,   2,   4,   8,   16

Factors usually occur in pairs:
$1 \times 16 = 16$, $2 \times 8 = 16$, $4 \times 4 = 16$

A factor is sometimes called a divisor.

To find all the factors of a number, look for factor pairs.

For example,   20 = 1 × 20   so 1 and 20 are factors of 20
20 = 2 × 10   so 2 and 10 are factors of 20
20 = 4 × 5   so 4 and 5 are factors of 20.

The factors of 20 are 1, 2, 4, 5, 10, 20.

The **common factors** of two or more numbers are the factors that they have in common.

The **highest common factor (HCF)** of two or more numbers is the highest factor that they have in common.

> **Study tip**
>
> Be systematic so you don't lose any factors.

> **Study tip**
>
> Remember, 1 is a factor of all numbers.

Example: Find the highest common factor (HCF) of 20 and 24.

Solution: A factor is something that goes into the number.

The factors of 20 are **1**, **2**, **4**, 5, 10, 20.
The factors of 24 are **1**, **2**, 3, **4**, 6, 8, 12, 24.

The common factors are the numbers that are in both lists.

The common factors are **1**, **2**, **4**.
The highest common factor is **4**.

The **multiples** of a number are the products in its multiplication table.

For example, $1 \times 3 = 3$, $2 \times 3 = 6$, $3 \times 3 = 9$, ... The answers 3, 6, 9, ... are the multiples of 3.

So the multiples of 3 are   3   6   9   12   15   18   21   ... (goes on forever)

Adding the digits of each multiple   3   6   9   3   6   9   3

You can check whether a number is a multiple of 3 by adding the digits to see if you get 3, 6 or 9.

For example, adding the digits of 957 gives $9 + 5 + 7 = 21$ then $2 + 1 = 3$

So 957 is a multiple of 3.

Note this test works for multiples of 3, but not for others such as multiples of 4 or 5.

The **least common multiple (LCM)** of two or more numbers is the smallest multiple that they have in common.

Example: Find the least common multiple (LCM) of 6, 8 and 12.

Solution: A multiple is something the number goes into.

The multiples of 6 are   6, 12, 18, **24**, 30, 36, 42, **48**, 54, 60, 66, **72**, ...

The multiples of 8 are   8, 16, **24**, 32, 40, **48**, 56, 64, **72**, ...

The multiples of 12 are   12, **24**, 36, **48**, 60, **72**, ...

The common multiples are the numbers that are in all three lists.

The common multiples are **24**, **48**, **72**, ...
The least common multiple is **24**.

Practise... 2.7 Factors and multiples    G F E D C

G

1 Here is a list of numbers: 2   3   4   5   6   7

Which of these numbers are factors of:

a   8   **c**   20   **e**   84

b   12   **d**   28   **f**   420?

2 Find all the factors of:

a   4   **c**   10   **e**   25

b   9   **d**   18   **f**   60

3 Write down the first five multiples of:

a   4   **b**   6   **c**   7   **d**   8

4   **a**   **i**   Write down the first six multiples of 10.

   ii   How can you tell whether a number is a multiple of 10?

b   **i**   Write down the first six multiples of 5.

   ii   How can you tell whether a number is a multiple of 5?

c   Here is a list of numbers: 90   105   210   306   495   570

   Which of these are multiples of: **i**   10   **ii**   5   **iii**   3?

5   **a**   Write down the first 12 multiples of 9. Then find their digit sums.

   b   Here is a list of numbers: 153   207   378   452   574   3789
         Which of these do you think are multiples of 9?

   c   Check your answers to part **b** by dividing by 9.

   d   How can you tell whether a number is a multiple of 9?

6   Find the common factors of:

   a   6 and 9   **c**   14 and 35   **e**   15 and 35

   b   8 and 28   **d**   24 and 36   **f**   12 and 30.

7   Find the common factors of 42 and 70 and write down the highest common factor.

8   Find the factors then the highest common factor of the following pairs of numbers:

   a   6 and 15   **c**   24 and 32   **e**   50 and 75

   b   12 and 18   **d**   48 and 60   **f**   42 and 70.

9   The highest common factor of two numbers is 7. Give three possible pairs of numbers.

10   Find the least common multiple of the following sets of numbers:

   a   4 and 6   **d**   12 and 20

   b   7 and 5   **e**   2, 3 and 5

   c   6 and 8   **f**   3, 4 and 5.

11   Tracy says that the least common multiple of 12 and 30 is 6.
       Is she correct? Explain your answer.

12   Find the highest common factor of:

   a   6, 18 and 24   **b**   36, 45 and 54   **c**   14, 56 and 84.

13   Find the least common multiple of the following sets of numbers:

   a   8, 10 and 12   **b**   6, 8 and 32   **c**   15, 20 and 25.

14   A planet has moons called Titania and Oberon.
       Titania goes round the planet every 9 days.
       Oberon goes round the planet every 13 days.
       On one evening the moons are in line with the planet.
       How many days will it be before they are in line again?

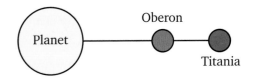

15   **a**   A shop is open every day. The farm delivers milk to it every 2 days and
             butter every 3 days. Today they had a delivery of milk and butter.
             How many days will it be before the deliveries **next** arrive on the
             same day?

   b   A different shop is open every day. The farm delivers milk to it every 2 days,
         butter every 3 days and eggs every 7 days. Today they had a delivery of milk,
         butter and eggs. How many days will it be before all the deliveries **next**
         arrive on the **same** day?

Learn... 2.8 Prime numbers and prime factors

A prime number is a positive whole number that has **exactly two factors**.

The first 7 prime numbers are:

2	3	5	7	11	13	17
Factors	Factors	Factors	Factors	Factors	Factors	Factors
1 & 2	1 & 3	1 & 5	1 & 7	1 & 11	1 & 13	1 & 17

1 is not a prime number because it has only one factor.

2 is the only even prime number. All other even numbers have factors of 1, themselves and 2.

All the other missing odd numbers have three or more factors.
For example, the factors of 15 are 1, 3, 5 and 15.

Index form

Prime numbers are the 'building blocks' of mathematics.
All other numbers can be written as products of prime numbers.

This is sometimes called prime factor decomposition.

For example, $12 = 2 \times 2 \times 3 = 2^2 \times 3$

product   **index**

and $81 = 9 \times 9 = 3 \times 3 \times 3 \times 3 = 3^4$

This is called index form.   index

It is more difficult to find the prime factors of larger numbers.

You can use the **tree method** to do this. See the example below.

Example: Write 280 as a product of its prime factors in index form.

Solution: Two 'trees' are shown below. The first starts by splitting 280 into 28×10.

The numbers are then split again and again until you get to prime numbers.

The second tree starts by splitting 280 into 2×140.

This shows that whichever tree you use, you end with three 2s, a 5 and a 7.

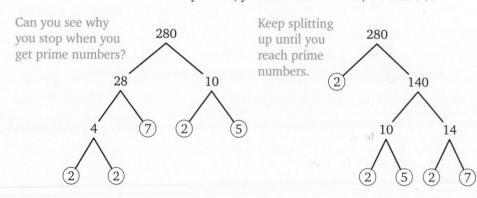

Can you see why you stop when you get prime numbers?

Keep splitting up until you reach prime numbers.

280 written as a product of its prime factors is $2 \times 2 \times 2 \times 5 \times 7$

In index form $280 = 2^3 \times 5 \times 7$

The index, 3, means that 3 twos are multiplied together.

Practise...

2.8 Prime numbers and prime factors

G F E D C

D

C

1 Write down all the prime numbers between 20 and 30.

2 Which of these numbers are **not** prime numbers? 31 33 35 37 39 41
Explain your answers.

3 Write each number as a product of prime factors.
  a 14   **b** 30   **c** 33   **d** 42   **e** 65   **f** 91

4 Write each number as a product of prime factors.
Write your answers using index notation.
  a 24   **b** 36   **c** 45   **d** 64   **e** 84   **f** 96

5 Ruth says that if you write 40 as a product of prime factors, the answer is $1 \times 2^3 \times 5$.
Is she correct? Explain your answer.

6 Write each number as a product of prime factors. Use index notation.
  a 100   **b** 132   **c** 144   **d** 153   **e** 216   **f** 520

7 Which of these numbers **cannot** be prime? 895 356 3457 5739
Explain your answers.

8 **a** Write each number as a product of prime factors, using index notation.
    i 27   **ii** 45

  b Use your answers to part **a** to find:
    i the HCF of 27 and 45   **ii** the LCM of 27 and 45.

9 **a** Write each number as a product of prime factors, using index notation.
    i 42   **ii** 60   **iii** 72

  b Use your answers to part **a** to find:
    i the HCF of 42, 60 and 72   **ii** the LCM of 42, 60 and 72.

10 The product of two prime numbers is sometimes used as a security device.
To 'break the code' you need to find two prime numbers that give a particular product.

Find two prime numbers that multiply to give:
  a 111   **b** 221   **c** 319   **d** 437   **e** 767

Why are even numbers not very useful in this situation?

11 Find the mystery number in each part.

  a It is a prime number. It is a factor of 35. It is not a factor of 25.

  b It is less than 50. It is a multiple of 3. It is also a multiple of 5.
    The sum of its digits is a prime number.

  c It is a prime number less than 100.
    It is one more than a multiple of 8 and its digits add up to 10.

Make up number descriptions of your own. Ask a friend to find the numbers.

2 Assess (k)

G

1 The price of a new car is £18 490.

   a Write the number 18 490 in words.

   b In the number 18 490, write down the value of

      i the digit 9   **ii** the digit 8.

   c The number 18 490 is divided by 10.
      In the new number, what does the digit 8 represent?

2 Work out:

   a $354 + 289$ **c** 86×7 **e** $245 \div 5$

   b $600 - 138$ **d** 46×29 **f** $900 \div 8$

> **Hint**
> You could use inverse operations or your calculator to check.

3 Write down all the factors of 40.

**G
E**

4 Here is a list of numbers: 3   5   6   8   16   23   27

From this list, write down:

   a two numbers that add up to 31   **d** a factor of 9

   b two numbers that have a difference of 7   **e** three numbers with a product of 240

   c a multiple of 9   **f** three prime numbers.

**F
E**

5 The table below gives the temperatures of some cities at dawn.

City	Birmingham	Bristol	Leeds	Manchester	Newcastle
Temperature	−1 °C	2 °C	−4 °C	−3 °C	−5 °C

   a Which city has   **i** the lowest temperature   **ii** the highest temperature?

   b Which cities have temperatures below −1 °C?

6 Copy and complete the following table.

Temperature	Change	New temperature
3 °C	+4 °C	
2 °C	−5 °C	
−4 °C	+9 °C	
−1 °C	−5 °C	
7 °C		11 °C
12 °C		8 °C
−3 °C		7 °C
−1 °C		−4 °C
	+6 °C	9 °C
	−5 °C	4 °C
	+13 °C	10 °C
	−2 °C	−7 °C

7   The first five terms of a sequence are 160, −80, 40, −20.
Find the next four terms.

8   **a**   Find the highest common factor of 45 and 75.

b   Find the least common multiple of 45 and 75.

9   Write 392 as a product of its prime factors in index form.

10   James races two model cars around a track.
The first car takes 42 seconds to complete each circuit.
The second car takes 1 minute to complete each circuit.
The cars start together from the starting line.
How long will it be before they are together on the
starting line again?

Practice questions

1   Here is a list of numbers:

3   4   6   8   9   12   18

a   Write down **four** different numbers from the list that add up to 30.   *(1 mark)*

b   Write down **one** number in the list that is a multiple of 6.   *(1 mark)*

c   Write down **all** the numbers in the list that are factors of 18.   *(2 marks)*

d   There are two square numbers in the list. Work out the difference between them.   *(2 marks)*

AQA 2008

2   Find a multiple of 4 and a multiple of 5 that add to make a multiple of 6.   *(2 marks)*

AQA 2008

3   **a**   Write 36 as the product of prime factors.
Give your answer in index form.   *(3 marks)*

b   What is the Least Common Multiple (LCM) of 12 and 36?   *(1 mark)*

AQA 2008

Objectives

Examiners would normally expect students who get these grades to be able to:

G

design and use tally charts for discrete and grouped data

D

understand and name different types of data

design and use data collection sheets, surveys and questionnaires

design and use two-way tables for discrete and grouped data

understand and name other types of data collection methods

C

identify possible sources of bias in the design and use of data collection sheets and questionnaires

understand the data-handling cycle

understand that increasing sample size generally leads to better estimates.

You should already know:

✓ how to count in fives for tally charts.

Did you know?

Recording and collecting information

Q: How do you know what has happened in the past and what is happening now?

A: This is because someone has recorded it.

They have then written about it, talked about it, filmed it or collected data about it.

This has always been the case. You may have heard of the Great Fire of London from 1666. This is probably due to a man called Samuel Pepys. He kept a diary for many decades about life in London.

Below is an extract from 2nd September 1666.

'So down [I went], with my heart full of trouble, to the Lieutenant of the Tower, who tells me that it began this morning in the King's baker's house in Pudding Lane, and that it hath burned St. Magnus's Church and most part of Fish Street already. So I rode down to the waterside, . . . and there saw a lamentable fire. . . . Everybody endeavouring to remove their goods, and flinging into the river or bringing them into lighters that lay off; poor people staying in their houses as long as till the very fire touched them, and then running into boats, or clambering from one pair of stairs by the waterside to another. And among other things, the poor pigeons, I perceive, were loth to leave their houses, but hovered about the windows and balconies, till they some of them burned their wings and fell down.'

In statistics you need to think about how data can be collected, recorded and sorted.

Key terms

hypothesis	population	observation
raw data	sample	controlled experiment
primary data	sample size	data logging
secondary data	questionnaire	tally chart
qualitative data	survey	frequency table
quantitative data	open questions	data collection sheet
discrete data	closed questions	observation sheet
continuous data	pilot survey	two-way table

Learn... 3.1 Types of data

The data-handling cycle is the framework for work in statistics. It has four stages.

The data-handling cycle

Stage 1
Specify the question
What are you trying to find out?
This leads to your hypothesis.

Stage 2
Collect the data
What data do you need?
How and where will
you collect them?

Stage 3
Process and represent the data
Calculate statistics and use
diagrams to represent data.

Stage 4
Interpret and discuss
What does your data tell you?
Have you answered your
question? Do you have enough
data to answer it? You may
need to pose a new question
and begin the cycle again.

Evaluate

In any statistical project it is usual to go through the data-handling cycle at least once.

The first stage is to decide on what you are trying to find out. This leads to the **hypothesis**, a statement that you want to investigate.

The second stage is to think about what data you need and how to collect it.

The third stage is to make calculations and summarise the collected data using tables and diagrams.

The fourth stage involves interpreting the diagrams and calculations you have produced. This should lead to an indication of whether the hypothesis has been supported or not.

After completing the full cycle, it may be necessary to refine the original hypothesis and begin the cycle again.

The way you collect the data, and how you represent it, may depend on the type of data you want.

When data is first collected it is called **raw data**. Raw data is data before it has been sorted.

Data can be **primary data** or **secondary data**.
Primary data are data which are collected to investigate the hypothesis.
Secondary data are data which have already been collected, usually for another purpose.

Data can be **qualitative** or **quantitative**.
Qualitative data are not numerical (a quality). These data measure a quality such as taste or colour.
Quantitative data involve numbers of some kind.

Quantitative data can be **discrete** or **continuous**.
Discrete data means exact values such as number of people in a car. It is numerical data that can only take certain values.
Continuous data are numerical data that are always measurements, such as distance or time, that have to be rounded to be recorded. They can take any value.

Example: Draw a table and tick the correct boxes to show whether the following data are qualitative or quantitative, discrete or continuous, and primary or secondary.

a   Sammi collects information about hair colour from the internet.

b   Kaye measures the height of 100 people.

c   Ashad spots the numbers on the sides of trains in the station.

Solution:

Person	Qualitative	Quantitative	Discrete	Continuous	Primary	Secondary
Sammi	✓		✓			✓
Kaye		✓		✓	✓	
Ashad		✓	✓		✓	

Study tip

Many students do not know these words and what they mean.
They often appear in questions so it is important to learn them!

Data are collected to answer questions.

For example, how many miles can a Formula 1 racing car run on one set of tyres?

The **population** of tyres is all the tyres that are the same type.

At some point a **sample** of the tyres will have been tested.

A sample is a small part of the population.

Information about the sample should be true for the population.

The **sample size** is important.

The bigger the sample then the more reliable the information.

So, the more tyres in the sample the more reliable the information.

However, it can be too expensive or time consuming to collect data on a very large sample.

You cannot test tyres then sell them.

Example: Ellie is investigating the question 'What is the average height of a Year 10 girl?'

    a   What is the population for her question?

    b   Give an advantage of a large sample.

    c   Give a disadvantage of a large sample.

Solution: **a**   All Year 10 girls (in the world).

    b   The larger the sample the more reliable the results.

    c   Trying to get too many results will be very time consuming.

Practise... 3.1 Types of data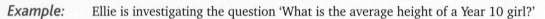

G F E D C

D

1   Copy the table and tick the correct boxes for these data.

    a   Nat finds out the cost of a cruise holiday in the newspaper.

    b   Prita counts the number of red jelly babies in 100 bags.

    c   Niles records the weather at his home every day for one month.

Person	Qualitative	Quantitative	Discrete	Continuous	Primary	Secondary
Nat						
Prita						
Niles						

2   For each of the following say whether the data are quantitative or qualitative.

    a   The number of people at a cricket test match.

    b   The weights of newborn babies.

    c   How many cars a garage sells.

    d   Peoples' opinions of the latest Hollywood blockbuster.

    e   The best dog at Crufts.

    f   The time it takes to run the London Marathon.

    g   The colour of baked beans.

    h   How well your favourite football team played in their last match.

    i   The number of text messages received in a day.

3 For each of the following say whether the data are discrete or continuous.

    a The number of votes for a party at a general election.

    b The number of beans in a tin.

    c The weight of recycling each household produces each week.

    d How many people watch the Nine O'Clock news.

    e How long it takes to walk to school.

    f The number of sheep Farmer Angus has.

    g The weights of Farmer Angus' sheep.

    h The heights of Year 10 students in your school.

    i The number of eggs laid by a hen.

4 Copy and complete the diagram by connecting the statements to their proper description. Use a different colour for each type of data.

The first one has been done for you.

| Lengths of fish caught in a competition |
| Number of goals scored by a football team |
| Ages of teachers at a school |
| Favourite colours in the tutor group |
| Number of sweets in a bag |
| Favourite type of music |
| Person's foot length |
| Person's shoe size |
| Cost of stamps |
| Best player in the Wales rugby team |

Quantitative and discrete

Qualitative

Quantitative and continuous

5 For the questionnaire opposite, copy the details down and then identify whether the information requested is:

- quantitative and discrete
- quantitative and continuous
- qualitative.

6 **a** What is a sample?

    b Why are samples taken rather than looking at the whole population?

    c Give two reasons why a sample should not be too large.

Questionnaire

Age (years)	
Gender (M/F)	
Height (cm)	
Hand span (cm)	
Arm span (cm)	
Foot length (cm)	
Eye colour	
No. of brothers	
No. of sisters	
House number	
Favourite pet	

7 Write down some:

    a qualitative data about a jumper someone has knitted for you

    b quantitative discrete data about the football team you support

    c quantitative continuous data about the launch of a space rocket

    d primary data you might collect about your maths homework

    e secondary data you might collect about keeping a pet rat.

⚙ **8** A newspaper says that the majority of people support the removal of toll charges from the Humber Bridge.

The newspaper based their statement on some data. How do you think they obtained these data – from a sample or the whole population?

Explain your answer.

⚙ **9** A company produces energy-saving light bulbs.

They claim each bulb uses 90% less energy in its lifetime compared to traditional bulbs.

Explain how and why sampling will have been used in testing this claim.

Learn... 3.2 Data collection methods

Writing a good questionnaire

One method of obtaining data is to ask people questions using a **questionnaire**.

Surveys often use questionnaires to find out information.

Questions can be **open** or **closed**.

Open questions allow for any response to be made.

Closed questions control the responses by using options.

It is important that questionnaires:

* are easy to understand
* are short and do not ask for irrelevant information
* give option boxes where possible
* do not have overlap or omissions in them where options boxes are used
* are not biased (such as 'Do you agree that …?')
* avoid asking for personal information unless vital to the survey
* are tested before being used to show up errors or problems (this is called a **pilot survey**).

Example: A shop manager wants to know the age of his customers.

He considers using one of these questions in a questionnaire.

> **Q1.** How old are you?   Answer_____

or

> **Q2.** Tick the box that contains your age.
>
> 20 or under   20 – 40   over 50
>
> ☐   ☐   ☐

a What problems might there be with these questions?

b Write an improved question.

Solution: **a** Q1 is an open question so all kinds of different answers (responses) can be given.
e.g. $18\frac{1}{2}$, 45, not telling you, over 50
This would make the data very difficult to organise.

Also people may not wish to give their exact age.

Q2 is a closed question so people are more likely to answer it. However, the option boxes are badly designed.

Chapter 3 Collecting data

For example:

The groups overlap. If you are 20 which box do you tick?

Some ages are missing. There is no box for people in their 40s.

The groups are quite wide so details are vague about the ages.

b   Tick the box that contains your age.

☐   ☐   ☐   ☐

under 20   20–39   40–59   60 or over

Other methods of collecting data

Surveys (and questionnaires) can be carried out in many ways.

Here are the most common.

Each method has advantages and disadvantages.

Method	Description	Advantages	Disadvantages
Face to face interviews/ telephone surveys	This is the most common method of collecting data and involves asking questions of the interviewee.	Can explain more complex questions if necessary. Interviewer is likely to be more consistent when they record the responses. More likely to get responses than with postal or email surveys.	Takes a lot of time and can be expensive. The interviewer may cause bias by influencing answers. The interviewee is more likely to lie or to refuse to answer a question.
Postal or email surveys	These surveys involve people being selected and sent a questionnaire.	The interviewees can take their time answering and give more thought to the answer. The possibility of interviewer bias is avoided. The cost is usually low.	Low response rates which may cause bias. Can take a long time. Different people might interpret questions in different ways when giving their answers.
Observation	This means observing the situation directly. For example, counting cars at a motorway junction or observing someone to see what shopping they buy. It can take place over a short or a long period of time.	Usually can be relied upon as those being watched do not know they are being observed and so act naturally. Often has little cost involved.	For some experiments, people may act differently because they know they are being observed. Takes a lot of time. Outside influences out of your control can affect the observations. Different observers can view the same thing but record it differently.
Controlled experiment	An experiment is more general than you might think and is not just for science. For example, timing cars along a particular piece of road is an experiment.	Results should be reliable. Repeats of the same conditions are possible if more data is needed.	Getting the right conditions for the experiment may be difficult, costly or time consuming. The experiment may need special equipment or expertise.
Data logging	A 'dumb' machine collects data automatically such as in a shop or car park entrance. The machine could then prevent more cars trying to enter an already full car park.	Once set up, machines can work without needing human resources. Data collection is continued for as long as required.	Machines breaking down can cause problems. As the machine is 'dumb' there is no detail in the data collection.

Practise... 3.2 Data collection methods G F E D C

D

1 The following questions are taken from different surveys.

Write down one criticism of each question.

Rewrite the question in a more suitable form.

a How many hours of TV do you watch each week?

Less than one hour ☐   More than one hour ☐

b What is your favourite football team?

Real Madrid ☐   Luton Town ☐

c How do you spend your leisure time? (You can only tick one box.)

Doing homework ☐   Playing sport ☐   Reading ☐

Computer games ☐   On the internet ☐   Sleeping ☐

d You do like football, don't you?

Yes ☐   No ☐

e How much do you earn each year?

Less than £10 000 ☐   £10 000 to £20 000 ☐   More than £20 000 ☐

f How often do you go to the cinema?

Rarely ☐   Sometimes ☐   Often ☐

g Do you or do you not travel by taxi?

Yes ☐   No ☐

h I hate dogs. What do you think?

So do I ☐   They are OK ☐   Not sure ☐

2 Peter is writing questions for a research task.

This is one question from Peter's questionnaire.

> Skateboarding is an excellent pastime. Don't you agree? Tick one of the boxes.
> Strongly agree ☐   Agree ☐   Don't know ☐

Write down two criticisms of Peter's question.

D
C

3 Write down the data collection method being used in each of these situations giving one advantage and one disadvantage of each method.

a A machine counts entry to a nightclub to prevent it becoming overcrowded.

b Jez fills in some questions on his PC about his mobile phone contract.

c Doctor Jekyll records blood pressure rates of people watching horror films.

d Annie is stopped by a person with a clipboard on the High Street asking about perfume.

e Iona records where students sit in a classroom the first time they enter it.

C

4 Give **two** reasons why a pilot survey might be carried out.

5 For each of the following situations write a single:

a closed question   **b** open question.

    i To find out whether an adult is married or not

    ii To find out the cost of getting the train to Glasgow

c Explain, for each situation, whether your open or closed question is better for finding out the desired information.

6 Write a questionnaire which could be used to find out:

a where students have been on holiday in the last two years

b who likes Wayne Rooney

c the cost of newspapers bought by student families.

> **Study tip**
>
> Remember to allow for all possible responses in a question.

 Learn... 3.3 **Organising data**

Once you have collected data, you need to organise them.

Before being organised in any way, data are called raw data.

The simplest way of organising data is in a **tally chart**.

Each item is shown as a single stroke or 'tally' like this |

Five items are shown as four strokes with a line through like this ⦀⃒

A frequency column can then be used to give the total of the tallies for each value or group of values.

A table like this with total frequencies is called a **frequency table.**

Example: The following information, collected from newspapers, shows the numbers of words in sentences.

16	22	14	12	19	23	18	21	24	29	17
22	17	11	15	18	19	20	22	15	17	18
25	16	21	20	19	15	12	14	8	11	19

Show this information in a tally chart.

Solution: There are too many different values to have a row for each one, so they need to be tallied in groups.

Step 1 Use groups for the data

When choosing groups it is best to have between four and eight groups of the same size.

The tally chart before any tallying could then look like this.

Number of words	Tally	Frequency
5–9		
10–14		
15–19		
20–24		
25–29		

The first group of 5–9 was chosen because the lowest value is 8.

The last group of 25–29 was chosen because the highest value is 29.

The range of each group (a five number spread) was chosen to give between four and eight group rows in the table.

Note – there are other equally good answers, e.g. 6–10, 11–15 and so on.

Step 2 Tally the data into the groups

Now go through the data one by one and tally the values in the chart as shown below.

For example, the first value is 16 so a tally is made in the 15–19 row.

Number of words	Tally	Frequency
5–9	|	1
10–14	卌 |	6
15–19	卌 卌 卌	15
20–24	卌 ||||	9
25–29	||	2

Step 3 The tallies are counted for each group

Count the tallies for each group and put the total in the frequency column.

Step 4 Check frequency total

To check that you have not made any errors add up the frequency values.
Check this against the number of data values in the data set.

There were 33 data values given in the newspaper data set.

Frequency total = 1 + 6 + 15 + 9 + 2 = 33 ✓

Sometimes when collecting data you need to design a **data collection sheet** or **observation sheet**.

These can be very similar to a tally chart but can also be like the one in the following example.

Example: Quinlan is collecting data about the types of vehicles passing his house.

He wants to see if there are differences between weekdays and weekends.

Design an observation sheet that Quinlan could use.

Solution: Here is one possible answer.

	Car	Bus	Lorry	Bicycle	Other
Weekday					
Weekend					

> **Study tip**
>
> In examinations students often forget to include a section for 'other'. Data collection sheets must allow for all possible outcomes in the situation that you are observing.

The table in the example above is an example of a **two-way table.**

Two-way tables are used to show more than one aspect of the data at the same time (time of week and type of vehicle).

Two-way tables can show lots of information at once.

Example: Students in a school were asked whether they had school dinners or packed lunches.
Their results are shown in the table below.

	Boys	Girls
School dinner	24	16
Packed lunch	12	32

Write down nine facts that can be obtained from this two-way table.

Solution: 24 boys have school dinner.

16 girls have school dinner.

12 boys have packed lunch.

32 girls have packed lunch.

40 (24 + 16) students have school dinner.

44 (12 + 32) students have packed lunch.

36 (24 + 12) boys have either school dinner or packed lunch.

48 (16 + 32) girls have either school dinner or packed lunch.

84 (24 + 16 + 12 + 32) students have either school dinner or packed lunch.

Practise... 3.3 Organising data

1   Use the following information to copy and complete the tally chart.

3	2	2	1	3	4	0	1	3
0	2	1	1	4	3	2	2	1
3	2	3	1	1	0	4	3	2
2	0	1	0	1	1	0	2	3

Number	Tally	Frequency
0		
1		
2		
3		
4		

2   The tally chart in Question 1 shows the number of bedrooms in properties advertised in a newspaper. Use your table to provide the following data.

a   How many properties were surveyed altogether?

b   How many properties had three bedrooms?

3   The following information shows the marks obtained by a class in a test.

15	17	23	25	22	18	17	14	12	10	14	18	21	22
23	17	14	10	11	16	18	21	21	22	19	14	13	21

Use the information to copy and complete the tally chart below.

Number	Tally	Frequency
10–13		
14–17		
18–21		
22–25		

4   The tally chart shows the heights (in centimetres to the nearest centimetre) of bushes in a garden centre.

The interval $10 < h \leqslant 15$ includes all heights from 10 cm to 15 cm but not including 10 cm

Number	Tally	Frequency
$5 < h \leqslant 10$	⦀⦀ |||	
$10 < h \leqslant 15$	⦀⦀ ⦀⦀	
$15 < h \leqslant 20$	⦀⦀ ||	
$20 < h \leqslant 25$	⦀⦀	

Copy and complete the table and use it to answer the following questions.

a   How many bushes were surveyed in the garden centre?

b   How many bushes had heights between 10 cm and 15 cm?

c   How many bushes had heights above 15 cm?

D

5 The two-way table shows information about gender and wearing glasses.

	Boys	Girls
Glasses	8	17
No glasses	15	24

Use the table to answer the following questions.

a How many people wear glasses?

b How many girls were in the survey?

c How many boys do not wear glasses?

d What method of data collection could have been used to obtain these data?

⚠ 6 The table shows the different animals on a farm.

	Sheep	Cattle	Pigs
Male	80		90
Female		70	

The farmer has:

- 130 sheep in total
- 340 male animals
- 600 animals in total.

Copy and complete the table

⚠ 7 Mike thinks the weather is often better in the morning than the afternoon.

Design an observation sheet to collect data to investigate this.

 8 A school has 100 students. 52 boys play football.

Of the 33 girls, $\frac{6}{11}$ play football and the rest do not.

Copy and complete the two-way table.

	Play football	Do not play football
Boys		
Girls		

9 The two-way table shows the price of holidays.

Prices per person per week for Costa Packet

	7th April to 5th June	6th June to 21st July	22nd July to 5th Sept
Adult	£124	£168	£215
Child (6–16 years)	£89	£120	£199
Child (0–5 years)	Free	£12	£50

The Brown family consists of 2 adults and 2 children aged 3 and 12 years.

They have a maximum of £500 to spend on a one week holiday at Costa Packet.

a On which dates could they go on their holiday?

b Mr Brown says that if they save up another £200 they could have a two week holiday at Costa Packet.

Is he correct?

3 Assess

1 Use the following information to complete the tally chart.

3	1	2	4	3	2	0	2	3	3
2	0	4	2	2	3	1	1	0	3
2	1	1	3	2	4	2	1	0	0
3	4	3	2	2					

Number	Tally	Frequency
0		
1		
2		
3		
4		

2 The following information shows the marks obtained in a test.

16	18	19	23	24	25	22	15	16	11	10	19	22	25
25	18	10	15	16	19	17	25	23	20	18	12	16	18

Use this information to complete the tally chart below.

Number	Tally	Frequency
10–13		
14–17		
18–21		
22–25		

3 In a survey, 40 adults are asked if they are left-handed or right-handed.

	Men	Women
Left-handed	5	8
Right-handed	19	8

Use the table above to answer the following questions.

a How many men are in the survey?

b How many of the 40 adults are right-handed?

c What fraction of those asked are right-handed men?

d What percentage of women asked are left-handed?

4 Some teachers are asked to choose their favourite snack, chocolate or sweets.
Some of the results are shown in this table.

	Chocolate	Sweets
Male	24	
Female	16	

a A total of 50 male teachers are asked and 30 teachers choose sweets.
Copy and complete the table.

b How many females are asked?

c How many teachers are asked altogether?

d What fraction of the teachers who prefer chocolate are female?
Give your answer in its simplest form.

D **5** **a** Criticise each of the following questionnaire questions.

   i How many hours of television have you watched in the last two months?

   ii Do you or do you not watch news programmes?

b Criticise each of the following questionnaire questions and suggest better alternatives to find out the same information.

   i What do you think about our new improved fruit juice?

   ii How much do you earn?

   iii Do you or do you not agree with the new bypass?

   iv Would you prefer to sit in a non-smoking area?

   v How often do you have a shower?

C **6** Briefly explain a good method for collecting data in each of these situations.

a The average weight of sheep on a farm with 1000 sheep.

b The favourite building of people in your town.

c The average amount of time spent on homework each week by students in your school.

d The average hand span of students in a school.

e The views of villagers on a new shopping centre.

f Information on voting intentions at a general election.

g The number of people entering a shop in the month of December.

7 The owners of a small shop claim to have the cheapest prices for fruit and vegetables in a small town.

Discuss how this could be tested by explaining how the full data-handling cycle could be used in this investigation.

8 Mr and Mrs Khan and their three children (Ali aged 14, Ravi aged 12 and Sabina aged 3) are planning a two-week-long holiday to Spain. The table shows the cost:

	May	June	July
Adult	£152	£174	£225
Child (5–16)	£120	£140	£209
Child (under 5)	Free	£25	£30

How much cheaper is it if they go to Spain in May rather than in June?

Practice questions k

1   **a**   30 students from Year 7 are asked how they travel to school. Their replies, walk (W), bus (B) or car (C) are shown below.

    C   C   B   W   B   W   C   B   W   C

    B   B   W   W   W   C   W   C   C   B

    W   W   B   W   B   W   B   W   W   C

    i   Copy and complete the tally column and the frequency column in the table.   *(3 marks)*

	Tally	Frequency
Walk (W)		
Bus (B)		
Car (C)		
Total		30

    ii   Which reply is the most common?   *(1 mark)*

    iii   What fraction of the students travel by bus?   *(1 mark)*

b   30 students from Year 11 are also asked how they travel to school. Their results are shown in the table.

	Frequency
Walk (W)	13
Bus (B)	14
Car (C)	3
Total	30

Compare how Year 7 and Year 11 travel to school.

    i   Write down **one** difference.   *(1 mark)*

    ii   Write down **one** similarity.   *(1 mark)*

(AQA 2008)

4 Fractions

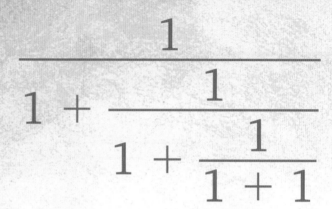

$$\cfrac{1}{1 + \cfrac{1}{1 + \cfrac{1}{1 + 1}}}$$

Did you know?

Continuing fractions

The word fraction comes from the Latin word *frangere* meaning 'to break into pieces'.

Here's an amazing fraction!

$$\cfrac{1}{1 + \cfrac{1}{1 + \cfrac{1}{1 + 1}}}$$

It is part of a series of fractions that starts:

$$1, \quad \cfrac{1}{1 + 1}, \quad \cfrac{1}{1 + \cfrac{1}{1 + 1}}, \quad \cfrac{1}{1 + \cfrac{1}{1 + \cfrac{1}{1 + 1}}}, \quad \cfrac{1}{1 + \cfrac{1}{1 + \cfrac{1}{1 + \cfrac{1}{1 + 1}}}}$$

This is a sequence of what are called continuing fractions. Can you see how the sequence could continue?

The fractions in the sequence simplify to $1, \frac{1}{2}, \frac{2}{3}, \frac{3}{5}, \frac{5}{8}, \dots$ Can you continue this sequence?

Do you recognise these numbers?

You may not be able to do it yet, but by the end of the chapter perhaps you will!

You should already know:

✔ how to add, subtract, multiply and divide simple numbers

✔ the meaning of 'sum', 'difference' and product'

✔ how to use simple fractions such as halves and quarters.

Learn... 4.1 Simple fractions (k)

Numbers between integers are expressed using fractions or decimals. They can be positive or negative.

The number lines below show the numbers from 0 to 5 expressed in different ways.

You could imagine these number lines are rulers. Compare them with your own ruler and with each other. Notice what is the same and what is different.

| 0 | 0.5 | 1 | 1.5 | 2 | 2.5 | 3 | 3.5 | 4 | 4.5 | 5 |

| 0 | $\frac{1}{2}$ | 1 | $1\frac{1}{2}$ | 2 | $2\frac{1}{2}$ | 3 | $3\frac{1}{2}$ | 4 | $4\frac{1}{2}$ | 5 |

| 0 | $\frac{5}{10}$ | 1 | $1\frac{5}{10}$ | 2 | $2\frac{5}{10}$ | 3 | $3\frac{5}{10}$ | 4 | $4\frac{5}{10}$ | 5 |

0 $\frac{1}{4}$ $\frac{1}{2}$ $\frac{3}{4}$ 1 $1\frac{1}{4}$ $1\frac{1}{2}$ $1\frac{3}{4}$ 2 $2\frac{1}{4}$ $2\frac{1}{2}$ $2\frac{3}{4}$ 3 $3\frac{1}{4}$ $3\frac{1}{2}$ $3\frac{3}{4}$ 4 $4\frac{1}{4}$ $4\frac{1}{2}$ $4\frac{3}{4}$ 5

> **Study tip**
>
> Numbers with a whole number and a fraction part are called **mixed numbers**.

Example: Use the number lines to write the following numbers in three different ways.

     a 2.5   **b** $1\frac{1}{2}$

Solution: Find the answers by looking at the same place on the different number lines to see different ways of writing the same number.

     a 2.5, $2\frac{1}{2}$, $2\frac{5}{10}$ **b** $1\frac{1}{2}$, 1.5, $1\frac{5}{10}$

Example: Use the number lines to work out:

     a $1\frac{1}{2} + \frac{3}{4}$ **c** $\frac{3}{4} \times 3$

     b $1\frac{1}{2} + 1\frac{1}{2} + 1\frac{1}{2}$ **d** $\frac{5}{10} + \frac{7}{10}$

Solution: The number line adjacent shows how to add $1\frac{1}{2}$ and $\frac{3}{4}$ to make $2\frac{1}{4}$

Go to $1\frac{1}{2}$ (red arrow), then move $\frac{3}{4}$ to the right (blue arrow).

The blue arrow ends at $2\frac{1}{4}$. So $1\frac{1}{2} + \frac{3}{4} = 2\frac{1}{4}$

So the answers are:

     a $2\frac{1}{4}$ **c** $2\frac{1}{4}$

     b $4\frac{1}{2}$ **d** $\frac{12}{10}$, which is $1\frac{2}{10}$ or $1\frac{1}{5}$

> **Study tip**
>
> Remember that $2\frac{1}{4}$ means two plus one-quarter and not two times one-quarter.

Practise... 4.1 Simple fractions (k)

1   **a** Arrange each list of numbers in order of size, starting with the smallest.

     i 4.5, 1.5, 0, 1, 0.5, 3.5, 4

     ii 1.6, 0.8, 3.2, 0.5, 5.0, 4.1

     iii 4.5, $2\frac{1}{2}$, 3.0, $1\frac{5}{10}$, 1.5, $3\frac{1}{2}$, $3\frac{1}{4}$

  b Which set of numbers has the largest range?

G
F

F

2 A fraction can be expressed as a percentage, for example, $\frac{1}{2} = 50\%$

Copy and complete the following:

$\frac{1}{4} = \underline{\quad}\%$ $\qquad\qquad$ $\frac{3}{4} = \underline{\quad}\%$

3 Work out these additions and subtractions. Look at the sequences of questions and answers to help you to understand the fractions.

a **i** $2\frac{1}{2} + \frac{1}{4}$ $\quad$ **ii** $2\frac{1}{2} + \frac{1}{2}$ $\quad$ **iii** $2\frac{1}{2} + \frac{3}{4}$ $\quad$ **iv** $2\frac{1}{2} + 1$ $\quad$ **v** $2\frac{1}{2} + 1\frac{1}{4}$

b **i** $2\frac{1}{2} + \frac{1}{10}$ $\quad$ **ii** $2\frac{1}{2} + \frac{2}{10}$ $\quad$ **iii** $2\frac{1}{2} + \frac{3}{10}$ $\quad$ **iv** $2\frac{1}{2} + \frac{4}{5}$ $\quad$ **v** $2\frac{1}{2} + \frac{5}{10}$

c **i** $2\frac{1}{2} - \frac{1}{4}$ $\quad$ **ii** $2\frac{1}{2} - \frac{1}{2}$ $\quad$ **iii** $2\frac{1}{2} - \frac{3}{4}$ $\quad$ **iv** $2\frac{1}{2} - 1$ $\quad$ **v** $2\frac{1}{2} - 1\frac{1}{4}$

d Write down the next two calculations in each sequence.

4 Write down three different addition and subtraction calculations that make each of these answers.

a 4.5 $\qquad$ **b** $3\frac{1}{2}$ $\qquad$ **c** $2\frac{1}{4}$ $\qquad$ **d** 0 $\qquad$ **e** $\frac{1}{10}$

5 Work out:

a **i** $3 \times \frac{1}{2}$ $\quad$ **ii** $3 \times 1\frac{1}{2}$ $\quad$ **iii** $3 \times 2\frac{1}{2}$ $\quad$ **iv** $3 \times 3\frac{1}{2}$

b **i** $1 \times \frac{3}{4}$ $\quad$ **ii** $2 \times \frac{3}{4}$ $\quad$ **iii** $3 \times \frac{3}{4}$ $\quad$ **iv** $4 \times \frac{3}{4}$ $\quad$ **v** $5 \times \frac{3}{4}$

c Jenny notices that in these multiplications the answers are smaller than the number being multiplied. Explain why.

6 Sort these fractions out into three sets: less than $\frac{1}{2}$, equal to $\frac{1}{2}$, greater than $\frac{1}{2}$

$\frac{5}{10}, \quad \frac{3}{4}, \quad 0.6, \quad \frac{3}{10}, \quad \frac{1}{4}, \quad \frac{4}{5}, \quad \frac{7}{10}, \quad \frac{2}{4}$

! 7 Complete these sets of fractions.

a $\dfrac{1}{2} = \dfrac{}{2x} = \dfrac{y}{} = \dfrac{}{z}$

b $\dfrac{}{} = \dfrac{2a}{3a} = \dfrac{2b}{} = \dfrac{}{6c} = \dfrac{}{d}$

8 The London Eye takes half an hour to travel the full 360° journey. How many degrees does it turn in quarter of an hour?

9 At the gym, Rick spends a quarter of an hour on weights, three-quarters of an hour on the running machine and half an hour in the pool.
How much time is this in total?

10 The lengths of notes in music are fractions of one another.

Whole note $\circ$ $\quad$ Half a note $\circ$ $\quad$ Quarter of a note $\bullet$ $\quad$ Eighth of a note $\bullet$

Add up the notes to find which of these sequences are equivalent to a whole note.
(For example, in **a** there are four quarter notes. This is equivalent to one whole note because $\frac{1}{4} + \frac{1}{4} + \frac{1}{4} + \frac{1}{4} = 1$)

a $\quad$ **b** $\quad$ **c** $\quad$ **d**

Invent a note sequence of your own equivalent to one whole note.

Learn... 4.2 Equivalent fractions

Equivalent fractions are fractions that are equal in value, such as $\frac{1}{2}$ and $\frac{2}{4}$

In the last section, the number lines showed many other equivalent fractions.

This diagram shows that $\frac{9}{12}$ is equivalent to $\frac{3}{4}$

0 ← $\frac{9}{12}$ → 1

$\frac{1}{12}$ $\frac{1}{12}$ $\frac{1}{12}$ $\frac{1}{12}$ $\frac{1}{12}$ $\frac{1}{12}$ $\frac{1}{12}$ $\frac{1}{12}$ $\frac{1}{12}$ $\frac{1}{12}$ $\frac{1}{12}$ $\frac{1}{12}$

$\frac{1}{4}$ $\frac{1}{4}$ $\frac{1}{4}$ $\frac{1}{4}$

← $\frac{3}{4}$ →

Equivalent fractions can be changed into one another. $\frac{9}{12} \underset{\div 3}{\overset{\div 3}{=}} \frac{3}{4}$ and $\frac{3}{4} \underset{\times 3}{\overset{\times 3}{=}} \frac{9}{12}$

The value of a fraction does not change when you multiply or divide the top (**numerator**) and the bottom (**denominator**) by the same number.

$\frac{9}{12}$ and $\frac{3}{4}$ have the same value even though they look different.

Example: Find three fractions equivalent to $\frac{3}{15}$

Solution: There is no end to the possible answers to this question.

Multiplying or dividing both the numerator and the denominator by any number gives a fraction equivalent to $\frac{3}{15}$

So, you can divide numerator and denominator by 3 to make $\frac{1}{5}$

You can multiply numerator and denominator by 2 to make $\frac{6}{30}$ or by 10 to give $\frac{30}{150}$

There are many other possibilities.

Practise... 4.2 Equivalent fractions

For Questions 1–3, use your calculator to simplify the fractions. Type in any fraction using the $\boxed{a\frac{b}{c}}$ or $\boxed{\Box}$ key and then press $\boxed{=}$ to find its simplest form.

1 **a** Write down the simplest equivalent fraction for each of these.

  i $\frac{2}{12}$ **iii** $\frac{4}{12}$ **v** $\frac{8}{12}$ **vii** $\frac{10}{12}$

  ii $\frac{3}{12}$ **iv** $\frac{6}{12}$ **vi** $\frac{9}{12}$ **viii** $\frac{12}{12}$

  b **i** List the fractions with a denominator of 12 that cannot be made simpler.

  ii Explain why they cannot be made simpler.

2 Find the odd fraction out in this list: $\frac{8}{10}, \frac{6}{8}, \frac{4}{5}, \frac{16}{20}$

Now do the question by changing each of the fractions to decimal form.

G

G

3 Jack says that $\frac{3}{5} = \frac{6}{8}$

Is he correct? Explain your answer.

4 Write down five fractions that are equivalent to $\frac{2}{3}$

5 Simplify these fractions.

a **i** $\frac{3}{9}$ **ii** $\frac{6}{9}$ **iii** $\frac{9}{9}$

b **i** $\frac{10}{100}$ **iii** $\frac{30}{100}$ **v** $\frac{50}{100}$ **vii** $\frac{70}{100}$ **ix** $\frac{90}{100}$

ii $\frac{20}{100}$ **iv** $\frac{40}{100}$ **vi** $\frac{60}{100}$ **viii** $\frac{80}{100}$ **x** $\frac{100}{100}$

c **i** $\frac{2}{18}$ **iii** $\frac{4}{18}$ **v** $\frac{8}{18}$ **vii** $\frac{10}{18}$ **ix** $\frac{14}{18}$ **xi** $\frac{18}{18}$

ii $\frac{3}{18}$ **iv** $\frac{6}{18}$ **vi** $\frac{9}{18}$ **viii** $\frac{12}{18}$ **x** $\frac{16}{18}$

d **i** $\frac{16}{24}$ **ii** $\frac{25}{30}$ **iii** $\frac{24}{36}$ **iv** $\frac{28}{24}$ **v** $\frac{36}{48}$ **vi** $\frac{24}{60}$

6 Simplify these fractions.

a $\frac{16}{24}$ **c** $\frac{24}{36}$ **e** $\frac{36}{48}$

b $\frac{25}{30}$ **d** $\frac{28}{42}$ **f** $\frac{24}{60}$

F

7 Find **a** two fractions with a denominator of 24 that can be simplified and **b** two fractions with a denominator of 24 that cannot be simplified.

8 Copy and complete these equivalent fraction statements.

a **i** $\frac{5}{9} = \frac{}{18}$ **ii** $\frac{8}{9} = \frac{}{18}$ **iii** $\frac{}{9} = \frac{4}{18}$ **iv** $\frac{}{9} = \frac{14}{18}$

b **i** $\frac{1}{6} = \frac{}{24}$ **ii** $\frac{5}{6} = \frac{}{24}$ **iii** $\frac{}{6} = \frac{4}{24}$ **iv** $\frac{}{6} = \frac{12}{24}$

c **i** $\frac{6}{12} = \frac{}{4} = \frac{}{2}$ **ii** $\frac{1}{4} = \frac{}{8} = \frac{}{16} = \frac{}{40} = \frac{50}{}$

9 This is a fraction wall diagram.

$\frac{1}{10}$	$\frac{1}{10}$	$\frac{1}{10}$	$\frac{1}{10}$	$\frac{1}{10}$	$\frac{1}{10}$	$\frac{1}{10}$	$\frac{1}{10}$	$\frac{1}{10}$	$\frac{1}{10}$
$\frac{1}{5}$		$\frac{1}{5}$		$\frac{1}{5}$		$\frac{1}{5}$		$\frac{1}{5}$	
$\frac{1}{2}$					$\frac{1}{2}$				

Use this diagram to copy and complete these equivalent fraction statements.

a $\frac{3}{5} = \frac{6}{}$ **b** $\frac{}{} = \frac{1}{2}$ **c** $\frac{}{10} = \frac{}{5} = \frac{}{2} = 1$

10 Write down three equivalent fraction statements about:

a sixths, twelfths and eighteenths

b tenths, twentieths and hundredths.

11 Fractions can be marked on a grid like this one. The dot shows $\frac{1}{4}$, because its numerator is 1 and its denominator is 4.

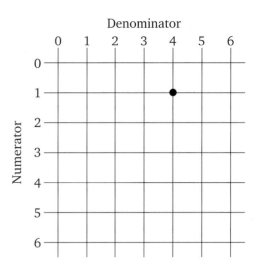

a Make a grid like this, going up to 12 in each direction.

b Mark all the fractions that are equivalent to 1 ($\frac{1}{1}$, $\frac{2}{2}$, $\frac{3}{3}$, etc). What do you notice?

c Mark two more sets of equivalent fractions on the grid. Compare one set with the other. What is the same and what is different?

d Where do top-heavy (improper) fractions appear on the grid?

e How can the grid help you to arrange fractions in order?

f How can the grid help you to simplify fractions?

12 This is a fraction wall diagram.

$\frac{1}{16}$	$\frac{1}{16}$	$\frac{1}{16}$	$\frac{1}{16}$	$\frac{1}{16}$	$\frac{1}{16}$	$\frac{1}{16}$	$\frac{1}{16}$	$\frac{1}{16}$	$\frac{1}{16}$	$\frac{1}{16}$	$\frac{1}{16}$	$\frac{1}{16}$	$\frac{1}{16}$	$\frac{1}{16}$	$\frac{1}{16}$
$\frac{1}{8}$		$\frac{1}{8}$		$\frac{1}{8}$		$\frac{1}{8}$		$\frac{1}{8}$		$\frac{1}{8}$		$\frac{1}{8}$		$\frac{1}{8}$	
$\frac{1}{4}$				$\frac{1}{4}$				$\frac{1}{4}$				$\frac{1}{4}$			
$\frac{1}{2}$								$\frac{1}{2}$							
$\frac{1}{1}$															

a Use the fraction wall to write down three equivalent fraction statements.

b **i** Use the fraction wall to write down three fractions that are equivalent to the whole number 1.

ii What can you say about the numerator and the denominator of a fraction that is equivalent to 1?

iii Which fractions in this list are equivalent to 1?

$$\frac{100}{100} \quad \frac{2\frac{1}{2}}{2\frac{1}{2}} \quad \frac{200}{100} \quad \frac{x}{x} \quad \frac{2x}{2x} \quad \frac{2x}{x} \quad \frac{x}{2x} \quad \frac{a}{a}$$

iv Which fractions in the list above are equivalent to 2?

13 A bar of chocolate is split into 24 equal pieces and Sam eats 4 of them.

Joe has another bar of chocolate the same size that is split into 30 equal pieces.

How many pieces of that bar should Joe eat so that he eats the same amount of chocolate as Sam?

14 Mrs Howes marks Year 9's homework. She changes marks out of 20 to marks out of 100 (percentages).

Copy and complete these statements about the marks.

a $\frac{10}{20} = \frac{\quad}{100} = 50\%$

c $\frac{16}{20} = \frac{\quad}{100} = \underline{\quad}\%$

b $\frac{5}{20} = \frac{\quad}{100} = \underline{\quad}\%$

d $\frac{\quad}{20} = \frac{\quad}{100} = 75\%$

Learn... 4.3 Arranging fractions in order

Equivalent fractions help you to put fractions in order of size.

Change the fractions to equivalent fractions all with the same denominator, then compare the size of the fractions by looking at the numerators.

Study tip

Another method of arranging fractions in order is to change each fraction to a decimal. You do this by dividing the numerator by the denominator (find out why this works). Then put the decimals in order.

Example: Arrange the following fractions in order of size, smallest first.

$$\frac{2}{3} \quad \frac{1}{4} \quad \frac{5}{6} \quad \frac{1}{12} \quad \frac{1}{2}$$

Solution: In order to put fractions in order of size, first change them all to the same denominator.

$$\frac{2}{3} \quad \frac{1}{4} \quad \frac{5}{6} \quad \frac{1}{12} \quad \frac{1}{2}$$

All the denominators go into 12 exactly, so 12 is a good number for the denominator.

Change the fractions to twelfths: $\frac{2}{3} = \frac{8}{12}$ and so on. ($\times 4$)

So the list $\frac{2}{3} \quad \frac{1}{4} \quad \frac{5}{6} \quad \frac{1}{12} \quad \frac{1}{2}$ becomes $\frac{8}{12} \quad \frac{3}{12} \quad \frac{10}{12} \quad \frac{1}{12} \quad \frac{6}{12}$

In order of size this is $\quad \frac{1}{12} \quad \frac{3}{12} \quad \frac{6}{12} \quad \frac{8}{12} \quad \frac{10}{12} \quad$ or $\quad \frac{1}{12} \quad \frac{1}{4} \quad \frac{1}{2} \quad \frac{2}{3} \quad \frac{5}{6}$

Practise... 4.3 Arranging fractions in order F

All these questions can be done without a calculator and you should make sure that you are able to do without. Also make sure that you can use your calculator to speed up and check your work, using your $\boxed{a\frac{b}{c}}$ or $\boxed{}$ key if you have one.

1 a Change these fractions to twelfths and arrange them in order from smallest to largest.

$$\frac{3}{4} \quad \frac{1}{3} \quad \frac{5}{12} \quad \frac{1}{6} \quad \frac{1}{2}$$

b Change these fractions to fifteenths and arrange them in order from smallest to largest.

$$\frac{3}{5} \quad \frac{2}{3} \quad \frac{7}{15} \quad \frac{4}{15}$$

c Change these fractions to hundredths and arrange them in order from smallest to largest.

$$\frac{3}{4} \quad \frac{1}{5} \quad \frac{7}{20} \quad \frac{3}{10} \quad \frac{1}{2} \quad \frac{57}{100} \quad \frac{8}{25} \quad \frac{13}{50}$$

Fractions with a denominator of 100 are percentages, for example $\frac{70}{100}$ is 70%

2 Arrange these fractions in order of size: $\frac{2}{3} \quad \frac{2}{5} \quad \frac{1}{2} \quad \frac{7}{10}$

3 **a** What is a good denominator for ordering each of the following?

  i Thirds, quarters and sixths

  ii Fifths, twentieths and fiftieths

 b Explain why it is not easy to change fifths to twelfths.

4 **a** Abby says 'Five-eighths is smaller than five-twelfths.' Is she correct?

 b Ali says 'Four-fifths is smaller than five-sixths.' Is he correct?

5 Find a fraction that is:

 a between one-half and three-quarters

 b between nine-tenths and one.

Learn... 4.4 Adding and subtracting fractions

To add fractions with different denominators you first have to change them so that they have the same denominator.

To find the sum of three-quarters and two-thirds you have to change the fractions to twelfths, because 12 is the smallest number that is a multiple of both 3 and 4.

$\frac{3}{4}$ is $\frac{9}{12}$

> **Hint**
>
> 24, or any other multiple of 12, would also have worked here, but 12 is better because it is smaller, and so easier to use. You can always find a number that is a multiple of two numbers by multiplying them together. (Here, $3 \times 4 = 12$)

$\frac{2}{3}$ is $\frac{8}{12}$

So $\frac{3}{4} + \frac{2}{3} = \frac{9}{12} + \frac{8}{12} = \frac{17}{12} = 1\frac{5}{12}$

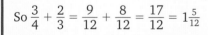
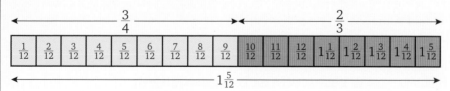

This is how to do the calculation without diagrams: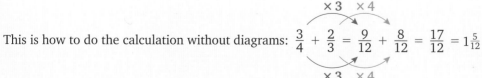

Subtracting is just the same: $\frac{3}{4} - \frac{2}{3} = \frac{9}{12} - \frac{8}{12} = \frac{1}{12}$

Mixed numbers are numbers that contain an **integer** (whole number) and a fraction.
To add mixed numbers, first change them to **improper** (top-heavy) fractions:

$$2\frac{2}{5} - 1\frac{2}{3} = \frac{12}{5} - \frac{5}{3}$$

Then subtract the fractions:

$$\overset{\times 3 \quad \times 5}{\frac{12}{5} - \frac{5}{3}} = \frac{36}{15} - \frac{25}{15} = \frac{11}{15}$$

$$\times 3 \quad \times 5$$

> **Hint**
>
> The denominator of the improper fraction is the same as the denominator in the fraction part of the mixed number. The easy way to find the numerator is to multiply the denominator by the integer part of the mixed number and add the numerator of the fraction part.
>
> So $1\frac{2}{3} = \frac{3 \times 1 + 2}{3} = \frac{5}{3}$

Example: Work out $3\frac{2}{3} - 2\frac{5}{6}$

Solution: Change the mixed numbers to improper fractions, then change them so that they have the same denominator.

$$3\frac{2}{3} - 2\frac{5}{6} = \frac{11}{3} - \frac{17}{6} = \frac{22}{6} - \frac{17}{6} = \frac{5}{6}$$

Practise...

4.4 Adding and subtracting fractions

G F E D C

D

1   Work out:

   a $\frac{4}{5} + \frac{3}{4}$ **d** $\frac{5}{8} - \frac{1}{3}$

   b $\frac{4}{5} - \frac{3}{4}$ **e** $\frac{5}{6} - \frac{4}{9}$

   c $\frac{5}{8} + \frac{1}{3}$ **f** $\frac{7}{20} + \frac{2}{5} + \frac{1}{4}$

> **Hint**
>
> Adding three fractions is just the same as adding two: just change the fractions so they all have the same denominator and then add all three numerators.

2   Fran says that:

$$\frac{1}{2} + \frac{1}{2} = \frac{1+1}{2+2} = \frac{2}{4} = \frac{1}{2}$$

   What has Fran done wrong?

3   Two glasses contain $\frac{9}{10}$ of a litre of water altogether.

   One glass contains $\frac{17}{20}$ of a litre.

   How much does the other contain?

4   Four of these calculations give the same answer and one gives a different answer. Which is the odd one out? Show how you worked it out.

   $\frac{1}{2} + \frac{1}{3} + \frac{1}{6}$

   $\frac{1}{2} + \frac{1}{2}$

   $\frac{2}{3} + \frac{1}{4} + \frac{1}{12}$

   $\frac{3}{4} + \frac{1}{8} + \frac{1}{16}$

   $\frac{3}{5} + \frac{1}{3} + \frac{1}{15}$

5 Work out:

a $\frac{3}{4} + \frac{3}{4}$

b $\frac{3}{4} + \frac{3}{4} + \frac{3}{4}$

c $\frac{3}{4} + \frac{3}{4} + \frac{3}{4} + \frac{3}{4}$

d $\frac{3}{4} + \frac{3}{4} + \frac{3}{4} + \frac{3}{4} + \frac{3}{4}$

6 Work out:

a $3\frac{3}{4} + 1\frac{4}{5}$ b $3\frac{3}{4} - 1\frac{4}{5}$

7 Anne's recipe needs $\frac{2}{3}$ of a cup of sugar. She has $\frac{3}{4}$ of a cup. How much will she have left?

June's recipes need $1\frac{1}{2}$ cups of sugar and $1\frac{2}{3}$ cups of sugar. How much sugar does June need altogether?

8 (In America, fabric is sold in yards and fractions of a yard rather than in metres and tenths of a metre as in the UK.)

A pair of trousers needs $1\frac{1}{2}$ yards of fabric and a jacket needs $2\frac{3}{8}$ yards. How much fabric is needed in total?

9 Amy mixes a fruit drink. It is made up of $\frac{1}{3}$ of a litre of orange juice, $\frac{2}{5}$ of a litre of apple juice and $\frac{7}{10}$ of a litre of blackcurrant juice. How much fruit drink is there in total? Amy adds some water to make it up to 3 litres. How much water has she added?

Learn... 4.5 Multiplying and dividing fractions

Multiplying fractions

To find the area of a rectangle you have to multiply two numbers: $2 \times 3 = 6$

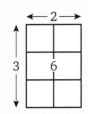

You can multiply fractions to find areas too.
The diagram shows that three-quarters times two-thirds is six-twelfths, which is a half.

$\frac{3}{4} \times \frac{2}{3} = \frac{6}{12} = \frac{1}{2}$

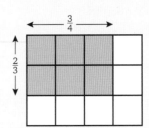

The diagram shows why the answer is smaller than both three-quarters and two-thirds.

The 6 in the sixth-twelfths comes from the shaded area – it is three units across and two units down, so contains six squares.

The 12 in the answer comes from the whole area – it is four units across and three units down, so contains 12 squares.

Six out of 12 squares are shaded, so the answer is $\frac{6}{12}$, which simplifies to $\frac{1}{2}$

This is how to do it without the diagram: multiply numerators $\quad \div 6$

$$\frac{3}{4} \times \frac{2}{3} = \frac{3 \times 2}{4 \times 3} = \frac{6}{12} = \frac{1}{2}$$

multiply denominators $\quad \div 6$

You can simplify before working out: $\frac{3}{4} \times \frac{2}{3} = \frac{{}^1\cancel{3} \times \cancel{2}^1}{{}_2\cancel{4} \times \cancel{3}_1} = \frac{1 \times 1}{2 \times 1} = \frac{1}{2}$

> **Study tip**
>
> Be careful not to mix up the method for adding fractions and the method for multiplying.

What about calculations such as $1\frac{3}{4} \times 2\frac{2}{3}$?

You can do this by changing the mixed numbers to improper fractions:

$$1\frac{3}{4} \times 2\frac{2}{3} = \frac{7}{4} \times \frac{8}{3}$$

Then simplify if possible and multiply to get the answer.

$$1\frac{3}{4} \times 2\frac{2}{3} = \frac{7}{{}_1\cancel{4}} \times \frac{\cancel{8}^2}{3} = \frac{7}{1} \times \frac{2}{3} = \frac{14}{3} = 4\frac{2}{3}$$

If the calculation involves integers, just write the integer as a fraction with a denominator of 1.

$$5 \times 4\frac{1}{3} = \frac{5}{1} \times \frac{13}{4} = \frac{65}{4} = 16\frac{1}{4}$$

Division of fractions

To divide by a fraction, you multiply by its **reciprocal.**

Dividing by $\frac{3}{4}$ is the same as multiplying by $\frac{4}{3}$:

$$\frac{2}{3} \div \frac{3}{4} = \frac{2}{3} \times \frac{4}{3} = \frac{8}{9}$$

> **Hint**
>
> You find the reciprocal of a fraction by turning it upside down. So the reciprocal of $\frac{3}{4}$ is $\frac{4}{3}$.

For mixed numbers, change them to improper fractions first:

$$1\frac{3}{4} \div 2\frac{2}{3} = \frac{7}{4} \div \frac{8}{3}$$

Then turn the second fraction to its reciprocal and multiply:

$$\frac{7}{4} \times \frac{3}{8} = \frac{21}{32}$$

> **Study tip**
>
> Make sure you understand all these fraction ideas so that you do not get them mixed up in the exam.

Example: Work out:

    a $3\frac{1}{2} \times 2\frac{5}{6}$

    b $4 \div 3\frac{2}{3}$

Solution: **a** Change the mixed numbers to improper fractions, then multiply numerators and denominators.

$$3\frac{1}{2} \times 2\frac{5}{6} = \frac{7}{2} \times \frac{17}{6} = \frac{119}{12} = 9\frac{11}{12}$$

    b Write the integer as a fraction with a denominator of 1, then change the mixed number to an improper fraction. Change dividing to multiplying by the reciprocal, then multiply numerators and denominators.

$$4 \div 3\frac{2}{3} = \frac{4}{1} \div \frac{11}{3} = \frac{4}{1} \times \frac{3}{11} = \frac{12}{11} = 1\frac{1}{11}$$

Practise... 4.5 Multiplying and dividing fractions (k) G F E D C

1 Work out:

  a **i** $\frac{2}{5} \div \frac{1}{3}$ **ii** $\frac{1}{3} \div \frac{2}{5}$

  b What do you notice about the answers?

  c Try another pair of fractions and compare answers.

  d Does the same thing happen with $5 \div 3$ and $3 \div 5$?

2 The reciprocal of a fraction is $3\frac{7}{8}$. What is the fraction?

3 These calculations can all be done very easily. How?

  a $3\frac{2}{5} \div 3\frac{2}{5}$ **b** $1\frac{1}{2} \times \frac{2}{3} \div \frac{2}{3}$ **c** $1\frac{1}{2} \times \frac{2}{3} \times \frac{3}{2}$

4 Work out:

  a $\frac{4}{5} \times \frac{3}{4}$ **e** $2\frac{1}{2} \times 6$ **i** $6\frac{1}{2} \times \frac{2}{5}$

  b $\frac{4}{5} \div \frac{3}{4}$ **f** $2\frac{1}{2} \div 5$ **j** $\frac{3}{4} \div 3\frac{1}{2}$

  c $\frac{5}{8} \times \frac{1}{3}$ **g** $10 \times 2\frac{3}{5}$ **k** $3\frac{3}{4} \times 2\frac{1}{2}$

  d $\frac{5}{8} \div \frac{1}{3}$ **h** $12 \div 1\frac{3}{4}$ **l** $2\frac{3}{5} \div 2\frac{1}{6}$

5 **a** How many times does $3\frac{1}{2}$ go into 21?

  b How many times does 21 go into $3\frac{1}{2}$?

6 Work out:

  a $\left(1\frac{1}{4}\right)^2$ **b** $\frac{3}{4} + 2\frac{1}{2} \times 1\frac{1}{2}$ **c** $\left(\frac{3}{4} + 2\frac{1}{2}\right) \times 1\frac{1}{2}$

7 **a** Which is bigger, $\frac{5}{6} \times \frac{2}{7}$ or $\frac{5}{6} + \frac{2}{7}$?
     Explain how you got your answer.

  b Which is bigger, $2\frac{1}{2} \times 1\frac{1}{4}$ or $2\frac{1}{2} + 1\frac{1}{4}$?
     Explain how you got your answer.

8 Jack has a dog that eats $\frac{2}{3}$ of a tin of food each day.
How many tins will be needed to feed the dog for five days?

9 A recipe for 16 biscuits needs $\frac{2}{3}$ of a cup of flour.
How much flour is needed for 48 biscuits?

10 Sanjay needs four curtains. Each curtain uses $3\frac{3}{4}$ yards of fabric.
How much fabric is that altogether?

11 A kilometre is about $\frac{5}{8}$ of a mile. How many miles are there in 16 km?
How many km in 100 miles?

12 Find the missing numbers. (These may be fractions or mixed numbers.)

  a $\frac{1}{2} \times \boxed{} = 1$ **c** $2\frac{1}{2} \times \boxed{} = 4$

  b $\frac{1}{2} \div \boxed{} = 1$ **d** $\boxed{} \div \frac{3}{4} = 6$

D

C

Learn... 4.6 Fractions of quantities

How do you work out three-quarters of something?

Without a calculator, a good way is to work out $\frac{1}{4}$ first, then find $\frac{3}{4}$.

Example: Find $\frac{3}{4}$ of £100.

Solution: $\frac{1}{4}$ of £100 = £100 ÷ 4 = £25

So $\frac{3}{4}$ of £100 = 3 × £25 = £75

Example: Five people have a meal and share the bill of £77.55 equally between them.

How much does each person pay?

Solution: The amount each person has to pay is one-fifth of the whole bill. To find one-fifth of something, divide it by 5.

$\frac{1}{5}$ of £77.55 = £77.55 ÷ 5 = £15.51 $\quad \frac{15.51}{5)77.55}$

Example: Suppose one of the people in the previous example pays for his friend as well. How much does he pay?

Solution: He pays $\frac{2}{5}$ of £77.55.

$\frac{1}{5}$ of £77.55 = £77.55 ÷ 5 = £15.51

So $\frac{2}{5}$ of £77.55 = 2 × £15.51 = £31.02

$$\begin{array}{r} 15.51 \\ \times \quad 2 \\ \hline 3_11.02 \end{array}$$

To find a fraction of a quantity, divide the quantity by the denominator of the fraction, then multiply the result by the numerator of the fraction. (Alternatively you can multiply the quantity by the numerator and divide by the denominator).

Hint

Another way is to multiply by 2, then divide by 5:

£77.55 × 2 = £155.10

£155.10 ÷ 5 = £31.02

This gives the same answer, so it does not matter whether you divide by 5 first and then multiply by 2, or multiply by 2 first, then divide by 5.

Study tip

This is a non-calculator unit, so you must know how to multiply and divide without a calculator.

Example: Find $\frac{5}{6}$ of 216.

Solution: $\frac{5}{6}$ of 216 = $\frac{216}{6}$ × 5 = 36 × 5 = 180

Study tip

This is an important process – make sure you really understand it and can use it in different circumstances, with and without a calculator.

Practise... **4.6 Fractions of quantities**

F

1   Work out:

   a   one-eighth of 32   **c**   one-tenth of 340

   b   one-sixth of 24   **d**   one-hundredth of £15

2   **a**   Find $\frac{2}{5}$ of these numbers.

   i   20   **ii**   25   **iii**   30   **iv**   35

   Explain why the answers go up by two each time.

   By how much would the answers go up each time if you calculated $\frac{4}{5}$ of the numbers instead of $\frac{2}{5}$?

3   Find:

   a   three-eighths of £200

   b   five-twelfths of 1200 kg

   c   four-ninths of £180

   d   six-elevenths of 33 km

4   Find three-quarters of these quantities.

   a   100 m   **c**   10 km   **e**   20 cm^2

   b   800 g   **d**   1 metre

5   Which is bigger, $\frac{4}{5}$ of 1 kg or $\frac{3}{4}$ of 1.2 kg?

6   Amy has £120. She gives one-quarter of it to her brother and two-thirds of the remainder to her sister. She spends £10 on a DVD.
   How much money does Amy have left?

7   Three-fifths of a number is 27.
   What is the number?

8   A pint is 20 fluid ounces. Chris uses $\frac{3}{4}$ of a pint of milk in a recipe.
   How many fluid ounces does she use?

9   A college has a grant of £9000 to spend on ICT equipment.
   Two-thirds of it is to be spent on laptops and one-third on software.
   How much is spent on laptops? How much is spent on software?

10   **a**   Work out what these prices are when reduced in a sale.

   i   A dress costing £48 is reduced by one-third.

   ii   A refrigerator costing £325 is reduced by a fifth.

   iii A CD player costing £55 is reduced by a quarter.

   iv   A television costing £325.40 is reduced by a tenth.

   b   In a sale the price of a coat is reduced by one-fifth to £80.
         What was the original price?

11   Three-quarters of one number is the same as half of another number.
   What could the two numbers be?

Learn... 4.7 One quantity as a fraction of another

One of the most useful fraction calculations is to work out one number or quantity as a fraction of another. In real life, it is usual to turn the fractions into decimals or percentages so that they can be easily compared.

To work out one quantity as a fraction of another, change both quantities to the same units if necessary. Write the first quantity as the numerator and the second quantity as the denominator and simplify the fraction.

Example: What fraction of £5 is 25p?

Solution: First change £5 to 500p.

$$\frac{25}{500} = \frac{1}{20}$$

$\div 25$ (numerator)
$\div 25$ (denominator)

Simplify the fraction by dividing the numerator and the denominator by the common factor 25.

> **Study tip**
>
> Make sure you divide the numerator by the denominator, not the other way round.

The fraction in its simplified form is $\frac{1}{20}$.

Example: Some patients are taking part in a medical trial. 150 of them with a disease are given Drug A and 102 of them get better. 120 of them are given Drug B and 80 of them get better.

Find the fraction of patients who get better with each drug and simplify the fractions.

Solution: The fraction of patients who get better with Drug A is $\frac{102}{150} = \frac{51}{75} = \frac{17}{25}$

$\div 2$ $\div 3$

> **Study tip**
>
> Simplify your fractions whenever possible.

The fraction of patients who get better with Drug B is $\frac{80}{120} = \frac{8}{12} = \frac{2}{3}$

$\div 10$ $\div 4$

(Note: in real life, doctors need to compare the fractions to see which drug seems to be more effective. They would change the fractions to decimals or percentages.)

Example: Three-tenths of a number is 90. What is the number?

Solution: Three-tenths of the number is 90, so one-tenth of the number is $90 \div 3 = 30$

So the whole of the number (ten tenths) is $30 \times 10 = 300$

Practise... 4.7 One quantity as a fraction of another

D

1 Work out the first number or quantity as a fraction of the second.

a 150, 250   **c** 800 g, 2 kg

b 50p, £4.50   **d** 75 cm, 120 m

2 At a football match, the crowd was 15 000. There were 10 500 home supporters. What fraction of the crowd was this?

3 Clare makes a cheesecake. She has 500 g of cream cheese and uses 350 g of it. What fraction of the cream cheese does she use?

4 Sue has 20 shirts to iron. What fraction of them has she done when she has ironed 12?

5 Mr Howes is marking 35 books. What fraction does he still have left to do when he has marked 14 books?

6 Sara's mark in one spelling test is 15 out of 20 and in the next is 20 out of 25. Which mark was better?

7 18 out of 20 in class 9Y passed a maths test and 25 out of 30 in class 9X passed. Which class did better?

8 In Kate's house, 16 of her 20 lightbulbs are low-energy ones. In Jane's house, 20 out of 24 bulbs are low-energy.

a Who has the higher fraction of low-energy light bulbs?

b There are 30 bulbs in Dipak's house. How many low-energy bulbs does Dipak need so that he has at least the same fraction as Jane?

4 Assess ⓚ

1 Write down what fraction of each shape is shaded.

a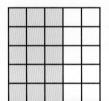

b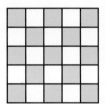

2 Simplify these fractions.

a $\frac{25}{100}$　　c $\frac{75}{100}$　　e $\frac{15}{45}$　　g $\frac{18}{81}$

b $\frac{50}{100}$　　d $\frac{100}{100}$　　f $\frac{56}{72}$　　h $\frac{12}{60}$

3 Find three-quarters of:

a £3　　c 1.8 kg　　e 0.5 metres

b $98　　d £1024

4 Find the calculations that give five-sixths of 48:

a $48 \div 6 \times 5$　　c $48 \times 6 \div 5$　　e $5 \times 48 \div 6$

b $48 \times 5 \div 6$　　d $5 \div 6 \times 48$　　f $\frac{48}{6} \times 5$

5 Four-fifths of a number is 88. What is the number?

6 Which fraction in this list is the greatest?

$\frac{2}{3}, \frac{7}{10}, \frac{3}{5}, \frac{8}{15}$

E

7 Write these fractions as decimals.

    a $\frac{3}{4}$ **b** $\frac{3}{5}$ **c** $\frac{7}{10}$ **d** $\frac{73}{100}$ **e** $\frac{5}{8}$

D

8 Work out the first quantity as a fraction of the second.

    a 24, 36   **c** 10 cm, 1 m

    b £2, £4.50   **d** 150 g, 1.5 kg

C

9 Lawn turf costs £12 a square metre.
What does a rectangle of lawn turf measuring $\frac{3}{4}$ metre by $\frac{5}{6}$ metre cost?

10 Sue makes trousers for her twin toddlers. Each pair of trousers needs three-eighths of a yard of fabric.
How much fabric is needed for four pairs of trousers?

11 Ali needs $1\frac{1}{3}$ cups of sugar to make fudge and $\frac{3}{4}$ of a cup of sugar to make biscuits. He has only 2 cups of sugar. How much more does he need?

12 How much bigger is $2\frac{3}{5} \times 1\frac{1}{2}$ than $2\frac{3}{5} \div 1\frac{1}{2}$?
Show how you worked it out.

Practice questions 🄺

1 There are 24 passengers on a bus.
$\frac{1}{4}$ of the passengers are men.
$\frac{1}{3}$ of the passengers are women.
The rest of the passengers are children.

    How many passengers are children?   *(3 marks)*

    AQA 2007

2 There are 175 pupils in Year 10 at a school.

    a $\frac{2}{5}$ of these pupils own a dog.

        How many pupils in Year 10 own a dog?   *(2 marks)*

    b Alice says that exactly half of the Year 10 pupils are boys.

        Explain why Alice must be wrong.   *(1 mark)*

    c The number of pupils in Year 10 is one-eighth of the total number of pupils in the school.

        Work out the total number of pupils in the school.   *(2 marks)*

    AQA 2008

5 Coordinates

Objectives

Examiners would normally expect students who get these grades to be able to:

G

use coordinates in the first quadrant

F

use coordinates in all four quadrants

E

draw lines such as $x = 3$ and $y = x$

C

find the coordinates of the midpoint of a line segment.

Key terms

coordinates
axis (pl. axes)
origin
horizontal axis
vertical axis
quadrant
line segment
midpoint

Did you know?

Cartesian coordinates

Cartesian coordinates were invented by the French mathematician, René Descartes. Descartes was born in France in 1596 and was known as the 'The Father of Modern Mathematics'.

One night, as he was lying in bed, he noticed a fly on the ceiling. He wondered how he might describe the position of the fly on the ceiling and invented Cartesian coordinates.

You should already know:

✔ negative numbers

✔ number lines

Learn...   5.1 Coordinates in four quadrants

In two dimensions, each point has two **coordinates**.

The first is the x-coordinate.

The second is the y-coordinate.

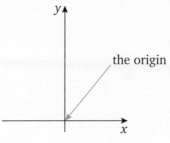

There are two **axes**: the x-**axis** and the y-**axis**.

They cross at the point $(0, 0)$, which is also called the **origin** (O).

The x-axis goes across the page – the **horizontal axis**.

The y-axis goes up the page – the **vertical axis**.

The axes divide the page into four **quadrants**.

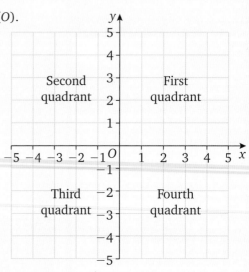

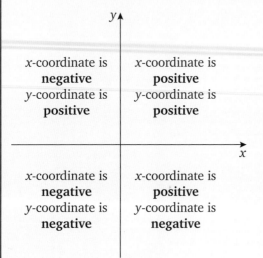

x-coordinate is **negative** y-coordinate is **positive**	x-coordinate is **positive** y-coordinate is **positive**
x-coordinate is **negative** y-coordinate is **negative**	x-coordinate is **positive** y-coordinate is **negative**

Example: Give the coordinates of the point drawn on this diagram.

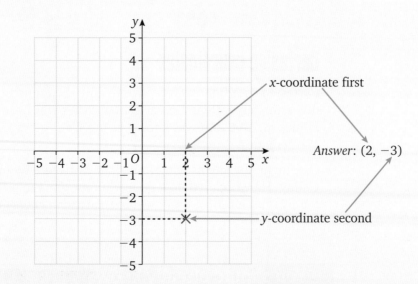

x-coordinate first

Answer: $(2, -3)$

y-coordinate second

Practise...   **5.1 Coordinates in four quadrants** G F E D C

1   Write down the coordinates of points A, B, C, D and E.

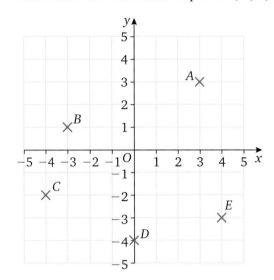

2   Draw a grid like the one in Question 1, with the x-axis and y-axis labelled from −5 to 5.

a   On your grid, mark the points A(2, 4), B(4, −1), C(−1, −3) and D(−3, 2).

b   Join A to B, B to C, C to D and D back to A.

c   What is the mathematical name of the shape you have drawn?

3   Paul says that the two points E and F marked on the grid below are (−2, −2) and (−4, −2). Is he right? Give a reason for your answer.

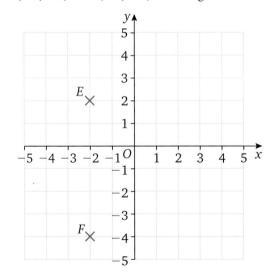

4   Write down the coordinates of:

a   the top left-hand corner of the hexagon

b   the bottom right-hand corner of the hexagon

c   the centre of the hexagon.

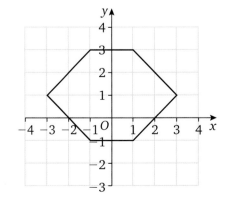

F

5 Judi says it is further from (−1, 3) to (5, 7) than it is from (0, −1) to (3, 5).

Plot the points on a grid and measure the distances to find out whether she is correct.

F
E

6 Draw a grid with the x-axis and the y-axis labelled from −6 to 6.

a On your grid, mark the points P(−2, −2), Q(−1, 2) and R(5, 2).

b Join P to Q and join Q to R.

c PQRS is a parallelogram.
Find the coordinates of S.

7 **a** A(2, 0) and B(2, 4) are two corners of a square, ABCD.
Write down the coordinates of C and D.
(There are two possible answers to this question.)

> **Study tip**
>
> Draw a set of axes and plot the positions of A and B.

b AB is a diagonal of the square APBQ.
Write down the coordinates of P and Q.

⚠ 8 Andy, Ben and Chris all draw a grid and mark the points (2, 3), (4, −1) and (0, 0).

Their teacher tells them to mark a fourth point so that they have the four corners of a parallelogram.

Andy marks (−2, 4).
Ben marks (2, −4).
Chris marks (6, 2).

a Who is correct?

b Plot all six points.
What do you notice?

⚙ **9** A yacht sends out a call for help.

Three boats, Pollyanna, Quicksilver and Roamer, are nearby and hear the call.

a Draw a grid with both axes labelled from −6 to 6.

b The yacht is at (0, 0).
Mark the position of the yacht.

c Pollyanna is at (5, 2).
Quicksilver is at (−4, 4).
Roamer is at (−3, 5).
Mark the positions of the three boats.

d Which boat is closest to the yacht?

Learn... 5.2 Introduction to straight-line graphs

Vertical lines

The points (2, 4), (2, 1), (2, −1), and (2, −4) are marked on the grid.

Any point on the line through these points will have an x-coordinate of 2.

The equation of this line is $x = 2$

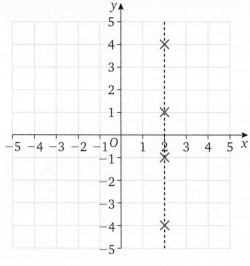

Horizontal lines

The points (−4, −4), (−2, −4), (0, −4) and (2, −4) are marked on the grid.

Any point on the line through these points will have a y-coordinate of −4.

The equation of this line is $y = −4$

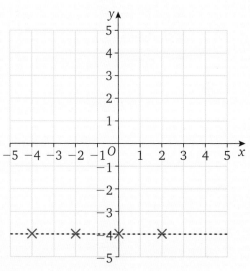

Practise... 5.2 Introduction to straight-line graphs

G F E D C

E

1   Use the vertical line graph above to write down the coordinates of two different points on the line $x = 2$

2   Use the horizontal line graph above to write down the coordinates of two different points on the line $y = −4$

3   Write down the coordinates of three points on the line $x = −3$

4   Write down the coordinates of three points on the line $y = 2$

5   Write down the coordinates of three points on the line $y = −1$

6   **a**   Write down the coordinates of three points on the x-axis.

     b   Wayne says that the x-axis is the line $x = 0$
          Use your answer to part **a** to explain why Wayne is wrong.

     c   What is the correct equation for the x-axis?

E

7   The line $x = 7$ crosses the line $y = 3$ at the point P.

Write down the coordinates of P.

Study tip

Drawing a sketch may help you to answer these questions.

8   The line $x = -5$ crosses the line $y = -4$ at the point Q.

Write down the coordinates of Q.

9   Write down the coordinates of the point where the line $y = -2$ crosses the y-axis.

10   Write down the coordinates of the point where the line $x = 4$ crosses the x-axis.

11   The line $x = -6$ does not cross the line $x = 1$. Why?

12   Write down the equations of:

a   the line PQ

b   the line ST

c   the line UV.

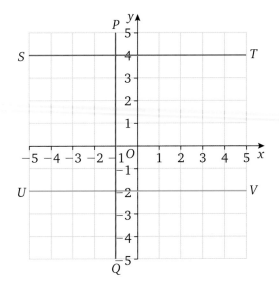

13   Draw a grid like the one in Question 12, with the axes numbered from -5 to 5.

On your grid, plot the points $A(-4, -4)$, $B(-1, -1)$ and $C(2, 2)$.

Draw the straight line through these three points.

a   Write down the coordinates of two other points on this line.

b   If you make the line longer, will it go through the point $(3, 4)$?
Give a reason for your answer.

c   Jodie says the equation of the line is $x = -4$
Geeta says its equation is $x = y$
Lily says its equation is $x = -y$
Who is correct?
Give a reason for your answer.

14   Draw a coordinate grid with both axes labelled from -6 to $+6$.

a   Draw a flag by joining $(2, 1)$ to $(2, 2)$ to $(2, 4)$ to $(4, 3)$ and back to $(2, 2)$.

b   **i**   Change the signs of the x-coordinates and draw the flag again.

ii   What happens to the flag?

c   **i**   Change the signs of both coordinates and draw the flag again.

ii   What happens to the flag?

Learn... 5.3 The midpoint of a line segment

A **line segment** is the part of a line joining two points.

The coordinates of the midpoint are the means of the coordinates of the end points.

Example: A line segment has been drawn from $A(-4, 1)$ to $B(2, 3)$.

Find the **midpoint** of AB.

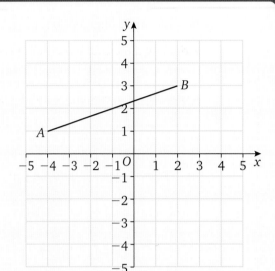

Solution:

Method 1

Measure halfway along the line.

The midpoint of the line is at $(-1, 2)$.

Method 2

Find the mean of the coordinates of the end points.

x: $\dfrac{-4 + 2}{2} = -1$ ◄ Add the two x-coordinates and divide by 2.

y: $\dfrac{1 + 3}{2} = 2$

Add the two y-coordinates and divide by 2.

Practise... 5.3 The midpoint of a line segment

G F E D C

C

1 **a** Work out the coordinates of the point halfway between $(2, 5)$ and $(-4, 1)$.

b Draw a grid with the x-axis and the y-axis labelled from -5 to 5.

Plot the points $(2, 5)$ and $(-4, 1)$.

Use your diagram to check your answer to part **a**.

2 Work out the coordinates of the point halfway between $(0, 4)$ and $(2, 6)$.

3 A is the point $(3, -1)$ and B is the point $(-5, -5)$.

Work out the coordinates of the midpoint of the line AB.

4 Lincoln says that the point $(1, 2\frac{1}{2})$ is halfway between $(-4, 3)$ and $(6, -8)$.

Is he correct?

Give a reason for your answer.

> **Study tip**
>
> It often helps to sketch a diagram and put the points on it. This also gives you a quick check on your calculations.

5 R is the midpoint of the line PQ.

The coordinates of Q are $(3, 2)$.

R is the point $(1, 1)$.

What are the coordinates of P?

C

6　$A(2, 5)$, $B(5, -2)$ and $C(-2, 2)$ are the vertices of a triangle.

   a　Find the coordinates of M, the midpoint of AB.

   b　Find the coordinates of N, the midpoint of BC.

   c　Draw a grid with the x-axis and y-axis labelled from -3 to 6.
      Plot the points A, B, C, M and N.

   d　Draw the lines MN and AC.
      What do you notice about them?

⚠ 7　A quadrilateral $PQRS$ has these coordinates:
    $P(0, 4)$; $Q(6, 2)$; $R(1, -3)$; $S(-5, -1)$.

   a　Find the midpoint of the diagonal PR.

   b　Find the midpoint of the diagonal QS.

   c　What do your results tell you about the quadrilateral $PQRS$?

⚠ 8　The quadrilateral $TUVW$ is a kite.
    Plot $T(1, 3)$, $U(3, 3)$ and $W(-4, -4)$ on a grid.
    Find the coordinates of the fourth vertex, V.

5 Assess ⓚ

G

1　Draw a grid with x- and y-axes labelled from 0 to 5.

   a　Plot the points $A(1, 4)$, $B(4, 4)$, $C(3, 2)$ and $D(0, 2)$.

   b　Join A to B, B to C, C to D and D to A.

   c　Which line is the same length as AB?

   d　Which line is parallel to AB?

F

2　Draw a grid with the x-axis labelled from -4 to 2 and the y-axis from -3 to 5.

   a　Plot the points $P(-1, 4)$, $Q(1, -2)$ and $R(-3, -2)$.

   b　Join PQ, QR and RP to form a triangle.

   c　Which two sides of your triangle are equal?

3 Ten points are marked on the grid below.

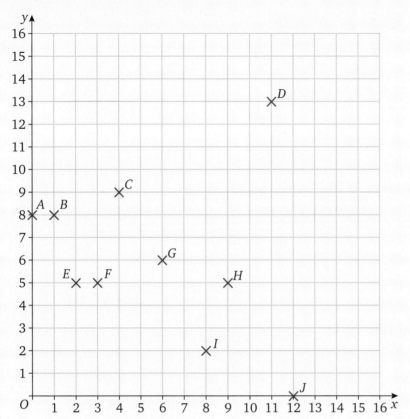

a Write down the coordinates of each of the ten points.

b Which point lies on the *x*-axis?

c Which point is furthest from the origin?

d Sean says that the points *E*, *F* and *H* lie on the line *x* = 5.
What mistake has Sean made?

e Which point lies on the line *y* = *x*?

4 The line *x* = 4 crosses the line *y* = −1 at the point *T*.

Write down the coordinates of *T*.

5 **a** Write down the coordinates of three points that lie on the *y*-axis.

b Write down the coordinates of three points that lie on the line *y* = −*x*

6 Draw a grid with the *x*-axis and the *y*-axis labelled from −4 to 5.

Plot the points *P*(−2, 2), *Q*(4, 4) and *R*(4, −1).

Join *P* to *Q* and *Q* to *R*.

a *PQRS* is a parallelogram.
S is a point in the third quadrant.
Find the position of *S* and write down its coordinates.

b Use your diagram to write down the coordinates of the midpoint of *PQ*.

C

7   Draw a grid with the *x*-axis and the *y*-axis labelled from −6 to 6.

Plot the points *A*(5, 2), *B*(2, −5) and *C*(−2, −1).

Join *AB*, *BC* and *AC* to form a triangle.

Find the midpoint of *BC* and label it *M*.

Write down the coordinates of *M*.

Join *AM*.

What is the angle between *AM* and *BC*?

8   *D* is the point (1, 4) and *E* is the point (3, −3).

What are the coordinates of the midpoint of *DE*?

9   *W* is the midpoint of the line *UV*.

U is the point (−3, 0).

W is the point (1, 2).

What are the coordinates of *V*?

Practice questions 🄚

1   A shape *ABCD* is drawn on the grid.

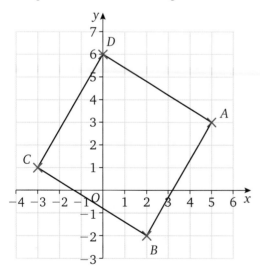

a   Write down the coordinates of *A*.   (*1 mark*)

b   Write down the coordinates of *C*.   (*1 mark*)

c   i   Draw the line *AC*. Mark the midpoint of *AC* and label it *M*.   (*1 mark*)
    ii Write down the coordinates of *M*.   (*1 mark*)

d   Explain why *M* is the same distance from *B* as it is from *D*.   (*1 mark*)

AQA 2008

Working with symbols

Objectives

Examiners would normally expect students who get these grades to be able to:

F

simplify an expression such as
$3x + 2x - x$

work out the value of an expression
such as $4x - 3y$ when $x = 1$ and $y = 2$

E

simplify an expression such as
$3x + 2 - 5x + 4$

understand the rules of arithmetic as
applied to algebra, such as $x - y$ is not
equal to $y - x$

work out the value of an expression
such as $5x - 3y$ when $x = -2$ and
$y = -3$

D

expand brackets such as $x(x + 2)$ in
context

factorise an expression such as $x^2 + 4x$

C

expand and simplify an expression
such as $x(2x + 1) - x(2x - 3)$.

Did you know?

Supermarket queuing theory

Supermarkets use queuing theory to decide how many
people they need to work at the checkout at any time.

There are mathematical formulae used in queuing
theory.

This is Little's theorem: $N = \lambda T$

Little's theorem is used in queuing theory.

 N stands for the average number of customers.

 λ is the average customer arrival rate.

 T is the average service time per customer.

Try testing out Little's theorem with real values to see if
it makes sense.

Key terms

expression
term
like terms
simplify
unlike terms
substitution
expand
multiply out
factorise

You should already know:

✓ number operations and BIDMAS

✓ how to add and subtract negative numbers

✓ how to multiply and divide negative numbers

✓ how to find common factors

✓ about angle properties

✓ how to find the perimeter and area of shapes.

Learn... 6.1 Collecting like terms

An **expression** is a collection of **terms** and does not have a solution, e.g.

$3x - 2 + 2y - 4x + 1 + 5y$

There is more than one way of collecting **like terms** in an expression.

One way is to separate each term with a line. This helps keep the + and − signs in the right place.

$3x \mid -2 \mid + 2y \mid - 4x \mid + 1 \mid + 5y$

Another way is to put circles around each term.

$(3x) (-2) (+2y) (-4x) (+1) (+5y)$

Another way is to write like terms in columns and add them up.

$3x - 2 + 2y - 4x + 1 + 5y$

$$
\begin{array}{rrr}
3x & -2 & +2y \\
-4x & +1 & +5y \\
\hline
-x & -1 & +7y
\end{array}
$$

Another way is to underline each like term in a different colour.

$3x - 2 + 2y - 4x + 1 + 5y$

When you **simplify** an expression, you collect like terms.

A common mistake is to think that an x^2 term is the same sort of term as an x term. x^2 and x are **unlike terms**. The power makes a difference.

Sometimes you may want to rewrite the expression putting the like terms next to each other first.

$4x^2 + 3x - 3x^2$

$4x^2 - 3x^2 + 3x$

$x^2 + 3x$

Example: Find an expression for the perimeter of this triangle.

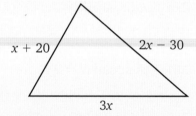

Solution: The sides add up to $x + 20 + 2x - 30 + 3x = 6x - 10$

> **Study tip**
>
> Use your own method for collecting terms that ensures you don't make mistakes with negative values. Remember, the sign is part of the term.

Practise... 6.1 Collecting like terms

G F E D C

F

1 Collect the like terms in each expression.

a $5p + 3p - p$

b $2a - 3a + 5a$

c $9c + 4c - c$

d $2x - 10x + 3x$

e $q - 11q + 8q$

f $20b - 7b - 13b$

g $6d - 3d + d - 5d$

h $10f - 4f - 3f - 2f$

2 Write down an expression for the perimeter of each shape.

a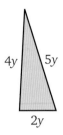

4y   5y

2y

c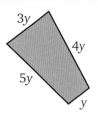

3y

4y

5y

y

e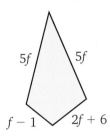

5f   5f

f − 1   2f + 6

b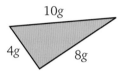

10g

4g   8g

d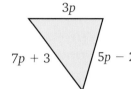

3p

7p + 3   5p − 2

f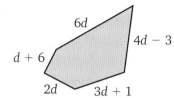

6d

4d − 3

d + 6

2d   3d + 1

Hint

The perimeter of a shape is the
total of the lengths of all the sides.

3 Write down an expression for the angles on each straight line.

a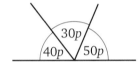

30p

40p   50p

b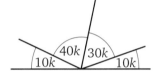

40k   30k

10k   10k

c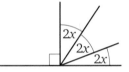

2x

2x

2x

4 Write down an expression for the angles around the point in each diagram.

a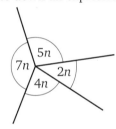

5n

7n   2n

4n

b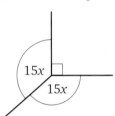

15x

15x

c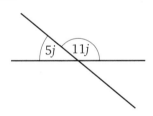

5j   11j

5 Simplify:

a $3d + 8d − 4d$

b $2x − 3x + 5x$

c $−3w + 10y − 5w + 3$

d $4c − 3 + 8d + c$

e $g + 2f − 3g − 4$

f $4fg − 3g + 2 − 5fg$

g $3b + 2a − 3b + a$

h $12x − 15y − 5 + 10x$

i $17 − 10m + 5 − 3n + 12$

6 **a** Show that $5x^2 − 4x^2 + x^2 = 2x^2$

b Show that $a^2 − a + 3a^2 − 5a = 4a^2 − 6a$

c **i** Find the mistake Shannon made when she collected the like terms in this expression:
$2f − 3f^2 − 2f^2 + 5f = 2f$

ii Give the correct answer to the simplification.

7 Simplify:

a $2x^2 − 3x^2 + x^2$

b $−5y^2 + y^2 − 2y − y$

c $2h − 5 + h^2 − h$

d $10v + 10v^2 − 15v^2 + v$

e $−3p^2 + 2p^2 + 4p^2 + 4t^2$

f $5t^2 + m^2 − 3m^2 − 6t^2$

F

E

8 Nilima collects one term from each column and simplifies her answer.
Her route is shown in the diagram.

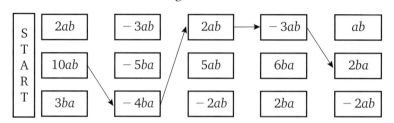

Nilima's route and simplified answer are: $10ab - 4ba + 2ab - 3ab + 2ba = 7ab$

a Choose your own route and simplify your expression in the same way as Nilima.

b Find a different route that gives the same answer as Nilima.

c Find a route that simplifies to give the answer ab.

Hint

Remember: ab and ba are equivalent.

Learn... 6.2 Substitution

When each of the letters in an expression represents a given number, you can find the value of that expression. This is called **substitution**.

If you are substituting negative numbers be careful to follow the rules for the addition, subtraction, multiplication and division of positive and negative numbers. The same rules apply in arithmetic and in algebra.

The rules of arithmetic and the rules of algebra

$x + y$ is the same as $y + x$

$x + -y$ is the same as $x - y$

$a \times b$ is the same as $b \times a$

$a \times -b = -ab$

$-a \times -b = ab$

$x - y$ is **not** the same as $y - x$

$x - -y$ is the same as $x + y$

$\dfrac{a}{b}$ is **not** the same as $\dfrac{b}{a}$

$\dfrac{-a}{b} = -\dfrac{a}{b}$

$\dfrac{-a}{-b} = \dfrac{a}{b}$

Example: Substitute the given values into the expression.
Simplify your answer.

a $p + q$ $p = 7$ $q = 2$

b $cd + 3c$ $c = 3$ $d = -4$

Solution: **a** $p + q = 7 + 2 = 9$

b $cd + 3c = 3 \times -4 + 3 \times 3$
$= -12 + 9 = -3$

Practise... 6.2 Substitution ⓚ

F

1 Substitute the values into each expression. Simplify your answer.

a $x + y$ $x = 2$ $y = 5$

b $a - b$ $a = 4$ $b = 7$

c $2p + q$ $p = 0.5$ $q = 1$

d $3m - 2t$ $m = 3$ $t = 4$

e ab $a = 4$ $b = 15$

f $3cd$ $c = 2$ $d = 7$

g $5gh + g$ $g = 2$ $h = 4$

h $10 - cd$ $c = 2$ $d = 0.5$

i $\dfrac{x}{2} + 2y$ $x = 10$ $y = 1$

j $ab + \dfrac{b}{2}$ $a = 3$ $b = 4$

2 Find the value of each expression, using the values given for x and y.

a $30° + 2x - 3y$ $x = 15°$ $y = 5°$

b $120° - 3y - x$ $x = 10°$ $y = 15°$

c $4x - 10° - 5y$ $x = 45°$ $y = 7°$

d $5y - 6x + 112°$ $x = 12°$ $y = 32°$

e $\dfrac{360°}{2x}$ $x = 5°$

f $\dfrac{180°}{(2x - y)}$ $x = 20°$ $y = 10°$

3 Chris has completed this pyramid puzzle by adding the expressions in the blocks next to each other and writing the result in the block above.

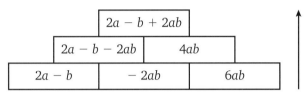

Use $a = 3$ and $b = 4$ to find the value of each block in the pyramid.

4 Tracey and Debbie are practising substitution. They have different expressions and values to substitute but their answers should be the same.

These are the first expressions they have worked out.

Tracey $2k + 4m$ $k = 5, m = -2$

         $2(5) + 4(-2)$

         $10 - 8$

         2

> **Hint**
> Put brackets in to help avoid mistakes with negative numbers.

Tracey and Debbie both get the answer 2.

Debbie $3k - 5m$ $k = 4, m = 2$

         $3(4) - 5(2)$

         $12 - 10$

         2

Now find the answers to Tracey and Debbie's questions to find out which give the same answers and which don't.

	Tracey		Debbie	
a	$3p - 2q$	$p = -2, q = 1$	$4p + q$	$p = 0.5, q = 1$
b	$4x - \dfrac{3y}{2}$	$x = 2, y = -1$	$7x - 2y$	$x = 0.5, y = -0.5$
c	cd	$c = -\frac{1}{2}, d = 4$	$\dfrac{4}{cd}$	$c = -1, d = 2$
d	$\dfrac{4a}{b}$	$a = 5, b = -2$	$2a - b$	$a = -6, b = -2$

5 Ali has been carrying out an investigation into area.

In this rectangle the length added to the width is 10 cm.

> **Hint**
> The area of a rectangle is width × length.

a Using whole numbers for the width and length, find the greatest area. Make sure you write down all the numbers you try.

b Ali wants to try negative numbers in his investigation. Why won't that work?

E

6

a   **i**   Write down and simplify an expression for the perimeter of this pentagon.

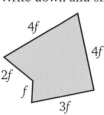

ii   Find the perimeter of the pentagon when $f = 2\,\text{cm}$.

> **Study tip**
>
> Remember to include the units in your answer if they are given in the question.

b   The length of each side of this pentagon is increased by 3 cm.

   i   Write an expression for the length of each side of the new pentagon.

   ii   Write down and simplify an expression for the perimeter of the new pentagon.

   iii   Find the perimeter if $f = 2\,\text{cm}$

D

7   Write an expression for the perimeter of each polygon.   Not drawn accurately

a

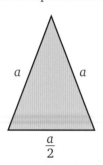

d

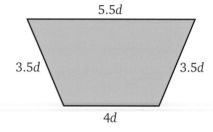

b

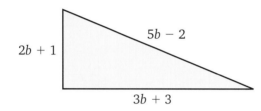

e

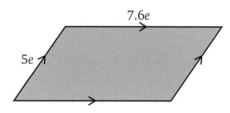

c

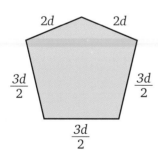

f

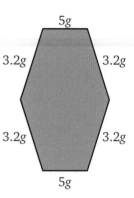

?   **8**   These two rectangles have the same area.
Both x and y are whole numbers.

A

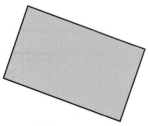

B

Not drawn accurately

width $= x + 1$

length $= x - 1$

If $x = 5$, find the value of y.

length $= 2y$

width $= y - 1$

? (9) In Kylie's pyramid puzzle, the expressions in blocks next to each other are added together to give the expression in the block above.

a Copy and complete the expressions in Kylie's pyramid puzzle.

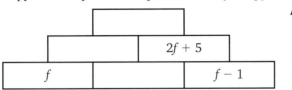

b Work out the value of each block in Kylie's pyramid if $f = 1.5$

c Design your own pyramid puzzle and try it out on your friends.

? (10) Here are three expression cards.

a Which card gives the greatest answer when:

  i $a = 2$ and $b = 3$?

  ii $a = 2$ and $b = -3$?

$a - b$	$\dfrac{a}{b}$	$3a$
card 1	card 2	card 3

b Can you find a pair of values for which cards 2 and 3 are equal?

? (11) In each of the following expressions the value of n is 5 and the value of m is -2.

Copy each pair of expressions and between them write $>$, $<$ or $=$ to make the statement correct.

a $m - n$ ..... $2m$ **c** $5m + 7$ ..... $10 - n$

b m^2 ..... $3n - 10$ **d** $n^2 - 10$ ..... $m^2 + 10$

Learn...   **6.3 Expanding brackets and collecting like terms**

When you **expand** brackets, **all** the terms inside the brackets must be multiplied by the term outside the brackets.

You will be given the instruction **expand** or **multiply out**.

If there is more than one bracket in the expression, each is done separately before collecting terms.

If there are terms not included in the bracket they are not included in the expansion.
They are collected after the brackets have been expanded.

Example: Expand $3(x - 2)$.

Solution: One method for expanding brackets is the grid method.

You have seen other methods in Unit 2.

$\times$	x	-2
3	$3x$	-6

x − 2 goes here. The terms are put into separate boxes.

3 goes here

$3(x - 2) = 3x - 6$

One way of checking your answer is to substitute a value for x into the expression before the expansion and the expression after the expansion. If you get the same answer then your expansion is correct.

e.g.   If $x = 5$
then $3(5 - 2) = 3 \times 3$ ⟵   Before the expansion
          $= 9$

and $3 \times 5 - 6 = 15 - 6$ ⟵   After the expansion
          $= 9$

Example: Multiply out $5a(2a + 1)$.

You can use other methods for expanding brackets.

Solution: Using the grid method:

×	2a	+ 1
5a	10a²	+ 5a

Remember that $a \times a = a^2$

$5a(2a + 1) = 10a^2 + 5a$

You can check your expansion by substituting values for x.

Example: Expand and simplify $9x - 2(x - 4)$.

Solution: Note that $9x$ is not included in the bracket.

The part of the expression that needs to be expanded is $- 2(x - 4)$.

Only use the grid to expand the brackets. $9x$ is not used at this point.

×	x	− 4
−2	−2x	+ 8

Remember the sign stays with the number.

$-2(x - 4) = -2x + 8$

Put the $9x$ back into the expression and then simplify.

$9x - 2(x - 4) = 9x - 2x + 8$

$\qquad\qquad\qquad = 7x + 8$

Example: Expand and simplify $4(3y + 2) - 5(y - 3)$.

Solution: Separate the expression into two brackets to carry out the expansion.

Expand $4(3y + 2)$

×	3y	+ 2
4	12y	+ 8

$4(3y + 2) = 12y + 8$

Expand $- 5(y - 3)$

Remember the minus sign is included here

×	y	− 3
−5	−5y	+ 15

$-3 \times -5 = +15$

$-5(y - 3) = -5y + 15$

Step 3: Put the two answers together and collect like terms.

$4(3y + 2) - 5(y - 3) = 12y + 8 - 5y + 15$

$\qquad\qquad\qquad\qquad = 7y + 23$

Example: Write an expression for the area of this rectangle. Expand your answer.

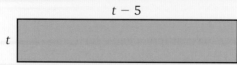

$t - 5$

t

Solution: Area of a rectangle is width × length.

$\text{Area} = t(t - 5)$

Put the length in a bracket so both terms are multiplied by t.

Study tip

You can use any successful method to expand brackets.

Expand the brackets using your own method.

$\text{Area} = t^2 - 5t$

There are no terms to simplify as t^2 and t are different types of term.

6.3 Expanding brackets and collecting like terms

Practise...

D

1 Expand:

a 3(x + 4)   c 8(2 − c)   e 5(5d − 1)   g 3(10v + 7)

b 5(y − 2)   d 3(2p + 5)   f 7(2 − 2f)   h 11(7 + 3m)

2 Write an expression for the area of each of these rectangles.
Expand your answer.

a
5a + 1
3

d
1.5d
d − 2

b
b − 5
2

e
2.5e
10 + e

c
4c + 3
6

f
3 − f
5.5f

Hint

Remember to use brackets and multiply out all the terms. Then collect like terms and simplify them.

3 Dora and Jim are writing number puzzles using symbols.
They use n to represent the missing number.

Dora says 'Think of a number, add two and then multiply the answer by 5.'

Jim writes his answer as n + 2 × 5.

a Write down the mistake Jim has made and re-write his answer correctly.

b Write each of these number puzzles as an expression, using n for the missing number.

i 'Think of a number, subtract 8 and then multiply the answer by 5.'

ii 'Begin with 10 and subtract the number, multiply the answer by 3 and then add 3 times the number.'

c Travis and his friends wrote these expressions for number puzzles. For each one, expand the brackets and collect like terms.

i 5(n + 2) − 10

ii 3n − 2(n − 1)

iii 5(n + 1) + 2(3 − n)

iv 7(3 − 2n) + 10n

v 3(2 + 3n) − 2(3 + 4n)

vi 2(n + 1) + 5(n − 2) − 4n

C

C

4 Find an expression for the shaded area of each shape. Expand and simplify your answer.

a

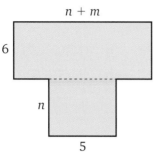

$n + m$

6

n

5

d

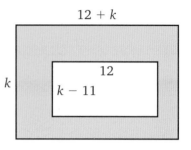

$12 + k$

12

k

$k - 11$

b

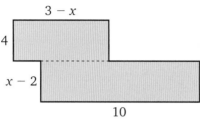

$3 - x$

4

$x - 2$

10

Hint
Remember the area of a triangle
$= \frac{1}{2}$ base × height

e

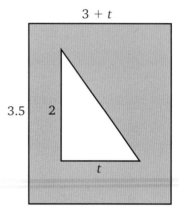

$3 + t$

3.5 2

t

c

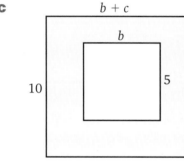

$b + c$

b

10   5

f

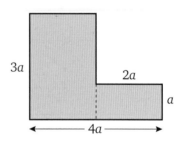

$3a$

$2a$

a

$4a$

5 Find the missing numbers to make each pair of expressions equal.

a $2(a + 4) + 3(a - 1)$ $?(a + 1)$ **d** $?(2x - 1) + 2(x - 3)$ $10(x - 1)$

b $5(1 - b) - 3(b - 3)$ $?(7 - 4b)$ **e** $5(1 - x) + ?(4x + 5)$ $3(x + 5)$

c $2(x + 1) - 5(x + ?)$ $-3(x + 6)$

? **6** In each diagram the value of the perimeter and the numerical value of the area are the same. In each question part, which value of x gives the same answer for the perimeter and the area?

a

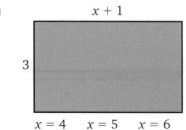

$x + 1$

3

$x = 4$ $x = 5$ $x = 6$

b

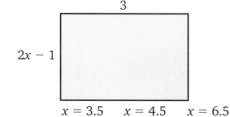

3

$2x - 1$

$x = 3.5$ $x = 4.5$ $x = 6.5$

c

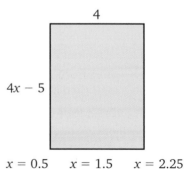

4

$4x - 5$

$x = 0.5$ $x = 1.5$ $x = 2.25$

Hint
Start by writing an expression for the perimeter and an expression for the area.

7   Here are two rectangles.

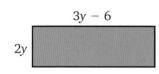

6y

3y − 6

2y

y − 2

Show that the two rectangles have equal area.

8   Row A | 3 | 4x | 2 | 3x | 5x | − 5 | 2x | − x |

Row B | 3 − 2x | x − 2 | 2x + 1 | 3 − x | x − 1 | x + 2 | 2 − x | 3x − 1 |

Jess chooses two terms from row A and two expressions from row B to make this expression:

$$3(3 − x) + 3x(x − 2)$$

Jess simplifies the expression in two steps:

$$9 − 3x + 3x^2 − 6x$$
$$3x^2 − 9x + 9$$

a   Choose your own four terms and expressions to make an expression and simplify it in the same way Jess has.

b   The following shows Jess's working when simplifying three other expressions.
Find the missing terms from the cards above, then copy and complete her working.

i $?(2x + 1) − 5(x + 2)$
$= 4x^2 + 2x − 5x − 10$
$=$

ii $4x(?) − x(2 − x)$
$= ? − ? − 2x + x^2$
$= 13x^2 − 6x$

iii $5x(x − 1) + ?(?)$
$= 5x^2 − ? + 6 − ?$
$= 5x^2 − ? + 6$

Learn...   6.4 Factorising expressions

Factorising is the opposite of expanding.

You will usually be given the instruction **factorise**.

Example: An expression for the area of this rectangle is $3xy + 6y$.
Factorise the expression to find possible dimensions of the rectangle.

Solution: You can use the grid method **in reverse** to factorise this expression.

Step 1: Find the common factor of the two terms in the expression.
   $3y$ is the common factor because 3 is a factor of 3 and 6, and y is a factor of xy and y.

| 3y | 3xy | + 6y |

Put 3y in the grid along with the two terms in the expression.

Step 2: Divide each term by the common factor.
   $3xy ÷ 3y = x$
   $6y ÷ 3y = 2$

| | x | + 2 |
| 3y | 3xy | + 6y |

Put x and + 2 into the grid.

Step 3: Read the values from the grid to give the answer.
   $3xy + 6y = 3y(x + 2)$

Practise... 6.4 Factorising expressions

D **C**

D

1 Factorise each expression.

a $8c + 4$ **e** $20x + x^2$ **i** $4n + 18n^2$

b $12d - 15$ **f** $y^2 - 5y$ **j** $15kl + 27k^2$

c $20 - 10p$ **g** $12xy - 9y^2$ **k** $13f^2 - 65fg$

d $24 + 18k$ **h** $b^2 + 9ab$ **l** $36j^2k - 30jk^2$

2 In each question, one side of the rectangle and the expression for the area has been given.

Use factorising to find an expression for the length of the other side.

a

area = $6x - 21$ 3

b

$5x$

area = $20x^2 - 25x$

c

area = $7p^2 - 5p$ p

> **Study tip**
>
> Always factorise fully. The highest common factor of all the terms in an expression should be outside the bracket.

d

$4t + 5$

area = $100t^2 + 125t$

e

k

area = $2kq - 3kr$

3 These expressions have been factorised.

Find the missing numbers or terms in each question part.

a $10p - 8 = ?(5p - 4)$ **d** $20pq - 15q = 5q(\ ? \ )$

b $12x - 15y = ?(4x - 5y)$ **e** $24x^2 + 9x = ?x(\ ? \ )$

c $11ab + 7bc = ?(? + 7c)$ **f** $19fh + 38fgh = 19fh \ (? + ?)$

4 Factorise fully the expressions for the area of these rectangles.

Use your answers to give possible dimensions of each rectangle.

a

area = $5g + 10gt^2$

D

b   area = $3x^2 + 21xy^2$

c

area = $6p^2q^2 - 2pq^3$

d   area = $5a^2bc^2 + 15ab^2c$

5   Chris and Sue both factorise this expression but get different answers.

$12xy^2 - 18x^2y$

Chris's answer is $2x(6y^2 - 9xy)$

Sue's answer is $6xy(2y - 3x)$

Who is correct? Give reasons for your answer.

6   These expressions have been factorised fully. Some are wrong and some are right.

For each question part, say whether the answer is wrong or right.

If it is wrong, give the correct answer.

a $3ap - 9p = 3p(a - 3)$

b $12f^2 - 18f = 3(4f^2 - 6f)$

c $36 - 4t^2 + 12t = 4(9 - t^2 + 3t)$

d $15x^2y^2 - 20x^2y = 5x(3xy^2 - 4xy)$

e $55k - 44klm^2 = 11k(5 - 4lm^2)$

7   In this factor puzzle the first expression is factorised. The factors are added.
This is repeated until the expression cannot be factorised again.

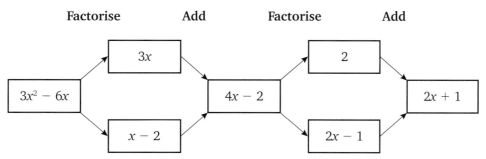

a   Copy and complete this factor puzzle.

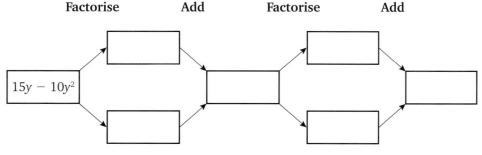

b   Complete a factor puzzle for each of these starting expressions.

i $7a^2 - 14a$ **ii** $4p^2 - 12p$ **iii** $28c - 35c^2$ **iv** $20q - 25q^2$

C

6 Assess (k)

F **1** Write down and simplify an expression for the perimeter of this triangle.

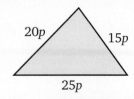

2 **a** Write down and simplify an expression for the perimeter of this pentagon.

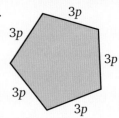

b Work out the perimeter when:

i $p = 2$ cm   **ii** $p = 10$ cm   **iii** $p = 0.5$ cm.

E **3** Work out the value of $2h - 3$ when:

a $h = 2$ **b** $h = 10$ **c** $h = -2$ **d** $h = -4$

4 Simplify:

a $3a - 5 + 4a + 2$ **b** $10ab - 3ab + 4ab - 2ab + ab$ **c** $3d + 2d^2 - 3 - 4d$

D **5** Write an expression in terms of b for the area of this rectangle. Write your expression in its expanded form.

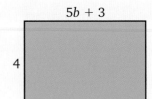

6 Expand and simplify:

a $12 + 4(x - 2)$ **b** $3(5 - 3p) - 2p$

7 Factorise fully:

a $14f + 21$ **b** $24x - 18xy$

8 Factorise fully:

a $5x + x^2$ **b** $y^2 - 3y$ **c** $7pq^2 - 56pq$

C **9** Expand and simplify $2(3x + 1) - 3(4 - x)$.

10 Write an expression for the yellow area of this shape.

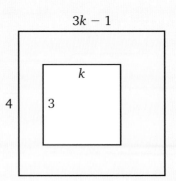

Practice questions (k)

1 **a** Multiply out $a(b + c)$. *(1 mark)*

b Work out the value of $xy + xz$ when $x = 27$, $y = 3$ and $z = 7$ *(3 marks)*

AQA 2008

7 Decimals

Objectives

Examiners would normally expect students who get these grades to be able to:

G

round to the nearest integer

F

write down the place value of a decimal digit such as the value of 3 in 0.63

order decimals to find the biggest and the smallest

round numbers to given powers of 10 and up to 3 decimal places

E

round a number to one significant figure

add and subtract decimals

estimate answers to calculations involving decimals

D

multiply decimals such as 2.4×0.7

convert simple fractions to decimals and decimals to fractions

C

divide a number by a decimal such as $1 \div 0.2$ and $2.8 \div 0.7$

recognise that recurring decimals are exact fractions and that some exact fractions are recurring decimals.

Did you know?

Photo finish

In many sports, gold medals are won by fractions of a second.
In the 100 m sprint, every hundredth of a second counts. Since 1975, official races have been timed electronically to a hundredth of a second.
In 2009, Jamaican athlete Usain Bolt set the world record for the 100 m at 9.58 seconds. This was an improvement of 0.11 seconds from his previous record a year earlier. This doesn't seem like much, but over 100 metres it really makes a difference!

Key terms

decimal	round
integer	decimal place
place value	numerator
digit	denominator
significant figure	recurring decimal

You should already know:

✓ how to arrange whole numbers in order of size

✓ how to add, subtract, multiply and divide whole numbers.

Learn... 7.1 Place value

The **decimal** point separates the whole number or **integer** part from the fraction part.

For example, the number 23.67 can be written in a place value table like this.

Thousands	Hundreds	Tens	Units	.	Tenths	Hundredths	Thousandths
		2	3	.	6	7	

The value of the **digit** 2 is 20. The digit 2 has the highest value so is the most important part of the number. It is called the most **significant figure**.

The value of the digit 3 is 3

The value of the digit 6 is 0.6

The value of the digit 7 is 0.07

Example: Write these numbers in order of size starting with the highest.

2.6   1.48   2.09   1.375

Solution: The numbers should be put into a place value table.

Thousands	Hundreds	Tens	Units	.	Tenths	Hundredths	Thousandths
			2	.	6		
			1	.	4	8	
			2	.	0	9	
			1	.	3	7	5

Compare the most significant values first. In this case this is the units.

There are two numbers starting with 2 so compare the tenths for these two numbers.

2.6 is higher than 2.09 as 6 tenths is higher than 0 tenths.

Compare the numbers starting with a 1 in the same way.

1.48 is higher than 1.375 as 4 tenths is higher than 3 tenths.

So this gives the order:

2.6   2.09   1.48   1.375

> **Study tip**
>
> Make sure you read carefully which order you are asked for. In this case you were asked to start with the highest.

Practise... 7.1 Place value

1   Write these numbers in a place value table.

17.65   231.4   5.961   0.35   54.702

2   Put each list of numbers in order of size, starting with the highest.

   a   3.4   3.16   3.27   3.19   3.08

   b   24.2   27.68   25.34   24.02   25.75

   c   0.426   0.57   0.623   0.64   0.421

3   Put each list of numbers in order of size, starting with the lowest.

   a   1.4   1.37   1.138   1.09   1.2

   b   15.46   16.54   15.49   17.3   15.0

   c   0.25   0.52   0.325   0.514   0.239

4   Write down the value of the digit 7 in each of these numbers.

   a   2.7   **c**   1.237   **e**   2.47   **g**   723.46

   b   7.34   **d**   2.714   **f**   0.176   **h**   7432.1

Learn...  7.2 Rounding 🔵

It is often sensible to **round** figures to give an approximate answer.

For example, using a calculator, an area is worked out to be 18.27146 square metres.

This could be rounded to 18 square metres to make the numbers more manageable.

Numbers can be rounded to the nearest integer, nearest 10, nearest 100, etc.

Numbers can also be rounded to decimals, for example 1 **decimal place**, depending on what the information is needed for.

Sometimes a number is exactly halfway between two others.

In this case it is always rounded up to the higher number.

So 17.5 would round up to 18.

Example: Round 17.8 to:

    a the nearest integer   **b** the nearest ten.

Solution: **a**

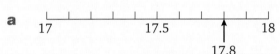

17.8 is closer to 18 than to 17 so 17.8 rounded to the nearest integer is 18.

    b

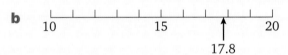

17.8 is closer to 20 than to 10 so 17.8 rounded to the nearest ten is 20.

Example: 🔵 Round 57.32 and 0.5732 to:

    a one decimal place

    b one significant figure.

Solution: **a** Rounding to one decimal place is rounding to the nearest tenth.

        57.32 is between 57.3 and 57.4

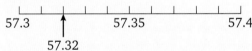

        57.32 is closer to 57.3 than 57.4 so 57.32 rounded to one decimal place is 57.3

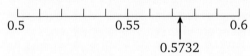

        0.5732 is between 0.5 and 0.6 but the **digit** 7 in the hundredths shows it is nearer to 0.6 so 0.5732 rounded to one decimal place is 0.6

    b Remember that the most significant figure is the one with the highest value.

        In 57.38 the 5 is the most significant figure as its value is 5 tens or 50.

        So rounding to one significant figure is rounding to the nearest ten.

        The number is between 50 and 60 but the 7 in the units shows it is nearer to 60.

        So 57.32 rounded to one significant figure is 60.

        In 0.5732 the 5 is still the most significant figure but its value is 5 tenths or 0.5. So rounding to one significant figure is the same as rounding to the nearest tenth or one decimal place.

        So 0.5732 rounded to one significant figure is 0.6

> Zeros at the beginning or end of a number are not significant. They are used to keep each digit in its correct position.

Practise... 7.2 Rounding (k)

G F E D C

G

1 Round these to the nearest whole number.
(Use a number line to help you.)

    a 4.2   **b** 7.8   **c** 34.6   **d** 0.7   **e** 0.3   **f** 76.5

F

2 **a** Julian says that 537 rounded to the nearest 10 is 54.
What has he done wrong?

    b Ravi says that 4.3 rounded to the nearest whole number is 5.
Is he correct?
Give a reason for your answer.

3 Round these numbers to **a** one decimal place **b** two decimal places and
c three decimal places.

    i 54.9235   **ii** 0.2741   **iii** 4.5291   **iv** 6.0381   **v** 12.4687

E

4 Round these numbers: **a** to the nearest 10   **b** to the nearest 100.

    i 776   **iii** 7089   **v** 14.3
    ii 346   **iv** 2578   **vi** 645

5 Round these numbers to one significant figure.

    a 256   **b** 324   **c** 5617   **d** 37.2   **e** 22.9   **f** 33 624

6 Give an example of a number that when rounded to the nearest 10 gives the same
answer as it does when rounded to the nearest hundred.

7 The number of spectators at an athletics
meeting is 23 278.

A local newspaper reported this as 24 000 to
the nearest thousand.

Is this correct?

Give a reason for your answer.

8 Give an example of a number that gives the same answer when rounded to the
nearest whole number as to one significant figure.

9 Give an example of a number that gives the same answer when rounded to the
nearest 10 as it does when rounded to one significant figure.

10 Give an example of a number that gives the same answer when rounded to
one decimal place as it does when rounded to one significant figure.

11 Bill bought three boxes which had a height of 20 cm each to the nearest whole number.
He tried to put them on a shelf which had a height of 60 cm but they would not fit. Why not?

12 What is the maximum difference when an integer is rounded to:

    a the nearest ten   **b** the nearest hundred   **c** two decimal places?

Learn... 7.3 Adding and subtracting decimals

In this unit you can use a calculator to add and subtract decimals.
However it is useful to know how to find the answer without a calculator.

To add and subtract decimals you must make sure the decimal points are lined up.
You can use a place value table to help you.

Example:　Work out:

　　　a　3.6 + 5.3　　**b**　7.2 − 4.9　　**c**　6.1 + 3.25　　**d**　5.3 − 4.26

Solution:　**a**　　　3.6　　　**b**　${}^6\!7.\!{}^1\!2$　　**c**　　　6.10　　**d**　　5.$\overset{2}{\cancel{3}}\overset{1}{0}$
　　　　　　　+ 5.3　　　　　　− 4.9　　　　　+ 3.25　　　　　− 4.26
　　　　　　　———　　　　　　———　　　　　———　　　　　———
　　　　　　　8.9　　　　　　　2.3　　　　　　9.35　　　　　1.04

> To avoid mistakes, put 0 in any 'spaces' to make both numbers line up on the right.

> **Study tip**
>
> To avoid mistakes, it is a good idea to work out an estimate of the answer.

Example:　Estimate the answer to 69.2 − 21.36 + 7.84

Solution:　Round all the numbers to 1 significant figure then work out the estimate.
　　　　　　This gives 70 − 20 + 8 = 58　(the actual answer is 55.68)

Practise...　7.3 Adding and subtracting decimals　(k)　G F E D C

E

1　Work these out without a calculator.

　　a　12.2 + 3.9　　　**c**　8.23 + 7.1　　　**e**　24.09 + 15.6

　　b　1.4 + 5.31　　　**d**　4.92 − 3.68　　　**f**　3.92 − 2.48 + 5.63

　　Check your answers with a calculator.

2　Yusef says that 3.2 + 1.34 = 4.36

　　Isaac says 3.2 + 1.34 = 4.54

　　Who is correct?

　　Give a reason for your answer.

3　Fill in the missing digits (shown as ☺) in these calculations.

　　a　2.4 + 1.3 = ☺.7　　**c**　☺.2 + 4.1 = 7.3　　**e**　☺.7 − 2.8 = 2.☺

　　b　3.☺ + 2.4 = 5.8　　**d**　5.4 − 1.2 = ☺.2　　**f**　9.☺ − 4.2 = ☺.5

4　Andy says that 7.4 − 5.32 = 2.08

　　Tom says that 7.4 − 5.32 = 2.12

　　Who made the mistake?

　　Explain the mistake he made.

5　Estimate the answers to these calculations by rounding to one significant figure.

　　Use a calculator to check that your estimated answers are close to the exact answers.

　　a　2.9 + 3.2　　　　**f**　69.46 − 22.7

　　b　7.9 + 2.2　　　　**g**　9.28 − 3.16

　　c　67.8 + 22.1　　　**h**　17.8 − 8.76

　　d　20.7 + 38.2　　　**i**　4.78 + 9.32 − 6.1

　　e　102.3 + 97.8　　**j**　87.4 − 31.6 + 42.9

6 A picture frame measures 30 cm by 20 cm.

Oliver drops it, and it breaks into eight pieces.

Here are the measurements of each piece.

4.6 cm	8.6 cm
12.6 cm	15.4 cm
8.6 cm	11.4 cm
17.4 cm	21.4 cm

a Can you pair up the pieces to rebuild the frame?
(You need to make two lengths of 20 cm and two lengths of 30 cm.)

b Can you use the same pieces to make a frame that measures 24 cm by 26 cm instead?

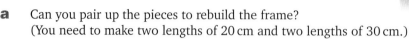

Learn... 7.4 Multiplying decimals

There are different ways to multiply two numbers together such as 32×17.

You can use the grid method:

×	30	2
10	300	20
7	210	14

$300 + 210 + 20 + 14 = 544$

You can use the column method:

$$\begin{array}{r} 32 \\ \times\ 17 \\ \hline 224 \\ 320 \\ \hline 544 \end{array}$$

These methods can also be used to multiply decimals.

Example: **a** Work out the exact value of 6.4×3.1

b Work out the exact value of 1.2×4

Solution: **a** First remove the decimal points: 64×31

Then multiply in your usual way.

Grid method

×	60	4
30	1800	120
1	60	4

$1800 + 120 + 60 + 4 = 1984$

Column method

$$\begin{array}{r} 64 \\ \times\ 31 \\ \hline 64 \\ 1920 \\ \hline 1984 \end{array}$$

Finally, put the decimal point back into the answer.

Estimate the answer by rounding each number to one significant figure.

So 6.4×3.1 is approximately $6 \times 3 = 18$

So the answer is 19.84
Or count up the number of decimal places in the question.

There are two decimal places in the question: 6.4×3.1

So you need two decimal places in the answer: 19.84

So $6.4 \times 3.1 = 19.84$

b   Remove the decimal point: 12×4

multiply the numbers: 48

replace the decimal point by either estimating 1.2×4 is approximately $1 \times 4 = 4$

or by counting the number of decimal points in the question: one decimal point in the question, so one decimal point in the answer.

So $1.2 \times 4 = 4.8$

Practise...   7.4 Multiplying decimals   G F E D C

1   Work out:

a	2.1×4	**e**	0.2×6
b	5×2	**f**	0.7×5
c	8.2×3	**g**	0.4×8
d	6.3×4	**h**	0.6×4

2   For each question, decide which is the best estimate.

		Estimate A	Estimate B	Estimate C
a	6.2×7.9	4.8	42	48
b	4.36×9.4	3.64	36	50
c	28.7×19.2	40.0	400	600

3   Work out:

a	0.3×0.3	**e**	0.05×0.1
b	2.3×0.2	**f**	3.1×0.3
c	0.4×0.6	**g**	$0.3 \times 0.2 \times 0.5$
d	0.15×0.3		

4   Use the multiplication $23 \times 52 = 1196$ to help you to complete these questions.

a	2.3×52	**e**	0.23×0.52
b	0.23×52	**f**	0.23×5.2
c	0.023×0.052	**g**	0.23×0.052
d	2.3×5.2		

5   Work out:

a	1.3×22	**e**	1.2×1.7
b	1.7×2.3	**f**	8.9×1.6
c	8.7×2.5	**g**	0.7×1.3
d	1.5×3.2	**h**	5.1×12.3

F

E

D

6 Using your answers to question 5, write down the answers to these.

a   0.13 × 0.22

b   0.17 × 0.23

c   0.087 × 0.025

d   1.5 × 0.032

e   0.012 × 0.17

f   0.0089 × 0.016

g   0.07 × 1.3

h   0.0051 × 0.123

7 Alex's kitchen floor is 4.2 metres long and 3.4 metres wide.
Alex wants to cover the floor of the kitchen with floor tiles.
The floor tiles are 0.5 m wide and 0.5 m long.
They are sold in boxes of four.

Work out the number of boxes Alex must buy.

Hint

To work out area, multiply length by width. Tiles can be cut to fit at the edges

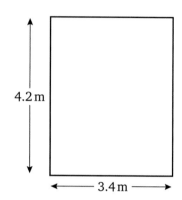

4.2 m

3.4 m

8 Alex is making some curtains. She has found this material online.

She needs four lengths of material each measuring 2.3 metres.
What is the total cost of the material she needs to buy?
Give your answer to the nearest penny.

£7.99 per metre

Learn... 7.5 Dividing decimals

To divide decimals without a calculator, you need to use numbers that are easier to work with.

First, write the division as a fraction. Then find an equivalent fraction that is easier to work with.
Multiply the numerator and denominator so that the denominator is a whole number.
You will need to multiply by 10 if there is one decimal place.
Then divide the numerator by the denominator to get your answer.

Study tip

Never try to divide by a decimal. **Always** make your divisor a whole number using equivalent fractions.

Example: a   Work out 26.4 ÷ 0.4   b   Work out 3.8 ÷ 0.02

Solution: a   First write the division as a fraction: $\frac{26.4}{0.4}$

Next, multiply the **numerator** and **denominator** by 10 so that the denominator is a whole number.

$$\overset{\times 10}{\underset{\times 10}{\frac{26.4}{0.4}}} = \frac{264}{4}$$

Finally divide the numerator by the denominator.

$4\overline{)264}$ with 66 above   So 26.4 ÷ 0.4 = 66

b $3.8 \div 0.02 = \frac{3.8}{0.02}$

This time you need to multiply by 100 so that the denominator is a whole number.

$$\overset{\times 100}{\underset{\times 100}{\frac{3.8}{0.02}}} = \frac{380}{2} = 190$$

Practise... 7.5 Dividing decimals (k)

G F E D C

1 Work out:

a 24 ÷ 0.4   c 81 ÷ 0.3   e 0.8 ÷ 0.2   g 48 ÷ 0.8

b 36 ÷ 0. 2   d 63 ÷ 0.7   f 70 ÷ 0.5   h 84 ÷ 0.4

2 Work out:

a 3.2 ÷ 0.4   d 25.4 ÷ 0.2   g 4.07 ÷ 1.1   j 25.3 ÷ 0.11

b 53.1 ÷ 0.3   e 1.74 ÷ 0.6   h 16.8 ÷ 0.12

c 0.56 ÷ 0.7   f 1.32 ÷ 0.04   i 22.8 ÷ 1.2

3 Carrie knows that 3.4 ÷ 0.4 = 8.5

Use this fact to copy and fill in the gaps in these questions.

a 34 ÷ 0.4 = ☐   c ☐ ÷ 0.04 = 8.5   e ☐ ÷ 4 = 0.85

b 340 ÷ ☐ = 8.5   d 3.4 ÷ 4 = ☐   f 0.34 ÷ 8.5 = ☐

4 Stu says that 36 ÷ 2 = 18, so 36 ÷ 0.2 = 1.8

Dean says 36 ÷ 2 = 18, so 3.6 ÷ 0.2 = 1.8

Jack says 36 ÷ 2 = 18, so 3.6 ÷ 2 = 1.8

Who is right? Give a reason for your answer.

5 Estimate the answers to each of these questions.

a $\dfrac{78.2 \times 2.8}{0.23}$ c $\dfrac{26.2 + 23.9}{0.89 - 0.72}$

b $\dfrac{107.6 + 92.1}{0.37}$ d $\dfrac{56.3 \times 9.7}{0.316}$

> **Study tip**
>
> When estimating, always round numbers to one significant figure first.

6 Jenny needs some pieces of ribbon of length 0.6 metres.

She has a roll of ribbon of length 4.3 metres.

How many pieces of ribbon can she cut from the roll?

7 A factory making 'Fizzypop' drink makes up batches of 2500 litres of 'Fizzypop' at a time.

A machine fills cans with the drink.

Each can holds 0.3 litres.

How many cans will be filled from one batch of 'Fizzypop'?

8 Loren is going on holiday to France for five days and five nights.

€1 is worth £0.80. Loren changes £400 into euros.

Her hotel costs €39 per night.

How many euros does she have left to spend per day?

9 Jamie says that when you divide one number by another the answer is always smaller.

Give an example to show that Jamie is wrong.

D

C

Learn... 7.6 Fractions and decimals

To change a fraction to a decimal, divide the numerator (top number) by the denominator (bottom number).

$$\frac{2}{5}$$ ←—— Numerator
←—— Denominator

Some fractions become **recurring decimals**.

This means that a number or group of numbers keeps repeating.

To change a decimal to a fraction, put the decimal into a place value table.

For example, you can write the number 0.37 in a place value table like this:

All fractions can be changed to a decimal. If the decimal keeps repeating it is a recurring decimal. If it does not, it is called a **terminating** decimal.

Units	.	Tenths	Hundredths
0	.	3	7

The least significant figure is hundredths, so this is the denominator of the fraction.

So $0.37 = \frac{37}{100}$

Example: **a** Write $\frac{2}{5}$ as a decimal. Is the answer a recurring decimal or a terminating decimal?

b Write $\frac{1}{3}$ as a decimal. Is the answer a recurring decimal or a terminating decimal?

Solution: **a** Divide 2 by 5: $5\overline{)2.0}^{\,0.4}$ Add zeros to the calculation.
Make sure the decimal points are lined up.

So $\frac{2}{5}= 0.4$

The decimal does not repeat, so this is a terminating decimal.

b Divide 1 by 3: $3\overline{)1.0000}^{\,0.3333}$ the '3' keeps repeating, so the answer is a recurring decimal.
This can be written as $0.\dot{3}$ (the dot shows which number is recurring).

Example: Write 0.6 as a fraction in its simplest form.

Solution:

Units	.	Tenths
0	.	6

The least significant figure is tenths, so this is the denominator of the fraction.

$0.6 = \frac{6}{10}$

This can be cancelled down to a simpler form by dividing both numbers by 2.

$\frac{6}{10} = \frac{3}{5}$ so $0.6 = \frac{3}{5}$

Practise... 7.6 Fractions and decimals   G F E D C

1 Change these fractions to decimals.

a $\frac{1}{5}$ **d** $\frac{3}{20}$ **g** $\frac{1}{50}$

b $\frac{7}{10}$ **e** $\frac{3}{4}$ **h** $\frac{3}{10}$

c $\frac{1}{8}$ **f** $\frac{3}{100}$

2 Which of these fractions is closest to 0.67?

a $\frac{3}{4}$ **b** $\frac{5}{8}$ **c** $\frac{3}{5}$

3   Write these decimals as fractions.

a   0.59   **c**   0.4   **e**   0.1   **g**   0.45

b   0.07   **d**   0.25   **f**   0.36   **h**   0.05

4   Write these fractions as recurring decimals.

a $\frac{1}{9}$ **b** $\frac{2}{3}$ **c** $\frac{1}{6}$

△ 5   Write these fractions as recurring decimals.

a $\frac{2}{9}$ **c** $\frac{5}{6}$

b $\frac{4}{15}$ **d** $\frac{1}{22}$

> **Hint**
> If there is more than one number in the recurring pattern, put a dot over the first and last numbers of the pattern.

6   On her birthday, Bridget is given a big box of small sweets called Little Diamonds.
She wants to find out how many sweets are in the box, but it would take too long to count them.
A label on the box tells her that the total weight is 500g.
She weighs 10 sweets. The weight of the 10 sweets is 0.4g.
How many sweets are there in the box?

7   Three identical blocks of wood are placed as shown, so that the top one rests with $\frac{1}{3}$ of its length on each of the other two.

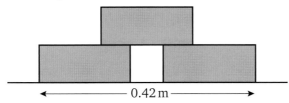

— 0.42 m —

Work out the length of one of the blocks.

Assess (k)

1   Round each number to the nearest integer.

a   37.2   **c**   4.295   **e**   13.526

b   9.7   **d**   3.71

2   Put each list of numbers in order of size, starting with the smallest.

a   7.2   7.02   7.16   7.28   7.025

b   84.72   83.9   83.531   84.709   84.8

c   0.46   0.64   0.446   0.464   0.466

3   Write down the value of the digit 8 in each of these numbers.

a   4.08   **c**   8.237   **e**   4.008   **g**   836.9

b   7.84   **d**   86.7   **f**   0.86   **h**   8342.1

4   32 917 people attend a concert. Write this number:

a   to the nearest 1000   **c**   to the nearest 10 000

b   to the nearest 10   **d**   to the nearest 100.

E

5   Ali drives 12.4 miles to get to work each day.
Petra drives 3.7 miles further than Ali to get to work.
How far does Petra drive?

6   Jon says that he and Carl are the same weight – to one significant figure.
Jon weighs 76 kilograms.
Carl weighs 82 kilograms.
Is Jon correct?
Explain your answer.

D

7   In a store room there are two piles of magazines.
One of the piles is 30 cm high.
The other pile is 12 cm high.
Each magazine is 0.6 cm thick.
How many magazines are in the store room?

C

8   Tom buys his electricity from Lowlec.
Lowlec charge the following prices:

Daytime electricity £0.20 per unit

Night-time electricity £0.04 per unit.

From June to September Tom uses 450 units of daytime electricity.
His total bill is £122.
Work out the number of night-time electricity units Tom used during this period.

Practice questions   *k*

1   You are making bookcases from planks of wood that are 20 cm wide and 20 mm thick.
The planks are sold in these lengths:
1.8 m   2.1 m   2.4 m   2.7 m   3 m

You make this bookcase.

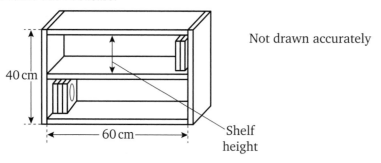

Not drawn accurately

40 cm

60 cm

Shelf
height

a   What is the total length of wood used to make the bookcase?   (*2 marks*)

b   The shelf height is the height of the gap between the shelves.
The two shelf heights are equal.
Work out the shelf height.   (*3 marks*)

AQA 2009

2   Sam has £1.65
Vicki has 7p
How much must Sam give Vicki so that they each end up with the same amount?   (*3 marks*)

AQA 2008

Objectives

Examiners would normally expect students who get these grades to be able to:

G

find the mode for a set of numbers

find the median for an odd set of numbers

F

work out the range for a set of numbers

calculate the mean for a set of numbers

find the median for an even set of numbers

E

calculate the 'fx' column for a frequency distribution

compare the mean and range of two distributions

D

calculate the mean for a frequency distribution

find the modal class for grouped data

C

find the mean for grouped data

find the median class for grouped data.

Key terms

average	grouped data
mean	discrete data
median	continuous data
mode	modal class
range	modal group
frequency table	class interval

Did you know?

The **average** student will:

- sleep for 7 hours per day during the week but 11 hours during the weekend

- spend two and a half hours on the internet after 6 pm on a weekday

- eat 1.7 burgers each week.

Averages

Facts like these can be interesting, but averages are useful in real life. For example, manufacturers need to know how many items to make. They could use data on sales from one month, but this is unlikely to be very reliable. Sales vary from one month to the next, so it's better to take an average over a longer period. Governments also use averages, so they can plan how many houses or hospitals will be needed in future. And if you want to avoid getting into debt it's a good idea to compare your average spending with your average income!

You should already know:

✓ how to use a calculator to work with the four rules of arithmetic.

Learn... 8.1 Basic measures

There are three basic measures of **average**.

Mean: To calculate the mean add up all the values and divide this total by the number of values.

Median: To find the median put the numbers in order and find the middle number.

(If there are two numbers in the middle, the median is the mean of these two numbers.)

Mode: To find the mode work out the number (or numbers) which occur most often.

There is one basic measure of spread.

Range: Take away the lowest value from the highest value.

> **Study tip**
>
> Students often confuse the different types of average. You must learn which is which and not mix them up.

> **Study tip**
>
> Data sets are usually compared using a measure of average and a measure of speed. If you are simply asked to compare two sets of data you have to work these out first.

Example: For this set of data find:

3   5   1   2   6   3   6   6

a the mode   **b** the mean   **c** the median   **d** the range.

Solution: **a** mode:

To find the mode work out the number (or numbers) which occur most often.

The number 6 occurs more than any other number, so the mode is 6.

b mean:

To calculate the mean add up all the values and divide the total by the number of values.

Add up all the values $3 + 5 + 1 + 2 + 6 + 3 + 6 + 6 = 32$

Divide this total by the number of values $32 \div 8 = 4$ so the mean = 4

c median:

To find the median put the numbers in order and find the middle number.

Put the numbers in order   1   2   3   3   5   6   6   6

Find the middle number   The middle number is the mean of 3 and 5

This is $\dfrac{3 + 5}{2} = 4$ so the median = 4

d range:

The highest value is 6. The lowest value is 1.

The range is the highest value minus the lowest value.

$6 - 1 = 5$ so the range = 5

> **Study tip**
>
> Notice how ordering the data helps with the range as well as the median.

Practise... 8.1 Basic measures

G
F

1 For the following sets of data, work out:

a the median

b the mode

c the mean

d the range.

i   4   6   14   5   1

ii   16   19   14   15   15   11

iii   7   5   7   5   7   5   4   8

G
F

F

E

2   Find the mode, median, mean and range for each of these situations.

a   A dice is rolled eleven times and these scores are recorded.

5   1   4   1   1   4   2   3   2   6   4

b   A group of twelve fathers were asked how many children they had.

3   1   4   3   1   2   1   1   1   3   2   1

c   A local football team plays ten matches and lets in these numbers of goals.

1   0   2   4   0   3   2   1   4   1

d   A shopkeeper keeps a record of the number of broken eggs found in eight deliveries.

5   1   5   1   2   0   5   2

3   Josh buys some toffees that cost 62p.

Nicola buys some mints that cost 48p.

Shelley buys some gums that cost 70p.

They share the sweets and share the cost of buying them.

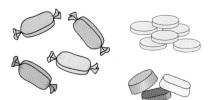

a   How much do they pay each?

b   What is the name of the average you have calculated?

4   The mean of four numbers is 10.

Three of the numbers are 8, 9 and 10.

Find the fourth number.

5   The median of five numbers is 25.

Four of the numbers are 34, 25, 28 and 17.

Write down a possible value for the fifth number.

6   The mode of five numbers is 8.

Three of the numbers are 6, 7 and 8.

The remaining two numbers are different to each other.

Write down a possible pair of values for the other two numbers.

7   Zoë was having a good year scoring goals in the hockey team.

After 10 matches she had scored: 1, 2, 2, 2, 0, 4, 3, 3, 1, 2 goals.

She said 'A mean of 2 goals is not bad.'

Is Zoë correct? You **must** show your working.

8   Mr Booth, the maths teacher, decided to give his class a test each day for two weeks.

a   Teddy's results were 4, 2, 4, 5, 5, 9, 6, 6, 8, 1
Calculate the mean and range of his marks.

b   Jasmin's results were 4, 4, 7, 5, 5, 7, 6, 4, 3, 5
Calculate the mean and range of her marks.

c   Compare the results of the two students.

9   Ivor is investigating whether teachers or lawyers are more intelligent.

Ivor uses a sample of teachers and a sample of lawyers.

He gives them all the same IQ test.

These are the data for the teachers.

124   116   108   122   117   118   120   131   103   125

These are the data for the lawyers.

121   100   118   129   112   103   102   110   105   119

Give a conclusion about Ivor's investigation.

You must show your working to justify your answer.

10   Write down a set of five numbers with all these features.

The mean is 10.   The median is 9.   The mode is 8.

11   The total of a set of numbers is 100.

The mode is 10.   The range is 5.

Write down a possible set of numbers which meet these conditions.

12   Look at this lift sign.

What does this suggest about the average weight of a person?

The average weight of a group of people in the lift is 90 kg.

> MAXIMUM LOAD
>
> 8 PERSONS
>
> 700 kg

What is the maximum number of people that can be in the lift without it being overloaded?

Learn... 8.2 Frequency distributions

A frequency distribution shows how often individual values occur (the frequency).

The information is usually shown in a frequency table.

A **frequency table** shows the values and their frequency.

The frequency table shows the number of pets for students at a school.

There are 5 students with no pets, 11 students with one pet, 8 students with 2 pets, ... and so on.
You can use the frequency table to calculate measures of average and measures of spread.

Number of pets (x)	Frequency (f)
0	5
1	11
2	8
3	5
4	2

The **mean** is the total of all the values divided by the number of values. In a frequency table you need to use the formula:

$$\text{Mean} = \frac{\text{the total of (frequencies} \times \text{values)}}{\text{the total of frequencies}} = \frac{\Sigma fx}{\Sigma f} \quad \text{where } \Sigma \text{ means the sum of}$$

The **mode** is the value which has the highest frequency (i.e. the value occurring most often).

The **median** is the middle value when the data are listed in order. It does not matter whether you go from smallest to highest or the other way round.

The **range** is the highest value minus the lowest value.

Example: For the frequency distribution above, find:

   a   the mean, mode and median

   b   the range.

> **Study tip**
>
> The average and the spread are useful measures to compare sets of data. You need to understand the difference between measures of average and measures of spread.

Solution: **a**   The mean is the total number of pets divided by the total number of students.

Number of pets (x)	Frequency (f)	Frequency × number of pets (fx)
0	5	0 × 5 = 0
1	11	1 × 11 = 11
2	8	2 × 8 = 16
3	5	3 × 5 = 15
4	2	4 × 2 = 8
	$\Sigma f = 5 + 11 + 8 + 5 + 2 = 31$	$\Sigma fx = 0 + 11 + 16 + 15 + 8 = 50$

$$\textbf{Mean} = \frac{\text{the total of (frequencies} \times \text{values)}}{\text{the total of frequencies}}$$

$$= \frac{\Sigma fx}{\Sigma f} \quad \text{where } \Sigma \text{ means 'the sum of'}$$

$$= \frac{50}{31}$$

$$= 1.6129$$

Mean = 1.6 (to 1 decimal place)

The mean is a useful measure of average.

> **Study tip**
>
> Always check that your answers are reasonable. Candidates often mistakenly divide by the number of rows instead of the total frequency. This will usually give a silly answer.

Mode

The mode is the number that occurs most frequently.

1 pet has a frequency of 11 and all the other frequencies are less than this.

Mode = 1

> **Study tip**
>
> When asked for the mode, make sure that you write down the value (in this case 1), not the frequency (in this case 11).

Median

The median is the middle value when the data are arranged in order.

The data have 31 values so the median is the $\frac{(31 + 1)}{2}$th value = 16th value. The data are already ordered in the table.

The first 5 values are 0, the next 11 are 1, so the 16th value is 1

0 0 0 0 0 1 1 1 1 1 1 1 1 1 1 1 2 2 2 …

$\uparrow$ 16th

Median = 1

The median can also be found using the 'running totals' of the frequencies as follows:

Number of pets (x)	Frequency (f)	Running total
0	5	5
1	11	5 + 11 = 16 ←
2	8	5 + 11 + 8 = 24
3	5	5 + 11 + 8 + 5 = 29
4	2	5 + 11 + 8 + 5 + 2 = 31

The 16th value will lie in this interval so the median is 1.

The range is the highest value minus the lowest value.

b   The range = 4 − 0 = 4

Range = 4

The range is a measure of how spread out the data are.

> **Study tip**
>
> Remember that the range should always be presented as a single answer (not a range!).

Practise... 8.2 Frequency distributions

E
D

1   A dice is thrown 100 times. The frequency distribution table shows the scores.

Score (x)	Frequency (f)	Score × frequency (fx)
1	18	
2	19	
3	16	
4	12	
5	15	
6	20	

Study tip

It is possible to use a calculator's statistical functions to find the mean of a frequency distribution. Make sure you are in statistical mode and enter the data value or midpoint followed by its frequency each time.

a   Find the mean score.

b   Find the median score.

c   What is the modal score?

d   Work out the range of scores from these 100 dice throws.

e   What fraction of the throws resulted in a 6?
        Give your answer in its simplest form.

2   The frequency table shows the speed limit of all the roads in one county.

Speed limit (mph)	Number of roads
20	8
30	88
40	52
50	23
60	150
70	3

a   How many roads have a speed limit of less than 40 miles per hour?

b   What percentage of roads have a 30 miles per hour speed limit?
        Give your answer to two decimal places.

c   What is the range of speed limits in this county?

d   For the data in the frequency table, work out:

  i   the modal speed limit

  ii   the median speed limit

  iii   the mean speed limit.

D

3   Andy keeps a record of his scores in tennis games.

The table shows results for 40 games he lost.

For the data work out:

a   the mean

b   the median

c   the mode

d   the range

e   the percentage of games where Andy scored 30 points.

Score	Frequency
0	5
15	8
30	20
40	7

4   The number of people in a sample of 100 cars is given in the frequency table.

Number of people	Frequency
1	60
2	32
3	6
4	2

a   Write down the median number of people in these cars.

b   Work out the mean number of people in these cars.

c   Which is more useful in predicting the number of people in the next car to come along?
Explain your answer.

 5   Fill in the frequencies so that the median is 10 and the mode is 9.

x	f
8	
9	
10	
11	

6

x	f
2	34
4	66
6	19
8	*

a   If the mode is 8, give a possible value for *. Explain your choice.

b   If the median is 4, give a possible value for *. Explain your choice.

7   The table shows the number of bedrooms in a sample of houses from a town centre and a village.

Number of bedrooms	Number of houses	
	Town centre	Village
1	8	3
2	19	9
3	6	10
4	2	8
5	0	5

> **Hint**
>
> As well as using measures of average and spread to make the comparisons you could also use percentages.

Compare the number of bedrooms in these two samples.

8   Two bus companies, Super Express and Big Bus, run a bus service between the same two towns along the same route.

George is investigating the punctuality of their buses on this route.

He records the number of minutes late, rounded to the nearest 5 minutes, for a sample of buses from each company over a one week period.

Here are the data George collects for Big Bus.

0	0	0	0	0	0	0	0	0	0
0	0	0	0	0	0	0	0	5	5
5	5	5	5	5	5	10	10	10	10
10	10	10	10	10	10	15	15	25	35

Here are the data George collects for Super Express.

0	0	0	0	5	5	5	5	5	5
5	5	5	5	5	5	5	5	5	5
5	5	5	10	10	15	15	15	15	15
15	15	15	15	15	15	15	15	15	15
15	20	20	20	20	20	20	20	20	20

> **Hint**
>
> When you are given sets of raw data, the first thing to do is sort out the data in a frequency table.

a   Compare the punctuality of the two bus companies.

b   Give a reason why you might be more interested in the range of the times late rather than the average.

Learn... 8.3 Grouped frequency distributions

A grouped frequency distribution shows how often **grouped data** values occur (the frequency).

A grouped frequency table shows the values and their frequency.

Grouped frequency distributions are usually used with **continuous data**.

Continuous data are data which can take any numerical value. Length and weight are common examples of continuous data.

Discrete data can only take individual values. Shoe sizes are an example.

You can use the grouped frequency table to calculate measures of average and measures of spread as before.

Mean

The mean is the total of all the values divided by the number of values.

$$\text{Mean} = \frac{\text{the total of (frequencies} \times \text{values)}}{\text{the total of frequencies}} = \frac{\Sigma fx}{\Sigma f} \quad \text{where } \Sigma \text{ means 'the sum of'}$$

As the data are grouped, you will need to use the midpoint of each group to represent the value.

Discrete data	Continuous data
To find the midpoint, add together the largest and smallest value of each group and divide the answer by two.	To find the midpoint, add together the smallest possible value (lower bound) and the largest possible value (upper bound) for each group and divide the answer by two.

Mode

The mode is the value which has the highest frequency next to it (i.e. the value occurring most often).

For grouped data it is more usual to find the modal class.

The **modal class** (or **modal group**) is the class (group) with the highest frequency.

Median

The median is the middle value when the data are listed in order.

For grouped data it is more usual to find the group containing the median.

Graphical work (see Chapter 7) is often used to find the median.

Range

The range is the difference between the highest value minus the lowest value.

For grouped data it is not always possible to identify the highest value and the lowest value. However, it can be estimated as:

Highest value in highest group − lowest value in lowest group.

Example: The table shows the time taken for students to solve a simple puzzle.

$20 \leqslant x < 30$ covers all the values between 20 and 30 seconds. The 20 is included in the group whereas the 30 will be in the $30 \leqslant x < 40$ group.

The range of values within a group is called a **class interval**.

Time in seconds (x)	Frequency
$10 \leqslant x < 20$	30
$20 \leqslant x < 30$	35
$30 \leqslant x < 40$	20
$40 \leqslant x < 50$	10
$50 \leqslant x < 60$	5

Use the information in the grouped frequency table to:

a write down the modal class

b work out the class which contains the median

c calculate an estimate of the mean time taken to solve the puzzle.

Solution:

a The **modal class** is the class with the highest frequency.

This is the class $20 \leqslant x < 30$ (as there are 35 students in this group).

b The median is the middle value when the data are listed in order. In this case the middle value is the 50th value.

The median can be found using the 'running totals' of the frequencies as follows.

The 50th value will lie in this interval so the median lies in the $20 \leqslant x < 30$ class.

Time in seconds (x)	Frequency	Running total
$10 \leqslant x < 20$	30	30
$20 \leqslant x < 30$	35	$30 + 35 = 65$
$30 \leqslant x < 40$	20	$30 + 35 + 20 = 85$
$40 \leqslant x < 50$	10	$30 + 35 + 20 + 10 = 95$
$50 \leqslant x < 60$	5	$30 + 35 + 20 + 10 + 5 = 100$

The $20 \leqslant x < 30$ class contains the median.

c As the data are grouped, you need to use the midpoint of each group.

An additional column should be added to the table for the midpoints.

Time in seconds	Frequency (f)	Midpoint (x)	Frequency × midpoint (fx)
$10 \leqslant x < 20$	30	15	$30 \times 15 = 450$
$20 \leqslant x < 30$	35	25	$35 \times 25 = 875$
$30 \leqslant x < 40$	20	35	$20 \times 35 = 700$
$40 \leqslant x < 50$	10	45	$10 \times 45 = 450$
$50 \leqslant x < 60$	5	55	$5 \times 55 = 275$
	$\Sigma f = 100$		$\Sigma fx = 2750$

$$\text{Mean} = \frac{\text{the total of (frequencies} \times \text{values)}}{\text{the total of frequencies}} = \frac{\Sigma fx}{\Sigma f} = \frac{2750}{100} = 27.5$$

Mean = 27.5

Remember that this is only an estimate of the mean as we do not know how the numbers are distributed within each group. Using the midpoint gives an approximation only.

Study tip

Remember to check that the answer you have obtained is sensible for the data. Your answer must lie within the range of the data. If it doesn't you have made a mistake.

Practise... 8.3 Grouped frequency distributions

1 The table shows how long people have to wait to be served in a restaurant.

Time, t (minutes)	Frequency
$0 \leqslant t < 2$	8
$2 \leqslant t < 4$	14
$4 \leqslant t < 6$	6
$6 \leqslant t < 8$	4
$8 \leqslant t < 10$	2

a Write down the modal class.

b In which group does the median lie?

c What percentage of people waited more than 8 minutes? Give your answer to one significant figure.

d Calculate an estimate of the mean waiting time. Explain why your answer is an estimate.

e Estimate the range of the waiting times.

D
C

D
C

2 The table shows the weekly wages of 40 staff in a small company.

a Work out:

   i the modal class

   ii the class that contains the median

   iii an estimate of the mean.

b Which average should you use to compare the wages with another company?
Give a reason for your answer.

Wages (£)	Frequency
$50 \leqslant x < 100$	5
$100 \leqslant x < 150$	13
$150 \leqslant x < 200$	11
$200 \leqslant x < 250$	9
$250 \leqslant x < 300$	0
$300 \leqslant x < 350$	2

C

3 The table shows test scores out of 50 for a class of 25 students.

Score	1–10	11–20	21–30	31–40	41–50
Number of students	2	3	12	6	2

Calculate an estimate of the mean weight of a score.

Hint
Apply the rule for discrete data in Learn 8.3.

4 A company produces three million packets of crisps each day. It states on each packet that the bag contains 25 grams of crisps. To test this, the crisps in a sample of 1000 bags are weighed.

The table shows the results.

Is the company justified in stating that each bag contains 25 grams of crisps?

You must show your working to justify your answer.

Weight, w (grams)	Frequency
$23.5 \leqslant t < 24.5$	20
$24.5 \leqslant t < 25.5$	733
$25.5 \leqslant t < 26.5$	194
$26.5 \leqslant t < 27.5$	53

Hint
To justify your answer you could:
1. Calculate an estimate of the mean weight of the crisps.
2. Estimate the percentage of packets that contain less than 25 grams.

5 Two machines are each designed to produce paper 0.3 mm thick. The tables below show the actual output of a sample from each machine.

	Machine A	Machine B
Thickness, t (mm)	Frequency	Frequency
$0.27 \leqslant t < 0.28$	2	1
$0.28 \leqslant t < 0.29$	7	50
$0.29 \leqslant t < 0.30$	32	42
$0.30 \leqslant t < 0.31$	50	5
$0.31 \leqslant t < 0.32$	9	2

Compare the output of the two machines using suitable calculations.

Which machine is producing paper closer to the required thickness?

6 A school has an attendance target of 95%.
Here are the percentage attendances of students in Class 7A and Class 7B.

Hint
Sort out the data into grouped frequencies before you start.

Class 7A

34	36	48	60	65	78	80	84	84	84
86	88	90	92	94	94	95	95	95	95
95	96	96	96	98	100	100	100	100	

Class 7B

42	42	46	48	48	52	64	68	76	80
86	86	94	94	94	94	94	94	94	94
94	94	96	96	96	98	98	100	100	100

Compare the attendance of each of these classes with the school target.

8   Assess

1   Find the mode, median, mean and range of the following sets of data.

   a   4, 4, 2, 2, 2, 7, 7, 7, 1, 8, 7, 3, 3, 6

   b   3, −3, −3, 2, −2, 1, −1, −1, 0, 0, 1, −1, 2, −1, −2, 3

2   Mr Patel records the marks of 10 students in his record book.

   28, 27, 32, 17, 23, 28, 29, 20, 27, 29

   a   Calculate:

       i   the mean mark   **iii**   the modal mark

       ii   the median mark   **iv**   the range.

   b   He realises that the mark recorded as 32 should have been 35.

       What effect will this have on the following?

       i   the mean mark   **iii**   the modal mark

       ii   the median mark   **iv**   the range.

3   A chart in the Health Centre shows that the average weight of a 6-month-old baby is 7.5 kg. There are six 6-month-old babies at the Health Centre. Their weights are:

Aneeta 7 kg   Sarah 8 kg   Chris 6.5 kg

Shivi 7.5 kg   Natalie 6 kg   Sam 8.5 kg

   a   What is the range of the babies' weights?

   b   What is the median weight?

   c   How many babies are over 7.5 kg?

   d   What is the mean weight of the six babies?

   e   Does this group of babies seem to share a similar average weight to those on the chart?
       Explain your answer.

4   The mean of three numbers is 21. Two numbers are smaller than the mean and one is bigger. Write down three possible numbers.

5   In a diving competition, Tom scores a mean mark of 5.3

   Seven of his eight marks are 4.9, 5.3, 5.5, 5.6, 5.8, 4.8, 4.9

   What is his eighth mark?

6   In a survey on the number of people in a household the information shown in the table was collected from 50 houses.

   a   Find the mean, median and mode of household sizes.

   b   Which average is the best one to use to represent the data?
       Explain your answer.

Number of people in a household	Number of households
1	9
2	19
3	9
4	8
5	4
6	1
Total	50

C

7 This table gives the number of years service by 50 teachers at the Clare School.

a   Find the modal class.

b   Calculate an estimate of the mean.

Number of years service	Number of teachers
0–4	11
5–9	15
10–14	4
15–19	10
20–24	6
25–29	4

8 In a science lesson 30 runner bean plants were measured. Here are the results correct to the nearest centimetre.

6.2	5.4	8.9	12.1	6.5	9.3	7.2	12.7	10.2	5.4
7.7	9.5	11.1	8.6	7.0	13.5	12.7	5.6	15.4	12.3
13.4	9.5	6.7	8.6	9.1	11.5	14.2	13.5	8.8	9.7

The teacher suggested putting the data into groups.

Length in centimetres	Tally	Total
5 but less than 7		
7 but less than 9		
9 but less than 11		
11 but less than 13		
13 but less than 15		
15 but less than 17		

a   Copy and complete the table.

b   Use the information to estimate the mean height of the plants.

c   Calculate the mean from the original data.

d   Why is your answer to part **b** only an estimate of the mean?

? **9** The weights of some apples are shown in the table.

Weight of apples, w grams	Frequency
$30 < w \leqslant 40$	25
$40 < w \leqslant 50$	28
$50 < w \leqslant 60$	21
$60 < w \leqslant 70$	6

Granny Smith apples have a mean weight of 45 grams and a range of 39 grams.

Compare these data with the table. Do the data in the table seem to be about Granny Smith apples?

Practice questions **k**

1   a   Here are four numbers.

4   2   1   7

Explain why the median is 3.   *(2 marks)*

b   Here are five numbers.

4   2   1   7   5

What fraction of the numbers is below the median?   *(2 marks)*

c   A set of six numbers has a median of 3. Only one of the numbers is below the median.

Write down a possible set of the six numbers.   *(2 marks)*

AQA 2008

9 Sequences

Objectives

Examiners would normally expect students who get these grades to be able to:

G
continue a sequence of diagrams or numbers

write the terms of a simple sequence

F
find a term in a sequence with positive numbers

write the term-to-term rule in a sequence with positive numbers

E
find a term in a sequence with negative or fractional numbers

write the term-to-term rule in a sequence with negative or fractional numbers

D
write the terms of a sequence or a series of diagrams given the nth term

C
write the nth term of a linear sequence or a series of diagrams.

Key terms

sequence
ascending
descending
term-to-term
linear sequence
nth term

Did you know?

Sequences in nature

Have you ever wondered why four-leaf clovers are so rare? It's because four isn't a number in the Fibonacci sequence.

The Fibonacci sequence 0, 1, 1, 2, 3, 5, 8, 13, ... is well known in nature and can be applied to seashell shapes, branching plants, flower petals, pine cones and pineapples.

If you count the number of petals on a daisy, you are most likely to find 13, 21, 34, 55 or 89 petals. These are all numbers in the Fibonacci sequence.

You should already know:

✓ how to identify odd and even numbers.

Learn... **9.1 The rules of a sequence**

A **sequence** is a set of numbers or patterns with a given rule.

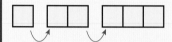 2, 4, 6, 8, 10, ... is the sequence of even numbers

The rule is **add two**.

Sequences can be

- **ascending** (going up) e.g. 2, 5, 8, 11, ...
- **descending** (going down) e.g. 5, 3, 1, −1, −3, ...

Sequences can also be patterns.

The rule is **add one square**.

Example: Write down the next two terms in this sequence.

5, 10, 15, 20, ...   The dots tell you that the sequence continues.

Solution: The rule to find the next number in the sequence is **+5**.

| 1st | 2nd | 3rd | 4th |
| term | term | term | term |

5,   10,   15,   20,

+5   +5   +5

The rule (called the **term-to-term** rule) can be used to find the next two terms.

The fifth term is 20 + 5 = 25

The sixth term is 25 + 5 = 30

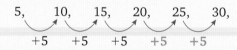
5,   10,   15,   20,   25,   30,

+5   +5   +5   +5   +5

Example: Write down the next two terms in this sequence.

5, 10, 20, 40, ...

Solution: The rule to find the next number in the sequence is ×2.

| 1st | 2nd | 3rd | 4th |
| term | term | term | term |

5,   10,   20,   40,

×2   ×2   ×2

The fifth term is 40 × 2 = 80

The sixth term is 80 × 2 = 160

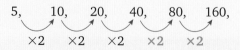
5,   10,   20,   40,   80,   160,

×2   ×2   ×2   ×2   ×2

Practise...   9.1 The rules of a sequence   G F E D C

1   Draw the next two diagrams in the following sequences.

a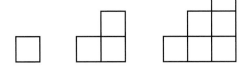

b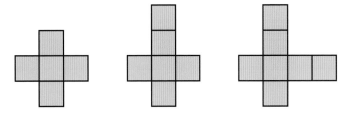

c

2   Write down the next two terms of the following sequences.

a   3, 7, 11, 15, …

b   4, 8, 12, 16, …

c   2, 10, 18, 26, …

d   0, 5, 10, 15, …

e   1, 2, 4, 8, 16, …

f   100, 1000, 10 000, 100 000, …

3   Copy and complete the following table.

Pattern (n)	Diagram	Number of matchsticks (m)
1		3
2		5
3		7
4		
5		

a   What do you notice about the pattern of matchsticks above?

b   How many matchsticks will there be in the fifth pattern?

c   How many matchsticks will there be in the tenth pattern?

d   There are 41 matchsticks in the 20th pattern.
How many matchsticks are there in the 21st pattern?
Give a reason for your answer.

F
E

4 Write down the term-to-term rule for the following sequences.

a   3, 7, 11, 15, ...   e   20, 16, 12, 8, ...

b   0, 5, 10, 15, ...   f   100, 1000, 10 000, ...

c   1, 2, 4, 8, 16, ...   g   2, 3, 4.5, 6.75, ...

d   3, 4.5, 6, 7.5, ...   h   54, 18, 6, 2, ...

D

5 The term-to-term rule is +4.
Write down five different sequences that fit this rule.

6 Here is a sequence of numbers.

3   5   9   17

The rule for continuing this sequence is: multiply by 2 and subtract 1.

a   What are the next two numbers in this sequence?

The same rule is used for a sequence that starts with the number −3.

b   What are the first four numbers in this sequence?

7 Here is a sequence of coordinates:

(2, 5), (3, 6), (4, 7), ...

What are the next two coordinates in this sequence?
What do you notice if you plot these points on a graph?

8 Jacob is exploring number patterns.

He writes down the following products in a table.

1×1	1
11×11	121
111×111	12 321
1111×1111	1 234 321
$11\,111 \times 11\,111$	
$111\,111 \times 111\,111$	

a   Copy and complete the next two rows of the table.

b   Jacob says he can use the table to work out 1 111 111 111 × 1 111 111 111
Is he correct? Give a reason for your answer.

9 Here are the first four terms of a sequence.

45, 31, 14, 15

Here is the rule for the sequence.
To get the next number, multiply the digits of the previous number and add 11 to the result.
Work out the 100th number of the sequence.

10 Investigate the following sequences. What are the rules and next terms?

a   1, 4, 9, 16, ...

b   1, 8, 27, 64, ...

c   1, 3, 6, 10, 15, ...

d   1, 1, 2, 3, 5, 8, ...

e   2, 3, 5, 7, 11, ...

Learn... 9.2 The nth term of a sequence

A **linear sequence** is one where the differences between the terms are all the same.

The sequence 5, 10, 15, 20, ... is a linear sequence because the differences are all the same.

5,   10,   15,   20,

+5   +5   +5

The sequence 5, 10, 20, 40, ... is NOT a linear sequence because the differences are not the same.

5,   10,   20,   40,

+5   +10   +20

To find the **nth term** of a linear sequence, you can use the formula:

nth term = difference $\times$ n + (first term $-$ difference)

$= dn + (a - d)$

For 7, 10, 13, 16 d is the difference = +3

a is the first term = 7

nth term = difference $\times$ n + (first term $-$ difference)

$= 3 \times n + (7 - 3)$

$= 3n + 4$

Example: The nth term of a sequence is $2n + 3$

Find the first four terms of the sequence.

Solution: 1st term = $2 \times 1 + 3 = 5$

2nd term = $2 \times 2 + 3 = 7$

3rd term = $2 \times 3 + 3 = 9$

4th term = $2 \times 4 + 3 = 11$

Similarly

100th term = $2 \times 100 + 3 = 203$

The first four terms are 5, 7, 9, 11.

The sequence is called a linear sequence because the differences between the terms are all the same.

5,   7,   9,   11, ...

+2   +2   +2

In this example, the differences are all +2.

The term-to-term rule is +2.

Example: The first four terms of a sequence are 7, 10, 13, 16.

Find the nth term.

> **Study tip**
>
> The nth term is sometimes called the general term.

Solution: 7,   10,   13,   16,

+3   +3   +3

The term-to-term rule is +3.

This tells you that the rule is of the form $3n + ...$

1st term = $3 \times 1 + ... = 7$

2nd term = $3 \times 2 + ... = 10$

3rd term = $3 \times 3 + ... = 13$

4th term = $3 \times 1 + ... = 16$

The sequence goes up in 3s, just like the 3 times table, so the rule begins $3 \times n$ ($3n$, for short).

From the above you can see that the nth term is $3n + 4$

$= 3n + (7 - 3)$ This method only works for linear sequences.

$= 3n + 4$

Practise... 9.2 The *n*th term of a sequence G F E D C

D

1 Write down the first five terms of the sequence whose *n*th term is:

   a $n + 5$ **c** $5n + 1$ **e** $n^2 + 2$ **g** $10 - 2n$

   b $3n$ **d** $2n - 7$ **f** $\frac{1}{2}n + 2$

2 Write down the 100th and the 101st terms of the sequence whose *n*th term is:

   a $n + 3$ **b** $3n - 10$ **c** $100 - 2n$ **d** $n^2 - 1$

3 Aisha writes down the sequence 2, 6, 10, 14, ...
She says that the *n*th term is $n + 4$

   Is she correct?
   Give a reason for your answer.

4 The *n*th term of a sequence is $3n - 1$

   a Colin says that 31 is a number in this sequence.
      Is Colin correct? Give a reason for your answer.

   b Diane says the 20th term is double the 10th term.
      Is Diana correct? Give a reason for your answer.

C

5 Write down the *n*th term for the following linear sequences.

   a 3, 7, 11, 15, ...   **e** −1, 1, 3, 5, ...

   b 0, 6, 12, 18, ...   **f** −5, −1, 3, 7, ...

   c 9, 15, 21, 27, ...   **g** 5, 6.5, 8, 9.5, ...

   d 8, 14, 20, 26, ...   **h** 23, 21, 19, 17, ...

6 Write down the 10th and the 100th terms of each of the sequences in Question 5.

7

Pattern (*n*)	Diagram	Number of matchsticks (*m*)
1		3
2		5
3		7

   a Write down the formula for the number of matchsticks (*m*) in the *n*th pattern.

   b There are 200 matchsticks. What pattern number can be made?

8 Write down the formula for the number of squares in the *n*th pattern.

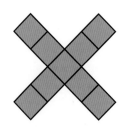

> **Study tip**
>
> Always check your *n*th term to see that it works for the sequence.

9 Stuart says that the number of cubes in the 100th pattern is 300.

How can you tell Stuart is wrong?

Give a reason for your answer.

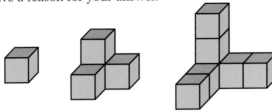

10 Write the *n*th term for these non-linear sequences.

a 1, 4, 9, 16, …

b 2, 5, 10, 17, …

c 2, 8, 18, 32, …

d 1, 8, 27, 64, 125, …

e 0, 7, 26, 63, 124, …

f 10, 100, 1000, …

> **Hint**
>
> Use your answer to part **a** to help you with parts **b** and **c**. Use your answer to part **d** to help you with parts **e** and **f**.

11 Write the *n*th term for the following sequences.

a $1 \times 2, 2 \times 3, 3 \times 4, …$

b $\frac{2}{3}, \frac{3}{4}, \frac{4}{5}, \frac{5}{6}, …$

c $1 \times 2 \times 5, 2 \times 3 \times 6, 3 \times 4 \times 7, 4 \times 5 \times 8, …$

d 0.1, 0.2, 0.3, 0.4, …

12 Jackie builds fencing from pieces of wood as shown below.

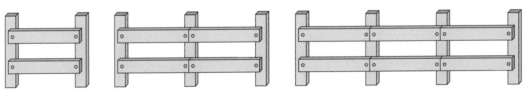

Diagram 1
4 pieces of wood

Diagram 2
7 pieces of wood

Diagram 3
10 pieces of wood

a How many pieces of wood will there be in Diagram *n*?

b Use your answer to part **a** to work out the number of pieces of wood needed for Diagram 10.

13 The table shows the stopping distances for cars travelling at different speeds.

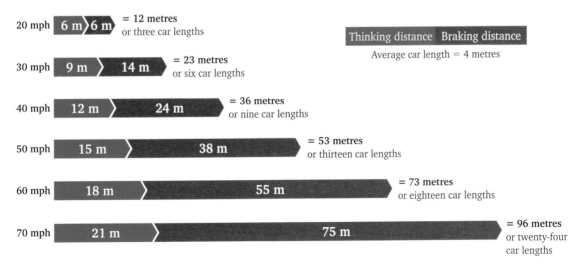

a Use the method of sequences to work out a formula for the thinking distance.

b Use the formula to work out the thinking distance for **i** 80 mph and **ii** 35 mph.

9 Assess

G
F

1 **a** Draw the next two diagrams in the following sequences.

   i

   ii

   iii

  b Write down the next two terms in the following sequences.

   i 2, 7, 12, 17, …
   iii 2, 6, 18, 54, …
   ii 1.2, 1.4, 1.6, 1.8, …
   iv 5, 50, 500, 5000, …

F

2 **a** Write down the 5th, 8th and 10th terms in the following sequences.

   i 2, 5, 8, 11, …
   iii 3, 6, 12, 24, …
   ii 1, 6, 11, 16, …

  b Write down the term-to-term rule in the following sequences.

   i 1, 5, 9, 13, …
   iii 1, 2, 5, 14, 41, …
   ii 2, 10, 50, 250, …

E
D

3 **a** Write down the 5th, 8th and 10th terms in the following sequences.

   i 20, 17, 14, 11, …
   iii 1, −2, 4, −8, …
   ii 64, 32, 16, …

  b Write down the term-to-term rule for the following sequences.

   i 8, 5, 2, −1, …
   iii 2, −2, 2, −2, 2, …
   ii −1, −4, −7, −10, …

D

4 The nth term of a sequence is $4n + 3$

Asha says that the 10th term is double the 5th term.

Is Asha correct?

Give reasons for your answer.

5 Information about some squares is shown.

  a Copy and complete the table.

  b Use the table to write down the nth term
in these sequences.

   i 2, 8, 18, 32, …
   ii −2, 1, 6, 13, …

Side of square (cm)	1	2	3	4	n
Area of square (cm²)	1	4	9	16	

6 Find the *n*th term in the following sequences.

    a   6, 8, 10, 12, …

    b   3, 13, 23, 3, …

    c   8, 6, 4, 2, …

7 The *n*th term of a sequence is $4n - 5$

    The *n*th term of a different sequence is $8 + 2n$

    Jo says that there are no numbers that are in both sequences.

    Show that Jo is correct.

8 Write down a linear sequence where the 4th term is twice the 2nd term.

    Jo says that that this is always true if the first term is equal to the difference.

    Is Jo correct?

    Give a reason for your answer.

Practice questions Ⓚ

1   **a**   The first term of a sequence is -2.
       The rule for continuing the sequence is:

> Add 7
> then multiply by 4

       What is the second term of the sequence?   *(1 mark)*

   b   This rule is used to continue a different sequence.

> Multiply by 2
> then add 5

       The **third** term of this sequence is 11.
       Work out the **first** term.   *(4 marks)*

AQA 2005

10 Percentages

Objectives

Examiners would normally expect students who get these grades to be able to:

F

understand that percentage means 'number of parts per 100'

change between percentages and fractions or decimals

E

compare percentages, fractions and decimals

work out a percentage of a given quantity

D

increase or decrease by a given percentage

express one quantity as a percentage of another

C

work out a percentage increase or decrease.

Try this!

Breakfast bits

Do you like bits in your orange juice?

A survey of British people found that:
- 15% won't touch orange juice with bits in it
- 7% won't have it without bits
- 7% won't eat the bits in marmalade or jam.

We have other loves and hates at breakfast time:
- 25% won't eat cereal that has gone soggy
- 14% demand to have matching cutlery
- 7% insist that the crusts are cut off their toast.

Carry out a survey to find out what students in your class love or hate at breakfast time. Surveys often give results in percentages. After working through this chapter you will be able to present the results of your own surveys in percentages.

Key terms

percentage	discount
amount	deposit
Value Added Tax (VAT)	balance
rate	credit
depreciation	interest
principal	

You should already know:

✓ place values in decimals

✓ how to put decimals in order of size

✓ how to simplify fractions

✓ how to write a fraction as a decimal and vice versa.

Learn... **10.1 Percentages, fractions and decimals**

1% (1 per cent) means '1 part out of 100'.
(In money this is '1p in the £1'.)

10% means '10 out of 100' or $\frac{10}{100}$

$1\% = \frac{1}{100} = 0.01$ $10\% = \frac{1}{10} = 0.1$

To write a **percentage** as a decimal or fraction, divide by 100.

As a fraction, $25\% = \frac{25}{100}$ Enter $\frac{25}{100}$ into your calculator
$= \frac{1}{4}$ then press [=] to simplify

As a decimal, $25\% = 25 \div 100$ Try this on your calculator, the
$= 0.25$ figures move 2 places to the right.

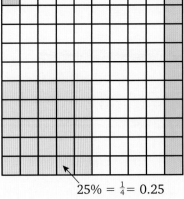

To write a decimal or fraction as a percentage, multiply by 100.

$0.25 = 0.25 \times 100\% = 25\%$ Try this on your calculator, the
figures move two places to the left.

$\frac{1}{4} = \frac{1}{4} \times 100\% = 25\%$ On your calculator, press $1 \div 4 \times 100 =$
or enter the fraction $\frac{1}{4}$ then press $\times 100 =$

$25\% = \frac{1}{4} = 0.25$

Example: Write these in order of size, starting with the smallest.
$0.87 \quad \frac{7}{8} \quad 78\%$

Solution: Write 0.87 as a percentage. $0.87 \times 100\% = 87\%$

Write $\frac{7}{8}$ as a percentage. $\frac{7}{8} \times 100\% = 87\frac{1}{2}\%$

(or $7 \div 8 \times 100\% = 87.5\%$)

In order of size, the values are: **78%, 0.87, $\frac{7}{8}$**

> **Study tip**
>
> When you are asked to compare fractions and decimals, change them all to percentages.

 Practise...   **10.1 Percentages, fractions and decimals**   G F E D C

1   For each of the 100 squares **a–d**:

    i   What percentage is shaded?

    ii   Write the percentage shaded as a decimal.

    iii   What fraction is **not** shaded?

    a   **b**   **c**   **d**

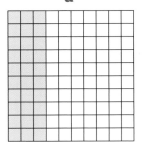 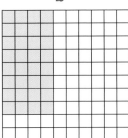 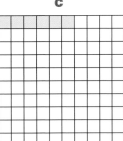 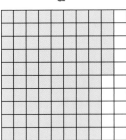

2   Change each decimal to a percentage.

    a   0.75   **c**   0.09   **e**   0.04   **g**   1.03   **i**   0.125

    b   0.16   **d**   0.9   **f**   0.4   **h**   2.5   **j**   0.026

3   Change each percentage to a decimal.

    a   30%   **c**   80%   **e**   32%   **g**   125%   **i**   7.5%

    b   47%   **d**   8%   **f**   3%   **h**   375%   **j**   62.5%

G

F

4   Change each fraction to a percentage.

a $\frac{27}{100}$ c $\frac{9}{10}$ e $\frac{1}{5}$ g $\frac{4}{5}$ i $\frac{9}{20}$

b $\frac{3}{100}$ d $\frac{7}{20}$ f $\frac{3}{4}$ h $\frac{16}{25}$ j $\frac{3}{8}$

5   Change each percentage to a fraction.
Give each fraction in its simplest form.

a   49%   c   36%   e   5%   g   2%   i   40%

b   70%   d   65%   f   60%   h   8%   j   24%

6   Write these in order of size, smallest first.

a $\frac{1}{5}$,   0.3,   25%   b   72%, $\frac{3}{4}$,   0.7   c   0.6,   58%, $\frac{13}{20}$

7   a   Which of these are greater than $\frac{1}{2}$?

     47%,   0.054, $\frac{4}{7}$,   8.5%,   0.62

     Give a reason for your answer.

   b   Which of these are less than $\frac{1}{4}$?

     24%,   0.3, $\frac{2}{9}$,   40%,   0.09

     Give a reason for your answer.

8   Tina says that 34% is less than a third. Is she right? Give a reason for your answer.

9   Tom says that five-eighths is 0.625%. What mistake has he made?

10   Which of the following fractions is nearest to 50%?

$\frac{4}{10}$ $\frac{9}{20}$ $\frac{14}{30}$ $\frac{19}{40}$

Show how you decided.

11   a   Copy the number square.

   b   Change each fraction to a percentage.

   c   Write the percentage answer with three digits down the centre.

   d   Use your other percentage answers to fill the rest of the square.

 $\frac{7}{10}$, $\frac{16}{25}$, $4\frac{3}{4}$, $\frac{9}{20}$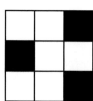

12   Write each percentage as a fraction in its simplest form.

a $7\frac{1}{2}\%$ b $12\frac{1}{2}\%$ c $6\frac{1}{4}\%$ d $3\frac{3}{4}\%$ e $66\frac{2}{3}\%$

> **Hint**
>
> Enter $7\frac{1}{2}$ into your calculator then divide by 100.

13   Amir, Emma and Duncan have saved some money.

Emma has saved 83% of the **amount** Amir has saved.

Duncan has saved $\frac{33}{40}$ of the amount Amir has saved.

Who has saved the most, Emma or Duncan?

Give a reason for your answer.

Learn... 10.2 Finding a percentage of a quantity

To find a percentage of a quantity:
- **find 1% by dividing by 100**
- then **multiply by the percentage** you need.

To find a percentage of a quantity using a decimal multiplier.
- To find 1% you multiply by 0.01 (1 ÷ 100)
- To find 10% you multiply by 0.10 (10 ÷ 100)
- To find 63% you multiply by 0.63 etc (63 ÷ 100).

Example:  Find:

    a   15% of £48

    b $42\frac{1}{2}$% of £6.35

Solution: **a**   15% of £48 = 48 ÷ 100 × 15 = £7.2

                   ↑   ↑
            Finds Finds
             1%   15%

Your calculator gives 7.2 which means £7.20

    b $42\frac{1}{2}$% of £6.35 = 6.35 ÷ 100 × $42\frac{1}{2}$ = £2.69875 ← Use 42.5 here if you wish.

                   ↑   ↑
            Finds Finds
             1% $42\frac{1}{2}$%

Your calculator gives 2.69875 which you should round to the nearest penny, £2.70.

Alternative method: using a decimal multiplier

    a   For 15% the decimal multiplier is 0.15   Decimal multiplier = 15 ÷ 100 = 0.15
        So 15% of £48 = 0.15 × £48 = £7.20

    b   For $42\frac{1}{2}$% the decimal multiplier is 0.425   Decimal multiplier = 42.5 ÷ 100 = 0.425
        So $42\frac{1}{2}$% of £6.35 = 0.425 × £6.35
                       = **£2.70** to nearest penny

Practise... 10.2 Finding a percentage of a quantity

G F E D C

1   Work out:

    a   25% of £140   **c**   20% of £190   **e**   70% of £280

    b   75% of £3000   **d**   30% of £8400   **f**   95% of £80

   Use a different method to check your answers.

2   Work out:

    a   15% of 240 m   **c**   32% of 4500 litres   **e**   23% of 800 g

    b   56% of 500 kg   **d**   45% of 80 km   **f**   74% of 250 ml

   Use a different method to check your answers.

F

3

a Write down the decimal multiplier for working out 20% of a quantity.

Hint

Decimal multiplier = 20 ÷ 100 (for 20%)

b Copy and complete this table of decimal multipliers.

To find	20%	1%	12%	35%	7%	4%	17.5%	2.5%	125%
Multiply by									

c Use the decimal multipliers from your table to work out:

i 20% of 150

ii 1% of 160

iii 12% of 320

iv 35% of £500

v 7% of £20

vi 4% of £220

vii 17.5% of £150

viii 2.5% of £32.50

ix 125% of £25.60

4 Work out:

a 5% of £37

b 15% of 678 cm

c 12% of £72.50

d 75% of 9.36 litres

e 7% of 892 miles

f 64% of 12.75 km

g 6% of 542 tonnes

h 29% of £6.75

i 74% of £135

5 Work out:

a $7\frac{1}{2}$% of 72

b 24.5% of 62 000

c $33\frac{1}{3}$% of 3150

d 1.25% of 980

e $8\frac{3}{4}$% of 3.6

f $66\frac{2}{3}$% of £16.95

6 A zoo has a herd of 120 zebras.
55% of the zebras are female.

How many male and female zebras are there in the herd?

7 The **Value Added Tax (VAT)** on these goods is 17.5% of their value.
Find the VAT on the following.

a
£460 + VAT

b
£58.60 + VAT

c
£75.99 + VAT

8 Gas and electricity companies charge 5% VAT on their bills.
Find the VAT on each of these bills.

a
```
Gas you've used
  (without VAT) = £217.62
```

b
```
Cost of electricity used
           (without VAT) = £113.76
```

9 Katie says '40% of £18 is seven pounds and two pence.'
Is she correct?

Explain your answer.

10 Tom has £2200.

He gives 15% to his son and 30% to his daughter.

He keeps the rest.

How much does Tom keep?

You **must** show your working.

11 Currently, the population of the UK is approximately 61 million.

About 13% of the population is between 5 and 15 years old.

By 2031 the population is expected to rise to 71 million.

About 12.4% of the population is expected to be between 5 and 15 years old.

How many more children between 5 and 15 years old are there expected to be in 2031?

12 In 2009 a TV set cost £650 **excluding** VAT.

During 2009 the **rate** of VAT was reduced from 17.5% to 15%

How much less was the cost of the TV set **including** VAT after the VAT rate was reduced?

13 Amie, Ben, Carrie, Dave, Emma and Fergus share £200 between them.

Amie gets 10% of the £200.

Ben gets 20% of what is left.

Carrie gets 30% of what is left after Amie and Ben take their share.

Dave gets 40% of what is left after Amie, Ben and Carrie take their share.

Emma and Fergus share the remainder.

Who gets the most?

14 Last year, 10% of the animals seen by a vet are cats.

The vet sees twice as many dogs as cats.

Last year, the vet saw 210 animals that were **not** cats or dogs.

How many animals did the vet see?

Learn... 10.3 Increasing or decreasing by a percentage

To increase or decrease by a given percentage:

- **Find 1% by dividing by 100.**
- Then **multiply by the percentage** you need.
- For a % increase, add to the original quantity. For a % decrease, subtract from the original quantity.

An alternative method is to use a decimal multiplier.

- Write the new quantity as a % of the original quantity.
- Convert this % to a decimal **multiplier**.
- Multiply by the original quantity.

Example: **a** Increase £84 by 20%

b Decrease 75 800 by 12.5%

Solution: **a** 20% of £84 $= \frac{84}{100} \times 20$

$= 16.8$

New amount $= 16.8 + 84$
$= £100.80$

b 12.5% of 75 800 $= \frac{12.5}{100} \times 75\,800$

$= 9475$

New amount $= 75\,800 - 9475$
$= 66\,325$

Study tip

Don't forget to add a zero to complete the pence.

Does your calculator have an ANS key?
You can use it here.

Alternative method: using a decimal multiplier

a New amount $= 100\% + 20\% = 120\%$
The multiplier $= 1.20$
New amount $= 1.2 \times 84$
$= £100.80$

b New amount $= 100\% - 12.5\% = 87.5\%$
The multiplier $= 0.875$
New amount $= 0.875 \times 75\,800$
$= 66\,325$

D

Practise...
10.3 Increasing or decreasing by a percentage

1
   a   Increase £40 by 25%
   c   Decrease £375 by 40%

   b   Increase £35 000 by 20%
   d   Decrease £7.60 by 75%

Use a different method to check your answers.

2
   a   Increase 120 m by 50%
   c   Decrease 8 miles by 15%

   b   Increase 70 kg by 30%
   d   Decrease 62.5 litres by 18%

Use a different method to check your answers.

3
   a   Increase £35.40 by 29%
   c   Decrease £75 by 5%

   b   Increase £260 by 12.5%
   d   Decrease £49.99 by $33\frac{1}{3}$%

4
   a   Write down the decimal multiplier for increasing a quantity by 20%

   b   Copy and complete these tables.

To increase by	20%	40%	8%	3.5%
Multiply by				

To decrease by	20%	40%	8%	3.5%
Multiply by				

> **Hint**
> This is how you work out the decimal multiplier for increasing a quantity by 20%
>
> Decimal multiplier = (100 + 20) ÷ 100

   c   Use the decimal multipliers from your table to work out the following.

     i   150 increased by 20%
     v   150 decreased by 20%

     ii   160 increased by 40%
     vi   160 decreased by 40%

     iii   320 increased by 8%
     vii   320 decreased by 8%

     iv   250 increased by 3.5%
     viii   250 decreased by 3.5%

5
The cost of a rail journey is £78.50.

What is the new price after a 4% increase?

Use a different method to check your answers.

> **Study tip**
> It is a good idea to always **check** your answers. One way of doing this is to use a different method if you know one.

6
The table gives the original prices of some clothes.

The shop reduces these prices by 30% in a sale.

Find the new prices.

Item	Original price
Trousers	£48.90
Shirt	£29.50
Jumper	£35.95
Gloves	£17.99

7
Gemma bought a car last year for £8900.

It has **depreciated** in value by 15%

What is it worth now?

> **Hint**
> Depreciation is a fall in value.

8
Paul opens a building society account with £2500.

The interest rate is 6% per year.

What is the amount in the account after:

   a   1 year
   b   2 years

> **Hint**
> £2500 is the **principal**.

D
C

9 This coat costs £95.50 before the sale.

Work out the price of the coat in the sale.

SALE
15% off

10 The prices of each of these items are given **excluding** VAT.
Find the cost of each item **including** VAT at the rate given.

a

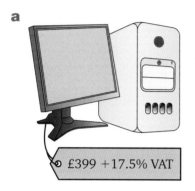

£399 +17.5% VAT

b

Cost of electricity
£246.38 + 5% VAT

c

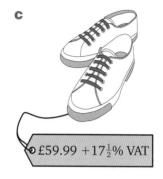

£59.99 +17½% VAT

11 The original price of a football is £6.95.
It is reduced by 40% in a sale.
Jake says the sale price is £2.78.

Is he correct? Explain your answer.

12 A zoo puts up its prices by 5%.
In the first week after the increase, it gives a **discount** of 5%.
Sunita says the cost will be back to the old price.

Do you agree? Explain your answer.

13 The table shows the salaries of some of a company's employees.

Job	Number of employees	Salary (per year)
Clerical assistant	5	£15 400
Factory worker	25	£16 900
Warehouse worker	8	£17 500
Delivery driver	4	£19 750

The company is discussing these two offers for a pay rise with the employees.

Offer 1
A salary increase of £350 for all employees

Offer 2
A 2% salary increase

a Tina and Afzal are clerical assistants.
Tina says Offer 1 gives her a bigger increase. Afzal disagrees.
Who is correct?
Give a reason for your answer.

b Which offer is best for each of the other workers?
Give a reason for each of your answers.

c Overall, which offer would cost the company less money?

14 Sally wants to buy a drum kit priced at £495.

She pays a **deposit** of £100.

There are two ways she can pay the rest of the price (the **balance**).

> **EasyPay Option**
> 7.5% **credit** charge on the balance
> 6 equal monthly payments
>
> **PayLess Option**
> 2.5% **interest** added each month to the amount owed
> pay £50 per month until the balance is paid off
> (In the last month Sally will only pay the remaining balance, not a full £50.)

Investigate these two options and advise Sally which one is best.

Would your advice be different if EasyPay charged 8% or PayLess charged 1.5% each month?

Learn... 10.4 Writing one quantity as a percentage of another

To write one quantity as a percentage of another:

- Divide the first quantity by the second. This gives you a decimal (or write the first quantity as a fraction of the second).
- Then multiply by 100, to change the decimal or fraction to a percentage.

Example: Write 80 pence as a percentage of £5.

Solution: $\dfrac{80}{500} \times 100 = 16$

£5 = 500p

> **Study tip**
> The quantities must be in the same units.

so 80 pence is 16% of £5. You can work in £ if you prefer.
$$0.80 \div 5 \times 100 = 16$$

Example: In one month, 108 baby boys and 96 baby girls are born in a maternity hospital.

What percentage of the babies are boys?

What percentage are girls?

> **Study tip**
> You must write each number as a percentage of the **total**.

Solution: The total number of babies = 108 + 96 = 204

Percentage that are boys = $\dfrac{108}{204} \times 100 = 52.9\%$ (to 1 d.p.)

Percentage that are girls = 100% − 52.9% = 47.1% (to 1 d.p.)

or 96 ÷ 204 × 100 = 47.1%. Then use 47.1% + 52.9% = 100% to check.

Example: The table shows the marks students get in a test.

a What percentage of students get less than 10?

b Students must get 20 or more to pass.

　　i What percentage of students pass?

　　ii What percentage of students fail?

Marks	Frequency
0–9	4
10–19	7
20–29	9
30–39	8
40–49	4

Solution:

a The total number of students = 4 + 7 + 9 + 8 + 4 = 32

4 out of 32 students get less than 10

Divide by the total

Percentage of students who get less than 10 = 4 ÷ 32 × 100 = **12.5%**

$$\text{or } \frac{4}{32} \times 100 = 12\tfrac{1}{2}\%$$

b The number of students who get 20 or more = 9 + 8 + 4 = 21

i Percentage of students who pass = $\frac{21}{32} \times 100$ = **65.6%**

ii Percentage of students who fail = 100% − 65.6% = **34.4%**

Alternatively: The number who fail = 32 − 21 = 11 then $\frac{11}{32} \times 100$ = 34.4%

10.4 Writing one quantity as a percentage of another

Practise...

When answers are not exact, round them to 1 decimal place.

1 Write:

a £32 as a percentage of £200

b 25p as a percentage of 80p

c 28p as a percentage of £3.50

d £325 as a percentage of £750

e 65p as a percentage of £5.20

f £18 500 as a percentage of £25 000

2 Express:

a 24 kg as a percentage of 50 kg

b 5 cm as a percentage of 200 cm

c 250 g as a percentage of 500 g

d 850 cm as a percentage of 500 cm

e 280 cm as a percentage of 250 cm

f 87 000 as a percentage of 1 million

3 In a survey, 28 out of 40 people say they prefer butter to margarine.
What percentage is this?

4 Out of 52 people who take a driving test, 34 pass.

a What percentage of the people pass? **b** What percentage of the people fail?

5 A class contains 15 boys and 17 girls.

10 out of the boys in the class have school dinners.

8 out of the girls in the class have school dinners.

a What percentage of the boys in the class has school dinners?

b What percentage of the girls in the class has school dinners?

c What percentage of the whole class has school dinners?

d What percentage of the whole class does not have school dinners?

6 The tally chart shows the hair colour of the students in a class.

Colour	Tally	Frequency
Blonde	ЖТ ЖТ	
Brown	ЖТ ЖТ |||	
Black	ЖТ	
Red	||	

> **Hint**
>
> Decide whether or not Ian is correct, then explain your decision.
>
> The explanation can include calculations as well as a few words.

Ian looks at the tally chart and says 10% of the class has blonde hair.

Is Ian correct?

Explain your answer.

D
C

7 The table gives the colours of the cars in a car park.

Colour	Number of cars
Red	9
Black	6
White	8
Blue	4
Other	1

  a What percentage of the cars are:

    i red

    ii black

    iii white

    iv blue

    v other colours?

  b Describe one way you can check your answers to part **a**.

D

8 The table gives the ages of the people who go on an activity holiday.

Age	Frequency
0–9	1
10–19	36
20–39	33
40–59	8
60 and over	2

  a What percentage of the people are under 20 years old?

  b People who are 40 or over must pay for extra insurance.

    What percentage of holidaymakers are 40 or over?

⚠ 9 Write:

  a 63 thousand as a percentage of 4 million

  b £92.5 million as a percentage of £3 billion

  c 745 cm as a percentage of 1.5 m

  d 640 cm as a percentage of 0.2 km

  e $1\frac{3}{4}$ hours as a percentage of 1 day.

Hint

1 billion = 1000 million

1 m = 100 cm

1 km = 1000 m

⚠ 10 The surface area of the earth is 510 million km².

149 million km² is land and the rest is sea.

  a What percentage of the earth's surface is land?

  b What percentage of the earth's surface is sea?

⚙ 11 A national travel survey asked people how often they cycled last year.

The results are shown in this table.

Cycled (number of times a week)	Number of people aged	
	5–15 years	16 years and over
once or more	1371	1576
less than once	792	2627
never	883	13 310

Study tip

When you are asked to compare sets of data with a different amount of data in each set, use percentages of the total amount of data in each set.

Use the data to compare the number of times that younger and older people cycle.

⚙ 12 The table gives the number of students in a class who are left-handed and right-handed.

	Girls	Boys
Left-handed	38	49
Right-handed	402	421
Total	440	470

Use percentages to compare left-handedness between the genders.

Learn... 10.5 Percentage increase and decrease

To write an increase or decrease as a percentage:

- Find the increase or decrease.
- Divide the increase (or decrease) by the original amount.
- Multiply by 100 to change to a percentage.

Example: A rail fare goes up from £48 to £54. Find the percentage increase.

Solution: Fare increase = £54 − £48 = £6

Percentage increase = $\frac{6}{48} \times 100 = 12.5\%$

So the fare increases by 12.5%

> **Study tip**
>
> Remember to divide by the **original** amount.

Example: A worker takes $1\frac{1}{4}$ minutes to pack a box.
After training he can do it in 50 seconds.

What is the percentage decrease in time?

> **Study tip**
>
> You must use the **same units**.

Solution: Before training, he takes 75 seconds ← $1\frac{1}{4} \times 60 = 75$

Decrease in time = 75 − 50 = 25 seconds   or $\frac{25}{75} \times 100 = 33\frac{1}{3}\%$

Percentage decrease = $\frac{25}{75} \times 100 = 33.3\%$ (to 1 d.p.)

Practise... 10.5 Percentage increase and decrease ⓚ

1 The price of a chocolate bar goes up from 80 pence to 86 pence.
Work out the percentage increase in the price of the chocolate bar.

2 A beekeeper had 25 hives last year.
This year she has only 21 hives.

What is the percentage decrease in
the number of hives?

3 A supermarket buys cauliflowers for 48 pence each.
It sells them for 85 pence each.
Work out the percentage profit.

The percentage profit is the
percentage increase in price.

4 Mike buys a car for £18 700.
He sells it a year later for £16 300.
Work out his percentage loss.

The percentage loss is the
percentage decrease in price.

C

5 The cost of a bus ride goes up from 95 pence to £1.05.

What is the percentage increase in the cost of a bus ticket?

6 A company employs fewer employees than 10 years ago.
The number of male workers has decreased from 8530 to 5380.
The number of female workers has decreased from 3150 to 1420.

   a Work out the percentage fall in:

      i the number of male workers

      ii the number of female workers.

   b Work out the percentage decrease for all workers.

7 The table gives the usual price and
sale price of a computer and printer.

   a Work out the percentage reduction in the price of:

      i the computer

      ii the printer.

   b Work out the percentage reduction in the total price.

	Usual price	Sale price
Computer	£549	£499
Printer	£89	£59

8 The rent of Sophie's flat has gone up from
£120 to £150 per week.
Sophie works out $30 \div 150 \times 100$
She says the rent has increased by 20%

   a What mistake has she made?

   b What is the actual percentage increase in Sophie's rent?

9 The table shows differences between what we drink now and four years ago.

Drink	Average consumption per person, per week	
	Four years ago	Now
Fruit juice	280 ml	340 ml
Low calorie soft drinks	442 ml	508 ml
Other soft drinks	1.39 litres	1.18 litres
Beverages (e.g. tea, coffee)	56	56
Alcoholic drinks	763 ml	772 ml

Hint
Use percentage changes.

Compare these results.

10 The table gives the UK population in millions.

Years	1971	1976	1981	1986	1991	1996	2001	2006
Population	55.9	56.2	56.4	56.7	57.4	58.2	59.1	60.6

   a In which five year interval was the percentage increase the greatest?

   b Use the data to estimate what the population will be in the following years.

      i 2011   **ii** 2016   **iii** 2021   **iv** 2026   **v** 2031

10 Assess

1 **a** What percentage of this shape is shaded?

   b What percentage of the shape is not shaded?

   c Another shape has 80% shaded.
   What fraction of that shape is shaded?

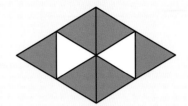

F

2 Copy and complete the table.
Write each fraction in its simplest form.

Decimal	Fraction	Percentage
0.7		
0.45		
0.625		
	$\frac{1}{4}$	
	$\frac{2}{5}$	
	$\frac{2}{3}$	
		5%
		12.5%
		$33\frac{1}{3}\%$
1.5		
	$2\frac{3}{5}$	
		375%

3 Which of these values are greater than $\frac{1}{2}$?

   47%   0.095   8% $\frac{3}{8}$ 0.64

E

4 Which is the larger amount?
You **must** show your working.   65% of £46 $\frac{3}{5}$ of £52

5 The table shows Carl's marks in two tests.

   In which test did Carl do better?
   You **must** show your working.

Test	Mark
A	52 out of 80
B	60 out of 100

D

6 The number of spectators at a football match is 14 594.
3825 of these spectators are season ticket holders.

   What percentage are season ticket holders?
   Give your answer to the nearest per cent.

7 There are 1246 students in Meera's school. Meera asks
250 of the students what they like to read.

   a What percentage of the school population does she ask?

   b The table shows her results.

      i   Why is the total more than 250?

      ii What percentage of the students in the survey
             like to read magazines?

      iii What percentage of the students in the survey
             like to read newspapers?

	Number of students
Books	102
Comics	146
Magazines	215
Newspapers	76
Other	85
Total	

D
C

D
C

8   The table shows the results of a cycling test.

	Boys	Girls
Pass	34	28
Fail	16	12

Compare the percentage of boys who passed with the percentage of girls who passed.

C

9   The cost of a flight increases from £175 to £210.

Calculate the percentage increase.

10   The population of a village decreases from 2476 to 1947.

Find the percentage decrease in the population.

11   Foollah scored 32 out of 60 in the first maths test.
The second maths test is out of 75.
Overall she needs to score 60% to get a pass in maths.

What mark does she need to score out of 75 in the second test?

	Mark	Maximum
Paper 1	32	60
Paper 2	?	75

12   A farmer has 275 sheep.
80% of the sheep had lambs.
35% of the sheep who had lambs had two lambs.
The rest of the sheep had one lamb.

How many lambs did the sheep have?

13   The table shows Debbie's English and maths test scores in Years 8 and 9.

In which subject has Debbie's test scores improved the most?
You **must** show your working.

	Year 8	Year 9
English	53%	75%
Maths	41%	63%

Practice questions ⓚ

1   **a**   The price of a mobile phone is £68.
In a sale the price is decreased by 15%
Work out the price of the mobile phone in the sale.   *(3 marks)*

b   The number of phones sold increased from 80 to 108.
Work out the percentage increase.   *(3 marks)*

AQA 2008

11 Perimeter and area

Objectives

Examiners would normally expect students who get these grades to be able to:

G

find the perimeter of a shape by counting sides of squares

find the area of a shape by counting squares

estimate the area of an irregular shape by counting squares and part squares

name the parts of a circle

F

work out the area and perimeter of a simple rectangle, such as 5 m by 4 m

E

work out the area and perimeter of a harder rectangle, such as 2.6 cm by 8.3 cm

D

find the area of a triangle and parallelogram

find the area and perimeter of shapes made from triangles and rectangles

calculate the circumference and area of a circle

C

work out the perimeter and area of a semicircle.

Key terms

perimeter
area
base
perpendicular height
circle
circumference
radius, radii

diameter
segment
tangent
arc
sector
chord

Did you know?

Surface area of the Earth

The Earth looks blue from space because about 70% of the Earth's surface area is water. Some of the larger countries in the world such as Russia, China and the USA take up a lot of the 30% of the Earth's surface area which is land.

Google Earth can be used to find where you live. Did you know that you can also use Google Earth to measure the perimeter and area of your house or your school grounds? Try it!

You should already know:

✓ how to add, subtract, multiply and divide whole numbers and decimals

✓ definitions of square, rectangle and triangle.

Learn...   11.1 Perimeter and area of a rectangle

The distance round the outside of a shape is called the **perimeter**.

This rectangle is 6 m long and 4 m wide.

To find the perimeter, imagine walking all the way round the edge.

The distance all the way round is **6 m + 4 m + 6 m + 4 m = 20 m**

So the perimeter of the rectangle is 20 m.

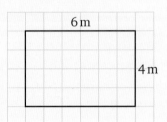

The **area** of a shape is the amount of space it covers.

Area is measured in square units.

The rectangle has been drawn on squared paper.

Counting the squares covered by the rectangle gives an area of 24 square units. As the measurements are in metres the area is 24 square metres or 24 m².

Counting squares can take a long time. In this rectangle, each row has 6 squares (the length). There are 4 rows (the width) so the total number of squares is 6 × 4 = 24

So:

Area of rectangle = length × width

Example: Find the perimeter and area of each shape.

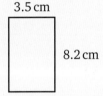

a 3.5 cm 8.2 cm

b 10 cm 5 cm 8 cm 4 cm

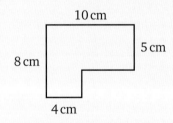

Solution: **a** Perimeter = 3.5 + 8.2 + 3.5 + 8.2 = 23.4 cm

Area = 3.5 × 8.2 = 28.7 cm²

b Perimeter method 1: To find the perimeter of this shape, first work out the missing lengths.

Missing width: 10 cm − 4 cm = 6 cm

Missing height: 8 cm − 5 cm = 3 cm

So the total perimeter = 10 + 5 + 6 + 3 + 4 + 8 = 36 cm

> **Study tip**
>
> Mark the corner you are starting from and imagine walking right round the shape. This will ensure that you don't miss out any sides.

Perimeter method 2: With L shapes, the perimeter is the same as the perimeter of a rectangle with length and width equal to the longest sides. Using this fact, you can find the perimeter without working out the missing lengths.

Perimeter = 10 + 8 + 10 + 8 = 36 cm

Area: To work out the area, divide the shape into rectangles, for example, A and B as shown.

Area of rectangle A = 10 × 5 = 50 cm²

Area of rectangle B = 4 × 3 = 12 cm²

Total area of shape = 50 + 12 = 62 cm²

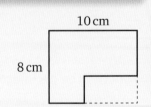

10 cm 8 cm

10 cm A 5 cm 8 cm B 4 cm

This length is 8 cm − 5 cm = 3 cm

> **Study tip**
>
> There is often more than one way to divide up a shape into rectangles.

Practise...   ## 11.1 Perimeter and area of a rectangle

G

1 These diagrams are drawn on centimetre squared paper.

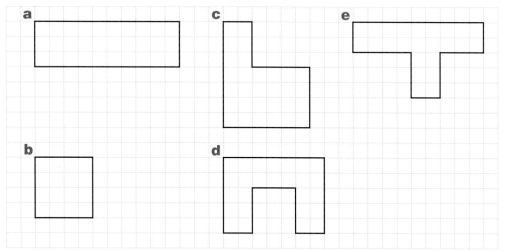

i Work out the perimeter of each shape.

ii Work out the area of each shape by counting squares.

2 Estimate the area of this shape.

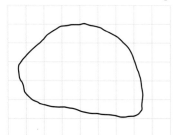

Hint

If more than half a square lies inside the shape, count it as a whole square.
If less than half the square lies inside the shape do **not** count it.

Study tip

On your copy, number the squares as you count them.

3 Look at these four rectangles.

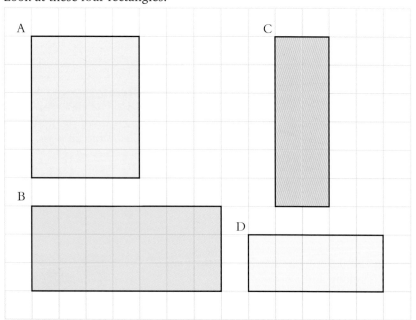

a Which rectangle has the largest perimeter?

b Which rectangle has the smallest perimeter?

c Which rectangle has the largest area?

d List the rectangles and their areas in decreasing order of size.

F

4 Work out the perimeter of squares with the following side lengths.

a   12 cm   c   4.6 cm   e   126.5 cm

b   20 cm   d   13.2 cm

5 On centimetre squared paper draw two different rectangles with a perimeter of 12 cm.

6 For each of these shapes, work out:

i   the perimeter

ii   the area.

a   2.7 cm
8.3 cm

e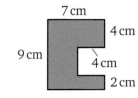
3 m
4 m
2 m
4.5 m

Not drawn accurately

b   1.4 cm   8.2 cm

f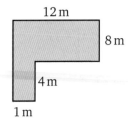
5 cm
6 cm
18 cm
5 cm

c   6 m

g   7 cm
9 cm   4 cm
4 cm
2 cm

d   5 cm

h   12 m
8 m
4 m
1 m

E

7 Find the area of rectangles with these measurements.

a   Length 3.7 cm, width 28 mm

b   Length 2.1 m, width 84 cm

> **Hint**
>
> Be aware of the units of length when calculating area and perimeter.

 8 A rectangle of length 40 cm and width 19.6 cm has the same area as a square.
Work out the length of the square.

9 A rug is 1.5 m long and 0.8 m wide. It is laid on the floor of a room which is 3.2 m long and 3 m wide.
Work out the percentage of the floor area that the rug will cover.

10 Andy and Katie would like name plaques for their bedroom doors.

The carpenter makes the letters by cutting and sticking together two types of rectangular pieces of wood.

Piece A – length 8 cm, width 4 cm

Piece B – length 6 cm, width 4 cm

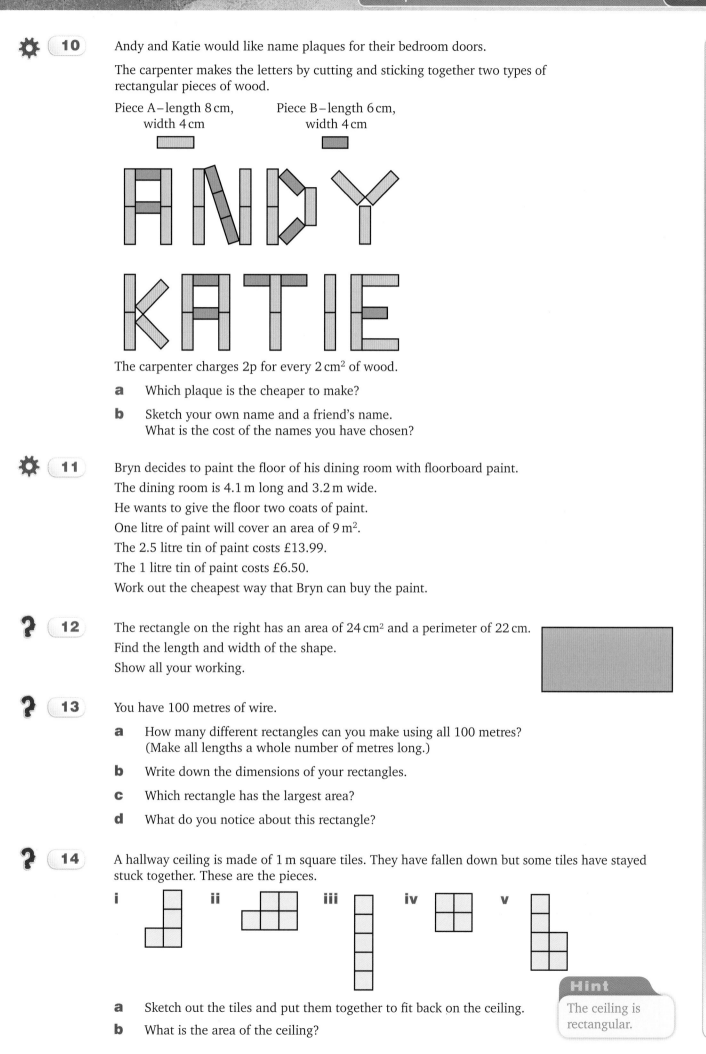

The carpenter charges 2p for every 2 cm² of wood.

a Which plaque is the cheaper to make?

b Sketch your own name and a friend's name.
What is the cost of the names you have chosen?

11 Bryn decides to paint the floor of his dining room with floorboard paint.
The dining room is 4.1 m long and 3.2 m wide.
He wants to give the floor two coats of paint.
One litre of paint will cover an area of 9 m².
The 2.5 litre tin of paint costs £13.99.
The 1 litre tin of paint costs £6.50.
Work out the cheapest way that Bryn can buy the paint.

12 The rectangle on the right has an area of 24 cm² and a perimeter of 22 cm.
Find the length and width of the shape.
Show all your working.

13 You have 100 metres of wire.

a How many different rectangles can you make using all 100 metres?
(Make all lengths a whole number of metres long.)

b Write down the dimensions of your rectangles.

c Which rectangle has the largest area?

d What do you notice about this rectangle?

14 A hallway ceiling is made of 1 m square tiles. They have fallen down but some tiles have stayed stuck together. These are the pieces.

i　　**ii**　　**iii**　　**iv**　　**v**

a Sketch out the tiles and put them together to fit back on the ceiling.

b What is the area of the ceiling?

Hint
The ceiling is rectangular.

Learn... **11.2 Area of parallelograms and triangles**

Area of a parallelogram

Here is a parallelogram drawn on squared paper.

If the shaded triangle is cut from one end of the parallelogram and put on to the other end, the shape becomes a rectangle.

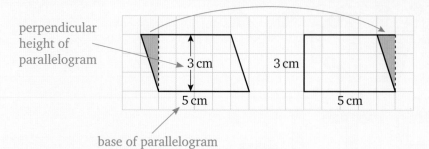

perpendicular height of parallelogram

3 cm   3 cm

5 cm   5 cm

base of parallelogram

The area of the parallelogram is the same as the area of the rectangle.

The **base** of the parallelogram is the same as the length of the rectangle.

The **perpendicular height** of the parallelogram is the same as the width of the rectangle.

Area of rectangle = $5 \times 3 = 15 \, \text{cm}^2$

Area of parallelogram = $5 \times 3 = 15 \, \text{cm}^2$

The area of any parallelogram can be calculated using the formula:

> Area of parallelogram = base × perpendicular height

Area of a triangle

If you draw a diagonal on the parallelogram, the parallelogram is divided into two equal triangles.

The area of each triangle is half the area of the parallelogram.

This gives the formula for the area of a triangle:

> Area of triangle = $\frac{1}{2} \times$ base × perpendicular height

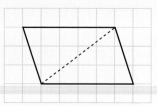

If a rectangle is divided into two triangles, then:

- the base of each triangle is the length of the rectangle
- the perpendicular height of each triangle is the width of the rectangle.

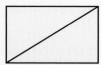

Example: Calculate the area of each triangle.

a

4 cm

9.5 cm

b

8 cm

6.4 cm

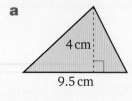

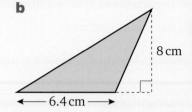

> **Study tip**
>
> Be careful to use the perpendicular height and not the length of the sloping sides of the triangle.

Solution: **a** From the diagram: base = 9.5 cm   perpendicular height = 4 cm

So area = $\frac{1}{2} \times$ base × perpendicular height

= $\frac{1}{2} \times 9.5 \times 4 = 19 \, \text{cm}^2$

b From the diagram: base = 6.4 cm   perpendicular height = 8 cm

So area = $\frac{1}{2} \times$ base × perpendicular height

= $\frac{1}{2} \times 6.4 \times 8 = 25.6 \, \text{cm}^2$

Example: A parallelogram has an area of 51 cm².

The perpendicular height of the parallelogram is 3 cm.

Work out the base of the parallelogram.

Solution: Using the formula, area = base × perpendicular height

51 = base × 3   Divide each side by 3.

$\frac{51}{3}$ = base

17 = base

The base of the parallelogram is 17 cm.

Practise...

11.2 Area of parallelograms and triangles

G F E D C

1 Work out the area of each parallelogram.

a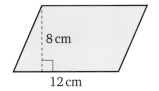

8 cm

12 cm

c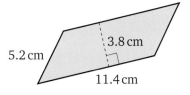

5.2 cm 3.8 cm

11.4 cm

b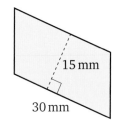

15 mm

30 mm

d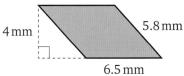

4 mm 5.8 mm

6.5 mm

2 Work out the area of each triangle.

a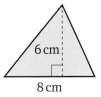

6 cm

8 cm

c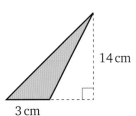

14 cm

3 cm

b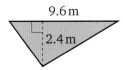

9.6 m

2.4 m

d

18 cm

5 cm

3 Which of the following shapes has the largest area? Show your working.

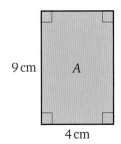

9 cm A

4 cm

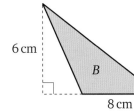

6 cm B

8 cm

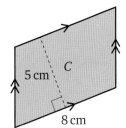

5 cm C

8 cm

D

D

4 A parallelogram of base 7.2 cm has an area of 97.2 cm².

Work out the height of the parallelogram.

5 Four students are trying to find the area of this triangle.

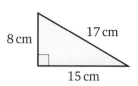

Kieran thinks the answer is 120 cm² because 8 × 15 = 120

Javed thinks the answer is 40 cm² because 8 + 15 + 17 = 40

Leanne thinks the answer is 60 cm² because $\frac{1}{2}$ × 15 × 8 = 60

Megan thinks the answer is 127.5 cm² because $\frac{1}{2}$ × 15 × 17 = 127.5

a Who is correct?

b What mistakes have the other students made?

6 Work out the perimeter and the area of these parallelograms.

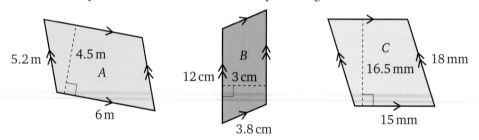

7 A triangle has a perpendicular height of 22 cm.

The area of the triangle is 308 cm².

Work out the length of the base of the triangle.

⚠ 8 Work out the area of each of these shapes.

a

9 cm

←7 cm→

b

17.2 cm

10 cm

 9 This club logo is to be made out of two metal triangles.

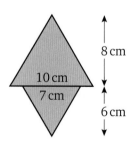

a Linda works out the dimensions of the smallest rectangle of metal from which the logo can be cut out are 10 cm by 14 cm.

Find a smaller rectangle from which the logo can be cut out.

b **i** What percentage of metal is wasted from Linda's rectangle?

ii What percentage of metal is wasted from the smallest rectangle?

 10 A company makes kites.

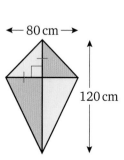

They cut triangles from yellow silk and blue silk as shown.

The yellow silk costs £5 per square metre and the blue silk costs £7 per square metre.

Assuming that the triangles for several kites can be cut from the material without wastage, find the cost of material used for each kite.

Learn... 11.3 Compound shapes

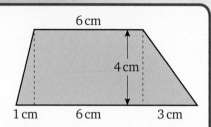

To find the area of a compound shape, divide up the shape into rectangles, parallelograms and triangles.

You can divide this shape into two triangles and a rectangle and work out the area of each smaller shape.

Total area =

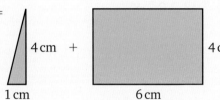

$$\text{area} = \tfrac{1}{2} \times 1 \times 4 \qquad \text{area} = 6 \times 4 \qquad \text{area} = \tfrac{1}{2} \times 3 \times 4$$
$$= 2\,\text{cm}^2 \qquad\qquad = 24\,\text{cm}^2 \qquad\qquad = 6\,\text{cm}^2$$

Total area = 2 + 24 + 6 = 32 cm²

The shape in this Learn is a trapezium.

The area of a trapezium can also be found by using the formula:

$$\text{area of trapezium} = \tfrac{1}{2}(a + b)h$$

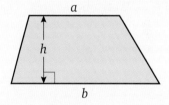

or in words, 'Add together the parallel sides and multiply by half the distance between them.'

You should try to use the formula for area of a trapezium whenever a compound shape includes a trapezium.

Example: Work out the perimeter and the area of this trapezium.

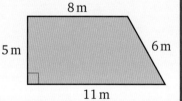

Solution: Perimeter = 8 + 6 + 11 + 5 = 30 m

Area $= \tfrac{1}{2}(a + b)h = \tfrac{1}{2}(8 + 11) \times 5 = \tfrac{1}{2} \times 19 \times 5 = 47.5\,\text{m}^2$

Example: Work out the area of this shape.

> **Study tip**
>
> Remember to state the units in your answers if the question asks for it.

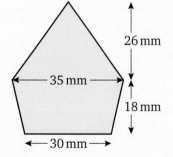

Solution: The shape can be split into a trapezium and a triangle.

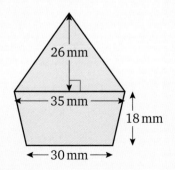

The area of the triangle is $\tfrac{1}{2} \times$ base $\times$ height $= \tfrac{1}{2} \times 35 \times 26$

$$= 455\,\text{mm}^2$$

The area of the trapezium is $\tfrac{1}{2}(a + b)h = \tfrac{1}{2}(35 + 30) \times 18$

$$= \tfrac{1}{2} \times 65 \times 18$$

$$= 585\,\text{mm}^2$$

The total area of the shape is 455 + 585 = 1040 mm²

Practise... **11.3 Compound shapes**

G F E D C

D

1 Each of these shapes is a trapezium.

Work out the area of each shape.

a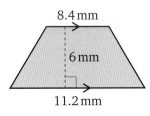
8.4 mm
6 mm
11.2 mm

b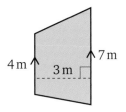
4 m
3 m
7 m

c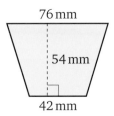
76 mm
54 mm
42 mm

d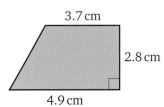
3.7 cm
2.8 cm
4.9 cm

2 Work out the area of each shape.

a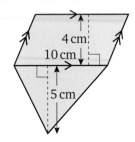
4 cm
10 cm
5 cm

c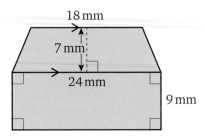
18 mm
7 mm
24 mm
9 mm

b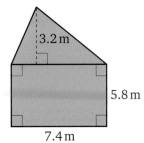
3.2 m
5.8 m
7.4 m

d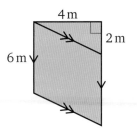
4 m
2 m
6 m

3 For each of these shapes, find:

i the perimeter

ii the area.

a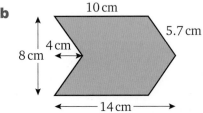
5.4 cm
2 cm
13 cm
10 cm
5 cm

c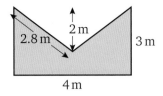
2.8 m
2 m
3 m
4 m

Not drawn accurately

e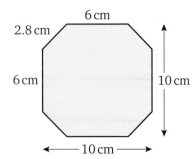
6 cm
2.8 cm
6 cm
10 cm
10 cm

b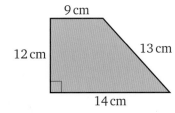
10 cm
5.7 cm
4 cm
8 cm
14 cm

d
9 cm
12 cm
13 cm
14 cm

4   **a**   Work out the area of the shaded part of each shape.

i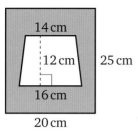

ii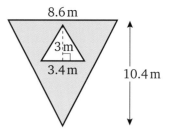

b   What fraction of diagram **i** is shaded?

 5   Sam is making badges using the design shown. He uses silver foil for the surround of the white centre shape.

Sam has one more badge to make. He has 10 cm² of silver foil left.

Does Sam have enough foil to complete the badge?

Show your working.

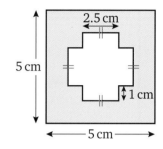

6   The diagram shows Joe's allotment which is in the shape of a trapezium.

a   Joe wants to build a new fence to go round the allotment leaving the gate in the same place. The fencing will cost Joe £9.60 per metre. Work out the cost of the new fencing.

b   Joe wants to plant vegetables in ¾ of his allotment. Work out the area of his allotment which will be used for vegetables.

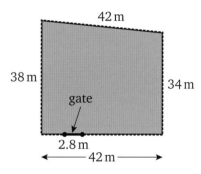

7   This is a sketch of Vikki's dining room.

a   Vikki wants to paint the floorboards which cover the whole of the floor. One tin of floorboard paint will cover 9.5 m² of floor. Vikki thinks that two tins will cover all her floor.

Is she correct?

You must show your working.

b   Vikki fits new skirting board all round the room except across the diagonal corner entrance. Skirting board is sold in 2.4 m lengths costing £7.99 each.

Work out the total cost of the skirting board.

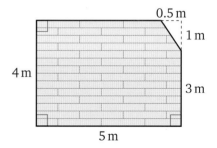

Learn... 11.4 Circumference and area of a circle ⓚ

In Learns 5.1, 5.2 and 5.3 you found perimeters and areas of various shapes. In this Learn you will find the perimeter (or **circumference**) and area of a **circle**.

First you will need to know the names of various parts of a circle.

circumference: the distance all the way round the circle

diameter: the distance from one side of the circle to the other, through the centre

radius: the distance from the centre of the circle to the circumference

Other parts of the circle are:

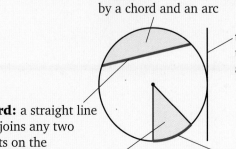

segment: an area enclosed by a chord and an arc

tangent: a straight line outside the circle that touches the circle at only one point

chord: a straight line that joins any two points on the circumference

arc: a section of the circumference

sector: an area between two radii and an arc

The importance of pi

π is the Greek letter pi and represents a value of 3.14159... (Look for the π button on your calculator.)

Circumference of a circle

The circumference, C, of a circle can be calculated using the formula:

$C = \pi d$ where d is the diameter of the circle   Remember that $d = 2 \times r$

Area of a circle

The area, A, of a circle with radius r can be calculated using the formula:

$A = \pi r^2$

Example: Find the circumference and area of a circle of diameter 12 cm.

Give your answers to one decimal place.

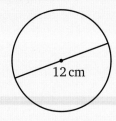

12 cm

Solution: $C = \pi d$ so $C = \pi \times 12$

Using the π button on a calculator gives $C = 37.69911...$

So the circumference of the circle is 37.7 cm (to 1 d.p.).

To find the area we must use the radius. If the diameter is 12 cm the radius is $\frac{12}{2} = 6$ cm.

$A = \pi r^2$ so $A = \pi \times 6^2$ or $\pi \times 6 \times 6$

Using the π button on a calculator gives $A = 113.0973...$

So the area of the circle is 113.1 cm^2 (to 1 d.p.).

> **Study tip**
>
> Always state the units of your answer and remember that area is always measured in square units.

Example: Find the diameter of a circle of circumference 22.3 cm.

Give your answer to one decimal place.

Solution: $C = \pi d$ so $22.3 = \pi \times d$

Divide both sides by π.

$d = \dfrac{22.3}{\pi} = 7.0983...$

The diameter is 7.1 cm (to 1 d.p.).

11.4 Circumference and area of a circle

Practise...

G

1 Name the parts of a circle labelled *A–D* on this diagram.

O is the centre of the circle.

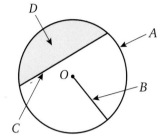

2 **a** Give the name for a line drawn from one side of a circle to the other, passing through the circle's centre.

b Give the name for the region between two radii and an arc of a circle.

c Give the name for a straight line outside a circle which touches the circle at only one point.

D

3 Calculate the circumference of each circle.

Give each answer to one decimal place.

a 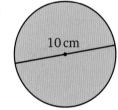 10 cm

b 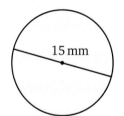 15 mm

c 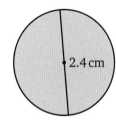 2.4 cm

d 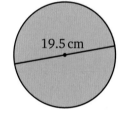 19.5 cm

4 Calculate the circumference of each circle.

Give each answer to one decimal place.

a 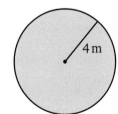 4 m

b 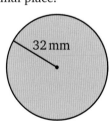 32 mm

c 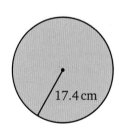 17.4 cm

d 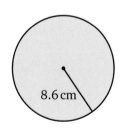 8.6 cm

5 A circle has a circumference of 62.8 cm.

Work out the diameter of this circle.

Give your answer to the nearest whole number.

6 Calculate the area of each circle.

Give each answer to two decimal places.

a 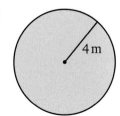 4 m

b 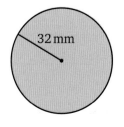 32 mm

c 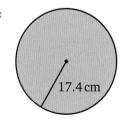 17.4 cm

d 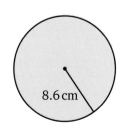 8.6 cm

D

7 Calculate the area of each circle.

Give each answer to two decimal places.

a 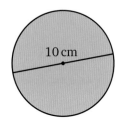 10 cm

b 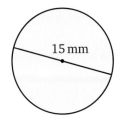 15 mm

c 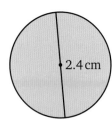 2.4 cm

d 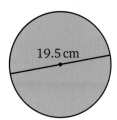 19.5 cm

C

8 For each semicircle, work out:

a the perimeter **b** the area.

Give each answer to one decimal place.

> **Hint**
>
> The area of a semicircle is half the area of a circle having the same diameter or radius. The perimeter of a semicircle is half the circumference of a circle having the same diameter or radius **plus** the diameter.

i 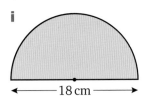 18 cm

ii 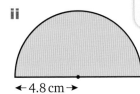 4.8 cm

9 A circle has an area of 201 mm².

Calculate the radius of the circle giving your answer to the nearest whole number.

10 For each of these shapes, calculate:

a the perimeter **b** the area.

i 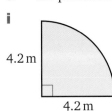 4.2 m 4.2 m

ii 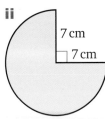 7 cm 7 cm

11 Teri is training for a fun run. She wants to run 10 000 m each week during her training.
The diagram shows the running track where she trains.

Teri says, 'If I run five times round this track each day from Monday to Friday, I will have run more than 10 000 m in a week.'

Is she correct? Show your working.

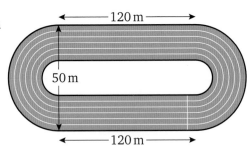 120 m 50 m 120 m

12 A circular cake tin has a diameter of 22.5 cm. The lid is sealed with tape. The ends of the tape overlap by 1.5 cm.

Calculate the length of tape needed to seal the tin.

 CAKE

13 The London Eye has a diameter of 135 m and takes approximately 30 minutes to complete one revolution.
Passengers travel in capsules.
How far does the base of a capsule travel every 5 minutes?

11   Assess (k)

1   Find the perimeter and the area of each of the following rectangles.

  a   Length 16 cm, width 12 cm

  b   Length 7.4 m, width 3.1 m

  c   Length 37 mm, width 15.2 mm

2   Find the area of each triangle.

  a
  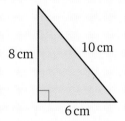

  c
  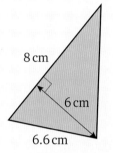
  Not drawn accurately

  b
  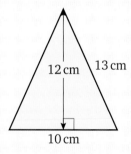

  d
  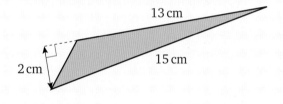

3   Find the area of each parallelogram.

Not drawn accurately

  a
  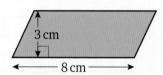

  c
  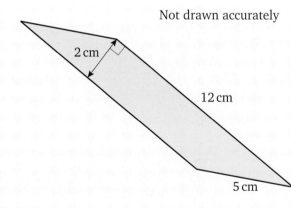

  b
  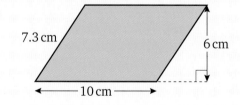

4   Find the circumference and the area of each circle.

  a
  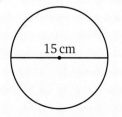

  b

  c
  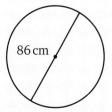

  d
  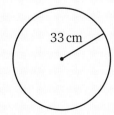

F
E

D

D

5   Work out the area of each of these shapes.

a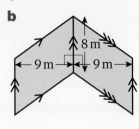

b   Not drawn accurately

C

6   A circle of diameter 45 cm is cut out of a square of side 50 cm.

Calculate the shaded area.

Not drawn accurately

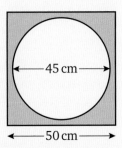

7   A shape is made from a square of side 6 cm surrounded by four semicircles of diameter 6 cm.

Work out the area of the shape.

Give your answer to one decimal place.

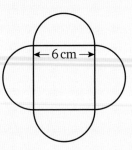

Practice questions

1   The diagram shows a plan view of a landfill site on a centimetre grid.

    a   Estimate the number of shaded squares in the diagram.
You **must** show your working.

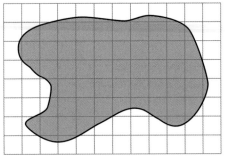

(2 marks)

    b   A landscape gardener is going to cover the site with turf (grass).
The table shows the cost of turf for different areas (m²).

Area of turf (m²)	Cost per square metre
40–59	£2.83
60–130	£2.33
131–240	£2.03
241–480	£1.78
481–640	£1.53
641–960	£1.40
961–1440	£1.23

On the diagram, one square represents 4 m².
The landscape gardener must buy enough turf to cover the landfill site.
Work out how much he has to pay. You **must** show your working.   *(3 marks)*

AQA 2009

2   Three identical rectangles fit together as shown.
Work out the total area.

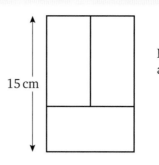

Not drawn
accurately

15 cm

(4 marks)

AQA 2008

3   The diagram shows five shapes, *A*, *B*, *C*, *D* and *E*,
drawn on a grid.

Put the shapes in order of area, starting with the
smallest (*D*) and ending with the largest (*A*).

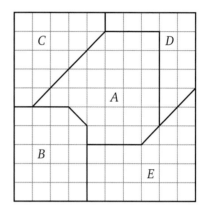

(2 marks)

AQA 2008

12 Real-life graphs

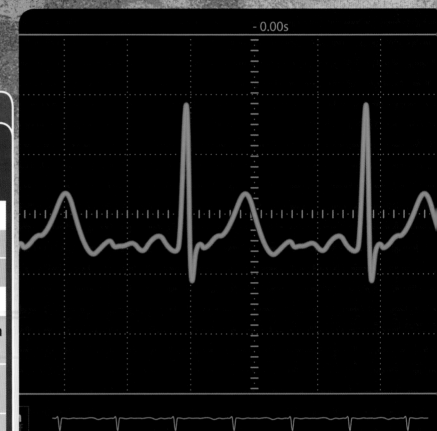

- 0.00s

Objectives

Examiners would normally expect students who get these grades to be able to:

F

plot points on conversion graphs

read values from conversion graphs

E

read a value from a conversion graph for a negative value

interpret horizontal lines on a distance–time graph

carry out simple interpretation of graphs such as finding a distance from distance–time graphs

D

carry out more advanced interpretation of real-life graphs, such as finding simple average speed from distance–time graphs and recognising when the fastest average speed takes place

construct linear functions from real-life situations and plot their corresponding graphs

C

find the average speed in km/h from a distance–time graph over time in minutes.

Key terms

axis
gradient
speed

Did you know?

... how important graphs can be?

Graphs that record information such as heart rate, heart beats and blood pressure are very important. Real-life graphs such as these are used in hospitals and can save lives.

You should already know:

✔ how to plot points on a graph

✔ how to draw, scale and label axes

✔ how to complete a table and use it to draw the graph of a straight line

✔ how to plot and interpret a line graph

✔ how to find the gradient of a straight line

✔ how to solve simple problems involving proportion

✔ common units for measuring distance, speed and time.

12.1 Conversion graphs and other linear real-life graphs

Conversion graphs are used to convert from one unit of measurement to another.

You need to plot two points to show where to draw your line, and a third point to check.

Study tip

It is usually up to you which points you plot, but try to use 'easy' values such as 0 or 1, 10 or 20 or 100. The units you are converting and the information you are given will often tell you which values to choose.

Example: Shane is converting between euros (€) and pounds (£). He knows that €10 = £8.60

   a Draw a conversion graph to convert euros (€) to pounds (£).

   b Use the graph to convert
       i   €4 to pounds
       ii £7.50 to euros.

Study tip

Draw lines on your diagram when you use conversion graphs.

Solution **a** Choose two points. The easiest are (0, 0) and (10, 8.6). A third point gives a good check. Since €5 = £4.30, (5, 4.3) is an easy point to work out and use. Plot these points and join them with a single straight line.

   b **i** Draw a line from 4 on the euros axis to the line, then from the line to the pounds axis. Read the value from there and write it down.
       €4 = £3.40

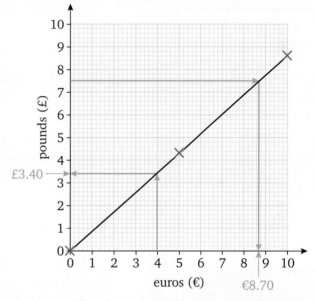

   ii Draw a line from 7.5 on the pounds axis to the line. From there draw a line to the euros axis. Read the value from there and write it down. £7.50 = €8.70

Example: Janette went to two hire shops to price the hire of a floor sander.

One shop charged a rate of £A per day. The other shop made a charge of £20 then a charge of £B per day.

   a How much does it cost to hire a floor sander for six days from:
       i   Tools-4-you
       ii Faster-hire?

   b Which shop charged a rate of £A per day?

   c What is the value of A?

   d What is the value of B?

   e For what length of time is the hire charge the same at both shops?

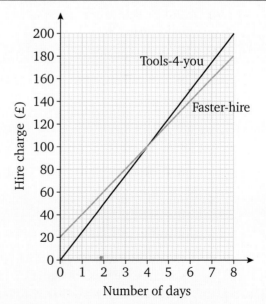

Solution:

a Read up from six days on the horizontal axis to each line, then across from the line to the vertical axis. Write down the values. These are shown on the graph:

    i The blue arrows show the cost of hiring from Tools-4-you is £150.

    ii The red arrows show the cost of hiring from Faster-hire is £140.

b Tools-4-you charge a rate of £A per day. You can tell this because the line for Tools-4-you goes through the origin (0, 0).

c The value of A is £25. You can read this from the graph – look for the cost of hiring for one day.

d The value of B is £20. You can read the cost of hiring for one day, then subtract the charge of £20. £40 − £20 = £20

e Both shops charge the same for four days. Look at the graph and find where the lines cross over. This is where the shops charge the same.

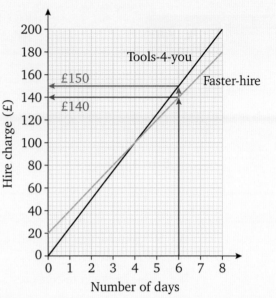

> **Study tip**
>
> Draw lines on your graph to show where you are reading from.

Practise...

12.1 Conversion graphs and other linear real-life graphs 🅚

G F E D C

1 This is a conversion graph for converting between gallons and litres.

  a Use the conversion graph to write the following in litres.

    i 10 gallons   **iii** 12 gallons

    ii 5 gallons   **iv** 2 gallons

  b Use the conversion graph to write the following in gallons.

    i 20 litres   **iii** 45 litres

    ii 70 litres   **iv** 42 litres

  c John bought some petrol at a filling station. He paid £35. Petrol was advertised at £1 per litre. How many gallons of petrol did he buy?

  d Charlie said that 20 gallons were the same as 4.4 litres. He was not correct. What mistake has Charlie made?

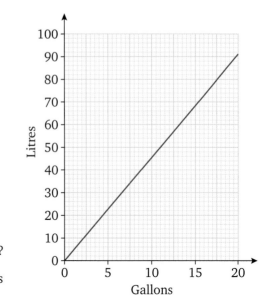

2 **a** Copy the set of **axes** shown on the right, using one large square to represent one unit.

b Rebecca knows that £10 = AUD $19
Use this information to draw a conversion graph for British pounds (£) to Australian dollars (AUD $).

c Use your conversion graph to convert the following amounts into Australian dollars.

   i £4   **iv** 50p

   ii £7   **v** £9.20

   iii £8.50

d Use your conversion graph to convert the following into British pounds.

   i A$12   **iv** A$6.50

   ii A$10   **v** A$0.50

   iii A$3

e Rebecca is on holiday in Australia.
She sends a postcard home.
The charge for postage is A$1.20.
She knows that the cost of sending a postcard from home to Australia is 56p. Which is cheaper?
Give a reason for your answer.

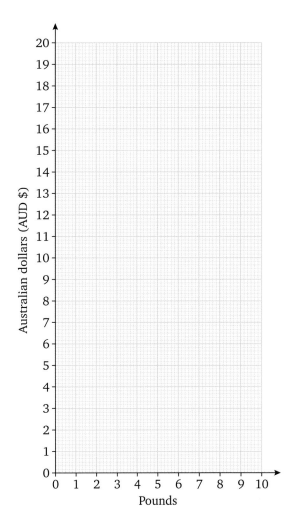

3 **a** At a filling station, diesel costs £1.10 per litre. Copy the table on the right, then use this information to complete it.

Number of litres	0	1	50
Cost		£1.10	

b Copy the set of axes shown below, using one large square to represent ten units.

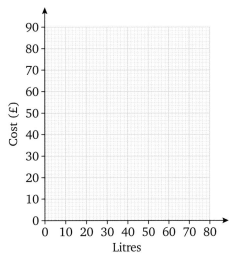

c Use the table to plot three points and draw a line.

d Use your graph to find the cost of:

   i 25 litres   **ii** 70 litres   **iii** 65 litres

e Use your graph to find the number of litres bought for:

   i £20   **ii** £65   **iii** £16

f Georgina filled up her car with diesel at this filling station. She spent £55.
Use your graph and the graph in Question 1 to find how many gallons of diesel she bought.

F
E

4

a Copy the axes shown on the right.
Use each large square to represent 20 units.

b 0°C is 32°F and 100°C is 212°F. Use this
information to draw a conversion graph for
Celsius (°C) to Fahrenheit (°F).

c Use your conversion graph to convert the
following temperatures to °F.

   i 20°C

   ii 70°C

   iii 90°C

   iv −20°C

   v −60°C

d Use your conversion graph to convert the
following temperatures to °C.

   i 100°F

   ii 80°F

   iii 0°F

   iv −20°F

   v −80°F

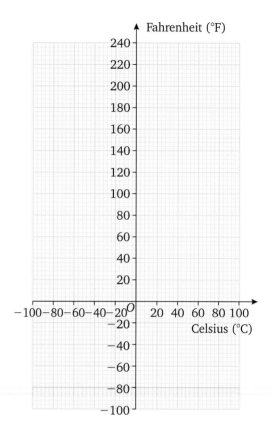

e The coldest air temperature ever recorded on
Earth is −89.2°C. It was recorded at Vostok
Station, Antarctica on 21 July 1983. Use your
conversion graph to find this temperature in °F .

f There is one temperature at which the number of °F is the same as the number of °C.
What is this temperature?

g The coldest temperature ever recorded in the UK was −27.2°C in Braemar, Scotland in
January 1982.
Use your conversion graph to find this temperature in °F

h The highest temperature ever recorded in the UK was 38.5°C on 10 August 2003, near
Faversham in Kent. Use your conversion graph to find this temperature in °F

5

a Copy the axes shown on the right.
Use 2 cm to represent ten units.

b Samantha knows that 32 km = 20 miles.
Use this information to draw a conversion
graph for miles to kilometres.

c Use your graph to convert the following
to km.

   i 50 miles

   ii 15 miles

   iii 4 miles

d Use your graph to convert the following to
miles.

   i 20 km

   ii 45 km

   iii 12 km

e Samantha is entering a 10 km race. How far
is this in miles?

f A marathon is 26 miles. Use your graph to
convert this to km.

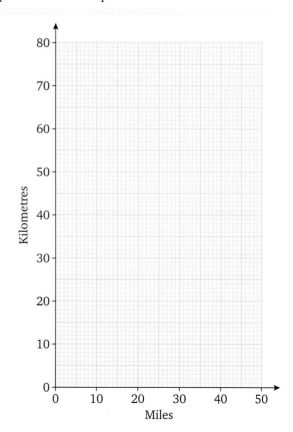

6   Ibrahim is filling his bath with water.

The sketch graph shows how the volume of water in the bath changes.

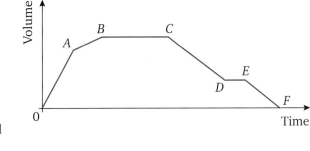

a   Which part of the graph shows when the bath was filling up at its fastest? How can you tell?

b   What do you think may have happened at *A*?

c   What happened at *B*?

d   Ibrahim cleaned the bath as the bath was emptying. Which part of the graph shows this?
How can you tell?

7   Sharon has a mobile phone.
The only charges she pays are for calls.
The graph shows her monthly charges for calls up to 300 minutes.

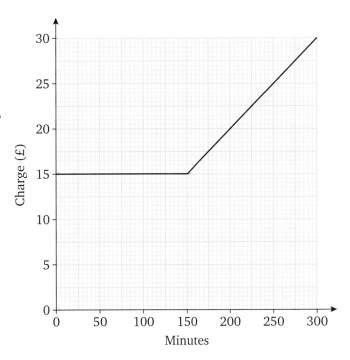

a   What is her basic monthly charge?

b   How many minutes are included in Sharon's basic monthly charge?

c   How much does Sharon pay per minute for her other calls?

8   Terence the plumber calculates the cost of a job as:
£50 call out fee plus £30 per hour.

a   Write down a formula for the price, £*P*, that Terence would charge for a job taking *H* hours.

b   Make a table for the price he would charge for jobs taking 1, 2, 3, 4 hours.

c   Draw a graph showing the price of jobs taking between 0 and 4 hours.

9   Stephen went to two hire shops to hire a bike when he was on holiday.
Fast Bikes charge a £30 hire fee plus £10 per day.
4 Bikers charge a flat rate of £16 per day.

a   Write down formulae for the cost, £*C*, of hiring a bike for *n* days from:
  i   Fast Bikes   **ii**   4 Bikers.

b   How much does it cost to hire a bike for one day from:
  i   Fast Bikes   **ii**   4 Bikers?

c   How much does it cost to hire a bike for 2 days from
  i   Fast bikes   **ii**   4 Bikers?

d   Draw a graph to show the costs of hiring a bike from each hire shop.

e   After how many days is it more expensive to hire from 4 Bikers than from Fast Bikes?

10 Harriet went to two hire shops to price hiring a mixer.
One shop charged £P per day, the other made a hire charge of £Q plus £R per day.

a How much does it cost to hire a mixer for 5 days from:

　i Hire 2 U?

　ii Hire Us?

b Which shop charged at a rate of £P per day? How can you tell?

c What are the values of:

　i P

　ii Q

　iii R?

d For what period of time is the hire charge the same from both shops?

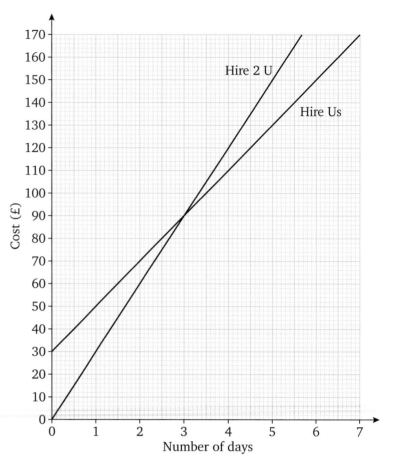

11 A car manufacturer advertises the following for a diesel car:

　100 km on only 3.9 litres of fuel, allowing it to cover almost 1500 km without refuelling

Use appropriate conversion graphs to answer the following questions.

a How many gallons does the fuel tank hold when full?

b How many miles per gallon will the car do?

c How much does a full tank of diesel cost for this car?

d How much does each mile cost?

e Jeremy is on holiday from Australia.
How much would Jeremy expect a 50-mile trip in this car to cost in Australian dollars?

Learn... 12.2 Distance–time graphs

Distance–time graphs tell you about a journey. They are used to compare speeds.

The diagrams show how far Sam and Richard have cycled over a race of 30 metres.

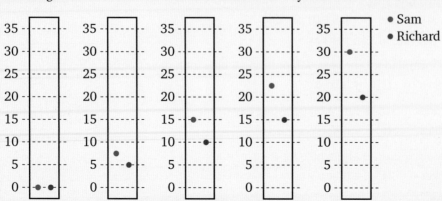

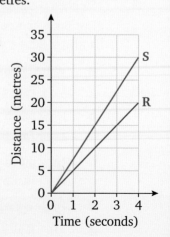

It is easy to compare the speed of the two cyclists.

The vertical **axis** is always distance. The horizontal axis is always time.

The distance is always from a particular point – usually the starting point. The higher up the graph, the further the distance from the starting point.

Time may be the actual time using am and pm or the 24-hour clock, or it could be the number of minutes or hours from the starting point.

If the graph goes back to the horizontal axis, it shows a return to the starting point.

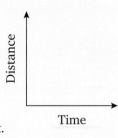

The **gradient** (steepness) of the line is a measure of **speed**. The steeper the line, the faster the speed. A horizontal line represents a speed of zero (i.e. stopped).

In Chapter 10 you learnt to find the gradient of a straight line. The same method is used to find speeds from a distance–time graph, i.e. use:

$$\text{Speed} = \frac{\text{distance travelled}}{\text{time taken}}$$

When the speed is in miles per hour, the distance must be in miles and the time in hours.

To find the average speed for a whole journey, use:

$$\text{Average speed} = \frac{\text{total distance travelled}}{\text{total time taken}}$$

Example: The distance–time graph shows Michael's journey to and from a supermarket.

a   Describe the journey, giving reasons for the shape of the graph.

b   How far is it to the supermarket?

c   During which part of the journey is Michael travelling the fastest?

d   During which part of the journey was Michael most likely to have been held up by roadworks?

e   Calculate Michael's speed in miles per hour for the following sections of the graph.

   i   AB   ii   BC   iii   CD   iv   EF

f   What was Michael's average speed for the journey to the supermarket?

g   What was Michael's average speed over the two hours?

Solution: a   Michael left home at A and travelled at a constant speed for $\frac{1}{4}$ hour to B.

He then travelled at a slower constant speed for $\frac{1}{2}$ hour from B to C.

He then travelled at a faster constant speed for $\frac{1}{4}$ hour from C to D.

He then stopped for $\frac{1}{2}$ hour.

Then it took $\frac{1}{2}$ hour to return home from E to F. The graph returns to the horizontal axis – this shows the return journey home.

b   The furthest distance Michael goes from A is 20 miles. This is the distance from A (home) to D (the supermarket).

c   Michael is travelling fastest between A and B, as the gradient (steepness) of the line is greatest then.

d   Michael is likely to have been held up by roadworks between B and C, as he is travelling much more slowly. The gradient (steepness) of the line is least then.

e **i** *AB*: In $\frac{1}{4}$ hour, he travels 12.5 miles. In 1 hour he would travel $4 \times 12.5 = 50$ miles His speed is 50 miles per hour (mph) (as he would travel 50 miles in 1 hour).

ii *BC*: In $\frac{1}{2}$ hour, he travels 2.5 miles. In 1 hour he would travel $2 \times 2.5 = 5$ miles His speed is 5 miles per hour (mph).

iii *CD*: In $\frac{1}{4}$ hour, he travels 5 miles. So in 1 hour he would travel $4 \times 5 = 20$ miles His speed is 20 miles per hour (mph).

iv *EF*: In $\frac{1}{2}$ hour, he travels 20 miles. So in 1 hour he would travel $2 \times 20 = 40$ miles His speed is 40 miles per hour (mph).

f In 1 hour, he travels 20 miles. His average speed is 20 miles per hour (mph).

g For the whole journey the distance travelled is 40 miles (there **and** back). The time taken is 2 hours.

Average speed = $\dfrac{\text{total distance}}{\text{total time}} = \dfrac{40}{2} = 20$ mph

> **Study tip**
>
> Remember to divide by the time **in hours** when you find the average speed in miles per hour, or km per hour.

Practise... 12.2 Distance–time graphs  **k** G F E D C

E D

1 Sam walks to town to buy a CD and then walks home. The distance–time graph shows his journey.

a How far does Sam walk altogether?

b Sam stops to talk to a friend on his way into town. How long does he stop for?

c When is Sam walking at his fastest? What is his average speed for this part of the journey?

> **Study tip**
>
> The horizontal axis has four squares for each hour – this tells you each square is $\frac{1}{4}$ hour. Remember, $\frac{1}{4}$ hour = 0.25 hours.

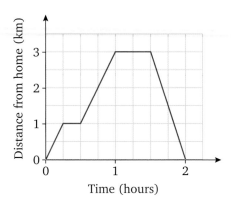

D C

2 Helen completed a short mountain bike trail. The distance–time graph shows her ride.

a What was the total distance Helen travelled?

b Helen enjoyed the ride, as there was a really fast section.

i Between which letters on the graph is this indicated?

ii How long was this section? Give your answer in km.

iii How long did it take Helen to ride this section?

c There was one very steep uphill section.

i Between which two letters on the graph is this indicated?

ii How long was this section?

iii How long did it take Helen to get up the hill?

d Calculate the average speed in km/h for each of the eight sections of the ride.

e Calculate Helen's average speed for the whole ride.

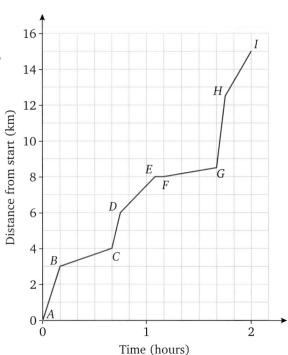

3 A coach travels from Kendal to Birmingham. The journey is shown in the distance–time graph.

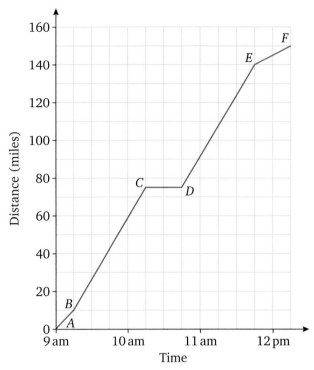

  a The coach stops at some services.

  i At what time does it stop at the services?

  ii How long does the coach stop for?

  iii How far are the services from Kendal?

  b At what stage on the graph does the coach join the motorway?

  c How far is the coach from Birmingham when it leaves the motorway?

  d Work out the average speed in mph for each of the five stages in the journey.

  e Find the average speed of the coach between Kendal and Birmingham.

4 Giovanni goes for a ride on his bike in the country. He starts from the car park and rides for 30 minutes at a steady 12 mph. He then goes up a hill at 8 mph for 15 minutes. At the top he stops to admire the view for 15 minutes. He then rides back down to the car park, which takes him 30 minutes.

Work out Giovanni's average speed in mph for the whole journey.

Hint

You may use a distance–time graph to help.

Study tip

When asked to find the average speed in km/h from a distance–time graph with time in minutes, remember to divide by the time taken in hours.

5 The graph below shows the journeys of four students to school in the morning.

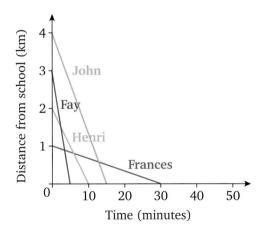

The four students used different ways to get to school.
One student walked, one cycled, one caught the bus and one used the train.

  a How did each student travel to school? Give reasons for your answers.

  b Calculate the speed of each student in km/h.

6 Hamish goes for a ride on his bike.
His journey is shown on the distance–time graph.

a Hamish fell off his bike at one point in his journey. When do you think this might have been? Explain your answer.

b When was Hamish going fastest?

c Describe his journey in words.

d What was his average speed for the whole journey?

e What could be changed in the graph for his average speed to have been 5 km/h?

f How would the graph be different if Hamish had been unable to cycle after he fell off?

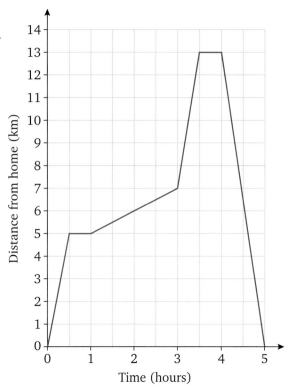

12 Assess (k)

F

1 This is a conversion graph for changing between pints and litres.

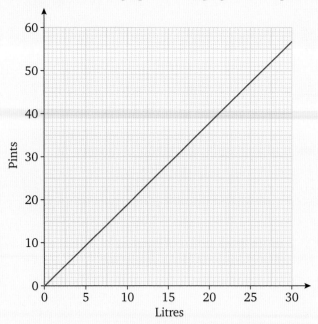

Use the graph to answer the following questions.

a Convert the following from litres to pints.
  i 10 litres **ii** 6 litres **iii** 24 litres **iv** 18 litres

b Convert the following from pints to litres.
  i 10 pints **ii** 45 pints **iii** 28 pints **iv** 32 pints

c Zachary sees two-pint bottles of milk in his local supermarket for 89p. Later he sees one-litre bottles of milk in his corner shop for 86p. Where would you advise Zachary to buy his milk? Give a reason for your answer.

2   **a**   Copy the set of axes below. Use one large square to represent five units.

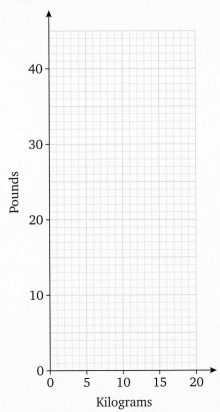

b   Sal knows that 1 kg ≈ 2.2 lb. Use this information to draw a conversion graph.

c   Use your graph to convert the following weights to kilograms.
   i   10 lb   **ii**   35 lb   **iii**   5 lb   **iv**   42 lb

d   Use your graph to convert the following weights to pounds.
   i   8 kg   **ii**   15 kg   **iii**   7.5 kg   **iv**   12 kg

e   John estimates his weight to be 140 pounds.
   Use your graph to convert his weight to kilograms.

f   Sal buys a bag of potatoes weighing 20 lb for £8. The shop advertises a price of £2.10 for 1 kg.
   Has Sal been charged correctly? Explain your answer.

3   Colin takes his dog Ben for a walk over Cartmel Fell. The distance–time graph shows his distance from home.

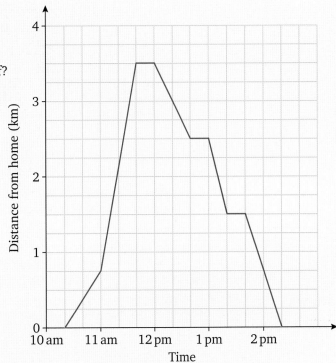

a   What time did Colin and Ben set off?

b   Colin had his lunch the first time they stopped.
   i   What time did Colin have lunch?
   ii   How long did they stop for lunch?

c   What was their average speed in km per hour before lunch?

d   On the way back they stopped several times for Colin to admire the view. At what times did Colin make these stops?

e   How far did they walk?

f   What was their average speed in km/h for the whole walk?

Practice questions ⓚ

1 The diagrams show two journeys *A* and *B*.

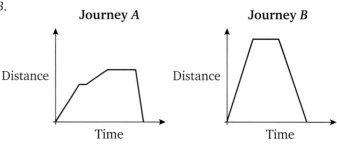
Journey A   **Journey B**

   a Which journey has two stops?
Explain your answer.   *(1 mark)*

   b Which part of journey A is the fastest?

Copy the diagram and mark the line with an arrow on the diagram.   *(1 mark)*

   c The times taken for all three parts of journey B are equal.

Jill says that the speed for the first and third parts of the journey must be equal.

Is she correct? Explain your answer.   *(2 marks)*

AQA 2008

2 Motorists should drive with a safe gap between their vehicle and the vehicle in front.
This graph shows the minimum safe gaps between vehicles at different speeds.
Different gaps are recommended for wet roads and dry roads.

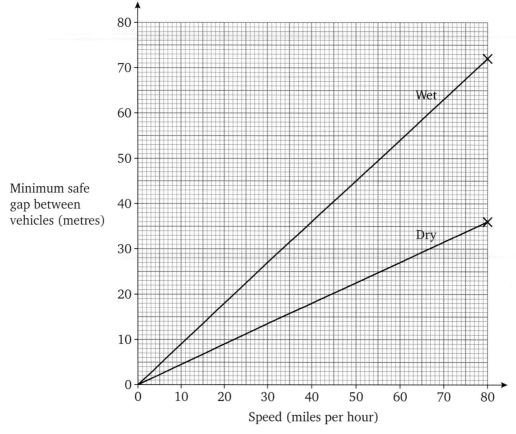

   a The road is dry.
A car is travelling at 30 miles per hour behind a lorry.

What is the minimum safe gap between the car and the lorry?   *(1 mark)*

   b Tim is driving at 60 miles per hour on a dry road.
He is driving with the minimum safe gap between his car and the car in front.
It starts to rain heavily and both cars slow down to 40 miles per hour.

Should Tim increase the gap between his car and the car in front to continue driving with the minimum safe gap?

You must show clearly how you obtain your answer.   *(3 marks)*

AQA 2008

13 Ratio and proportion

Objectives

Examiners would normally expect students who get these grades to be able to:

D

use ratio notation, including reduction to its simplest form and its links to fraction notation

divide a quantity in a given ratio

solve simple ratio and proportion problems, such as finding the ratio of teachers to students in a school

C

solve more complex ratio and proportion problems, such as sharing money in the ratio of people's ages

solve ratio and proportion problems using the unitary method.

Did you know?

A fair world?

Many African countries do not have good healthcare.

In Tanzania, the ratio of doctors to people is 0.02 to 1000. This means one doctor for every fifty thousand people!

People in other countries in the world have better access to a doctor. In Cuba, the ratio is 5.9 to 1000.

In the UK, it is 2.2 to 1000. Think about this next time you are in a surgery waiting room.

Key terms

ratio
proportion
unitary ratio
unitary method

You should already know:

✔ how to add, subtract, multiply and divide simple numbers by hand and all numbers with a calculator

✔ how to simplify fractions by hand and by calculator.

Learn... 13.1 Finding and simplifying ratios

Ratios are a good way of comparing quantities such as the number of teachers in a school with the number of students.

The colon symbol is used to express ratio.

In a school with 50 teachers and 800 students, the teacher : student ratio is 50 : 800

You read 50 : 800 as '50 to 800'.

Ratios can be simplified like fractions.

Ratio = 50 : 800
= 5 : 80   (dividing both numbers by 10)
= 1 : 16   (dividing both numbers by 5)

This is just like simplifying fractions $\frac{50}{800} = \frac{5}{80} = \frac{1}{16}$

$\div 10 \quad \div 5$

$\div 10 \quad \div 5$

Remember that you can use your calculator fraction key to simplify fractions.

The simplest form of the ratio is 1 : 16. This means there is one teacher for every 16 students, and $\frac{1}{16}$ of a teacher for every student.

The **proportion** of teachers in the school is $\frac{1}{17}$ and the proportion of students is $\frac{16}{17}$

For every 17 people, 1 will be a teacher and 16 will be students.
$\frac{1}{17}$ are teachers and $\frac{16}{17}$ are students.

Example: The total price of a meal is £6.16 which includes 66p service charge. What is the ratio of the original meal price to the service charge?

Solution: The original price is £6.16 − £0.66 = £5.50.

So the ratio of original price to service charge is

£5.50 : £0.66 = 550 : 66 (changing both amounts to pence)
= 50 : 6 (dividing both numbers by 11)
= 25 : 3 (dividing both numbers by 2)

> **Study tip**
>
> A common mistake is to write a ratio with different units. You need to make sure that the units are the same. In this example £5.50 has been changed to pence.

The ratio of the original price to the service charge in its simplest form is 25 : 3

So for every 25 pence of the original price there is 3 pence of service charge.

For every 25 pence of original price and every 3 pence of service charge there is 28 pence of total charge. The proportion of the total charge that is for service is $\frac{3}{28}$. The proportion of the total charge that is for meal is $\frac{25}{28}$

This means that the original price is $\frac{25}{28}$ of the total price and the service charge is $\frac{3}{28}$ of the total price. Make sure that you understand where these fractions have come from.

Example: A photo is 15 cm high and 25 cm wide. What is the ratio of height to width in its simplest form?

Solution: The ratio of height to width is 15 cm : 25 cm = 15 : 25 = 3 : 5 (dividing both numbers by 5).

Practise...   **13.1** Finding and simplifying ratios

1   Write each of these ratios as simply as possible.

a	$2:4$	**e**	$2:12$	**i**	$24:36$	**m**	$0.3:0.8$
b	$2:6$	**f**	$2:14$	**j**	$25:100$	**n**	$2\frac{1}{2}:7\frac{1}{2}$
c	$2:8$	**g**	$12:36$	**k**	$\frac{2}{3}:\frac{4}{9}$	**o**	$20\%:80\%$
d	$2:10$	**h**	$18:24$	**l**	$1.5:2.5$	**p**	$25:200$

2   **a**   Write down three different pairs of numbers that are in the ratio $1:2$

   b   Explain how you can tell that two numbers are in the ratio $1:2$

3   Three of these ratios are the same. Which three?

   $1:2.5$ $3:6$ $0.2:0.5$ $25:55$ $2:5$ $3:7.5$

4   Pippa writes the three pairs of numbers 6 and 9, 9 and 12, and 12 and 15.
She says these pairs of numbers are all in the same ratio.
What has Pippa done wrong?

5   A book reading group has men and women in
the ratio $2:7$

   a   There are 21 women in the group.
How many men are there?

   b   Two more men join the group.
How many more women are needed to keep
the ratio of men to women the same?

 6   On a music download site, a song costs 65p and an album costs £6.50.

   Find the ratio of the cost of a song to the cost of an album in its simplest form.

⚠ 7   The numbers a and b are in the ratio $2:3$

   a   If a is 4, what is b?   **d**   If b is 1, what is a?

   b   If b is 12, what is a?   **e**   If a and b add up to 10, what are a and b?

   c   If a is 1, what is b?

 8   When you enlarge a photograph, the ratio of the
height to width must stay the same. If the ratio is
different the objects in the photograph will look
stretched or squashed.

   a   A photo is 20 cm high and 30 cm wide.
What is the ratio of height to width in its
simplest form?

   b   Another photo measures 25 cm high and 35 cm wide.
Is the ratio of its width to its height the same as
the photo in part **a**?

D

9 A recipe for pastry needs 50 grams of butter and 100 grams of flour.

  a What is the ratio of butter to flour? What is the ratio of flour to butter?

  b How much butter is needed for 200 grams of flour?

  c How much flour is needed for 30 grams of butter?

  d What fraction is the butter's weight of the flour's weight?

10   **a** Find, in their simplest forms, the teacher : student ratios for these schools.

School	Number of teachers	Number of students
School 1	75	1500
School 2	15	240
School 3	22	374
School 4	120	1800
School 5	65	1365

  b **i** A school with 50 teachers has the same teacher : student ratio as School 1. How many students does it have?

     ii If a school with 2000 students had the same teacher : student ratio as School 1. How many teachers does it have?

  c Which school has the smallest number of students for each teacher?

11 Map scales are often expressed in ratio form, such as 1 : 100 000. (This is called a **unitary ratio** as it compares a unit length on the map with the real life length.)

  a Look at some maps (perhaps you can use examples from geography) and write down some examples of how the scales are shown.

  b A scale is written as '2 cm to 1 km'. Write this scale as a unitary ratio.

  c The scale 1 : 100 000 can be written as '1 cm to n km'. Work out the value of n.

  d What distance in real life does 3 cm represent on a 1 : 100 000 map?

Learn...   **13.2 Using ratios to find quantities**   k

You can use ratios to find numbers and amounts.

You can find
- the number of boys and the number of girls in a school

if you know
- the ratio of boys to girls

and
- the total number of students.

For example, in a school of 1000 students, the ratio of boys to girls is 9 : 11

This means that for every 9 boys there are 11 girls, whatever the size of the school.

The total number of parts is 9 + 11 = 20, so

9 out of every 20 students are boys and 11 out of every 20 students are girls.

The fraction of boys in the school is $\frac{9}{20}$ and the fraction of girls in the school is $\frac{11}{20}$

To find the number of boys, work out $\frac{9}{20}$ of 1000.

To find the number of girls, work out $\frac{11}{20}$ of 1000.

$\frac{1}{20}$ of 1000 = 1000 ÷ 20 = 50

Number of boys = 50 × 9 = 450

Number of girls = 50 × 11 = 550

Study tip

Check that the number of boys and the number of girls add up to the total number of students in the school.

Example: Jane is 6 years old and Karl is 10 years old.

Their grandmother gives them £24 to share between them in the ratio of their ages.

How much does each child receive?

Solution: The ratio of Jane's age to Karl's age is $6:10 = 3:5$. (You can use the fraction key on your calculator to simplify the ratio $6:10$).

The total number of parts is $3 + 5 = 8$, so Jane gets $\frac{3}{8}$ of £24 and Karl gets $\frac{5}{8}$ of £24.

$\frac{1}{8}$ of £24 is £24 $\div$ 8 = £3

So Jane gets $3 \times \frac{1}{8}$ of £24 = 3 $\times$ £3 = £9 and Karl gets $5 \times \frac{1}{8}$ of £24 = 5 $\times$ £3 = £15.

Practise... 13.2 Using ratios to find quantities k G F E D C

D

C

1   Divide these numbers and quantities in the ratio $1:2$

a   150   c   £4.50   e   £1.50

b   300   d   6 litres   f   1.5 litres

2   Divide the numbers and quantities in Question 1 in the following ratios.

a $1:4$ c $3:7$

b $2:3$ d $1:2:7$

3   In a savings account, the ratio of the amount invested to the interest paid is $50:1$

Approximately how much is the interest paid on a savings account that has £10 525 in it?

4   The angles of any pentagon add up to 540°.

The angles of one pentagon are in the ratio $2:3:4:5:6$

What is the size of the largest angle?

5   This table shows the ratio of carbohydrate to fat to protein in some foods.

Food	Carbohydrate : fat : protein
Chicken sandwich	1 : 1 : 1
Grilled salmon	0 : 1 : 1
Yoghurt (whole milk)	1 : 2 : 1
Taco chips	10 : 4 : 1
Bread	7 : 2 : 1
Milk	2 : 3 : 2

a   Work out the amount of fat in 150 g of each of the foods.

b   Which of these foods would you avoid if you were on a low-fat diet?

c   How many grams of yoghurt would you need to eat to have 100 g of protein?

d   Which of these foods would you avoid if you were on a low-carbohydrate diet?

6 Bronze for coins can be made of copper, tin and zinc in the ratio 95 : 4 : 1

    a How much of each metal is needed to make 1 kilogram of bronze?

    b How much of each metal is needed to make 10 kilograms of bronze?

    c How much of each metal is needed to make half a kilogram of bronze?

    d How much zinc would there be in a coin weighing 6 grams?

7 Leena invested £10 000 in a business and Kate invested £3 500.

At the end of the year, Leena and Kate share the profits of £70 000 in the ratio of their investments.

How much does each receive?

 8 The table shows the number of pupils in five schools together with the ratio of the number of boys to the number of girls.

School	Total number of students	Boy : girl ratio
School A	750	1 : 1
School B	900	4 : 5
School C	1800	4 : 5
School D	1326	6 : 7
School E	1184	301 : 291

    a Which school contains the greatest number of boys?
       Show working to justify your answer.

    b Which school has the greatest proportion of boys?
       Show working to justify your answer.

Learn... 13.3 Ratio and proportion: the unitary method

The **unitary method** is a very powerful mathematical tool.
The method is based on finding the amount or cost of **one** unit (hence the name 'unitary').

So if you know how much 20 litres of petrol cost, you can find the cost of one litre and then the cost of any number of litres.

> You can use the unitary method to do all types of percentages and well as ratio and proportion.

20 litres cost £20.60

So 1 litre costs $\frac{£20.60}{20}$ = £1.03 (divide the cost of 20 litres by 20)

Multiply by the cost of 1 litre to find the cost of any number of litres.

Example: A teacher pays £27.60 for 6 calculators.

How much does he pay for 15 calculators at the same price each?

> **Study tip**
>
> Check your answer is reasonable.

Solution: 6 calculators cost £27.60

So 1 calculator costs $\frac{£27.60}{6}$ = £4.60 (divide the cost of 6 calculators by 6)

So 15 calculators cost 15 × £4.60 (multiply the cost of 1 calculator by 15)

15 × £4.60 = £69

Practise...

13.3 Ratio and proportion: the unitary method

G F E D C

C

1 Abby travelled for three hours on the motorway and covered 190 miles.

   a How far would Abby travel in five hours at the same average speed?

   b How far would she travel in half an hour?

   c How long would it take her to travel 250 miles?

2 Dave drove 246 miles and used 25.4 litres of diesel.

   a How many litres of diesel does Dave need for a 400 mile journey?

   b How far can he go on 10 litres of diesel?

   c What assumptions do you have to make to answer these questions?

3 Here are prices for Minty toothpaste.

Size	Amount of toothpaste	Price
Small	50 ml	£0.99
Standard	75 ml	£1.10
Large	100 ml	£1.28

Which size gives the most toothpaste for one penny?
You **must** show your working.

4 These are prices for different packs of bird seed.

Pack size	Price
5.50 kg	£15.65
12.75 kg	£28.00
25.50 kg	£53.00

   a Find the cost of 1 kg of bird seed for each of the different pack sizes.

   b Which pack offers best value for money?

   c Find the cost of a 25.50 kg pack if the price per kg was the same as for the 5.50 kg pack.

   d Give one advantage and one disadvantage of buying a 25.50 kg pack.

⚠ 5 The weights of objects on other planets are proportional to their weights on Earth.
A person weighing 540 newtons on Earth would weigh 90 newtons on the moon and 1350 newtons on Jupiter.

a What would a teenager weighing 360 newtons on Earth weigh on Jupiter?

b What would a rock weighing 10 newtons on the moon weigh on Earth?

c What would an astronaut weighing 130 newtons on the moon weigh on Jupiter?

d Express the ratio 'weight of object on Earth : weight of object on moon : weight of object on Jupiter' in its simplest form.

⚙ 6 Sajid worked for 8 hours and was paid £30.

a How much will he be paid for working 10 hours at the same rate of pay?

b Complete a copy of this table. Plot the values in the table as points on a graph, using the numbers of hours worked as the *x*-coordinates and the money earned as the corresponding *y*-coordinates.

Number of hours worked	0	2	4	6	8	10
Money earned (£)						

c The points should lie in a straight line through (0, 0).
Explain why the parts should lie on a straight line and pas through (0, 0).

d Show how to use the graph to find out how much Sajid earns in 5 hours.

❓ 7 **a** 80% of a number is 16.
What is the number?

b 65% of a number is 195.
What is the number?

❓ 8 **a** 90% of a number is 27.
What is the number?

b A sweater is reduced by 10% in a sale. The sale price is £27.
What was the original price?

Learn...   **13.4 Dividing quantities in given ratios**

You can use ratios to find numbers and quantities. If you know the ratio of ingredients and the total, you can find how much of each ingredient you need.

Steak and kidney pudding needs steak and kidney in the ratio $3:1$

There must be 500 g of meat in total.

There are four parts altogether $(3 + 1 = 4)$.

$\frac{3}{4}$ of the meat must be steak and $\frac{1}{4}$ of it must be kidney.

$\frac{1}{4}$ of 500 g = 500 g ÷ 4 = 125 g
$$4\overline{)5^10^20}$$

$\frac{3}{4}$ of 500 g = 125 g × 3 = 375 g

$$\begin{array}{r} 125 \\ \times\quad 3 \\ \hline 375 \\ {\scriptstyle 1} \end{array}$$

Study tip

Check that the two amounts add up to the total amount you need.
125 g + 375 g = 500 g

So you need 125 g of kidney and 375 g of steak.

Example: This summer Jake and Kate have weeded their aunt's garden.
Jake filled 10 bags with weeds and Kate filled 15 bags.

Their aunt gives them £45 to share in the ratio of the number of bags they filled.
How much does each person receive?

Solution: The ratio of the number of bags Jake filled to the number Kate filled is $10:15 = 2:3$

There are five shares altogether $(2 + 3 = 5)$, so Jane gets $\frac{2}{5}$ of £45 and Kate gets $\frac{3}{5}$ of £45.

$\frac{1}{5}$ of £45 is £45 ÷ 5 = £9

So Jake gets £9 × 2 = £18 and Kate gets £9 × 3 = £27

Check the total: £18 + £27 = £45 (as it should be).

Practise...   **13.4 Dividing quantities in given ratios**   G F E D C

1   Divide these amounts in the ratio $1:2$

    a   £30   **c**   £60   **e**   £3000

    b   £24   **d**   £600

2   Divide the amounts in Question 1 in each of the ratios:

    a $1:4$ **c** $3:7$

    b $2:3$ **d** $1:2:7$

3   The ratio of staff : toddlers in a nursery should be $1:4$

    a   If there are 24 toddlers in the nursery, how many members of staff are needed?

    b   The ratio gives the minimum number of staff required for the number of toddlers. How many members of staff are needed for 28 toddlers?

D

D

4 **a** The ratio of full-colour pages to black and white in a magazine is 3 : 5

    i If there are 15 full-colour pages, how many black and white pages are there?

    ii If there are 20 black and white pages, how many pages are there in the magazine altogether?

  b A different production company has a magazine with 56 full-colour pages and 64 black and white pages. The next edition has 90 pages with the same ratio of full-colour to black and white pages. How many full-colour pages are there?

C

5 Find the numbers of boys and girls in these schools.

School	Number of students	Boy : girl ratio
School A	844	1 : 1
School B	960	2 : 3
School C	770	3 : 4
School D	810	4 : 5
School E	950	10 : 9

6 **a** The angles of one triangle are in the ratio 1 : 2 : 3

    i Find the size of the largest angle.

    ii What sort of triangle is it?

  b What sort of triangle is one whose angles are in the ratio 1 : 2 : 6?

> **Hint**
>
> In an **acute-angled** triangle, all three angles are less than 90°. A **right-angled triangle** has one angle of 90°. An **obtuse-angled triangle** has one angle over 90°.

7 Write an explanation to tell someone how to split a number in the ratio 2 : 3

8 The ratio of fat : sugar : flour in a crumble topping mixture is 1 : 1 : 2

  a How much flour do you need to make 200 g of crumble topping mixture?

  b How much crumble topping mixture can you make if you have plenty of flour and sugar but only 30 g of fat?

9 Waseem invested £3500 in a business and Ruksana invested £2500.

  a At the end of the year, Waseem and Ruksana share the profit of £30 000 in the ratio of their investments. How much does Waseem receive?

  b Next year, when the profit is shared in the same ratio, Ruksana gets £10 000. What is the total profit?

10 The bar chart shows the pupil : staff ratio in primary schools in various countries. For example, Denmark has the lowest pupil : staff ratio, with approximately 11 students for each teacher.

  a Approximately how many teachers would there be in a primary school in Denmark with 200 pupils?

  b Approximately how many teachers would there be in a primary school in Zimbabwe with the same number of pupils?

  c Approximately how many teachers would there be in a primary school in the United Kingdom with the same number of pupils?

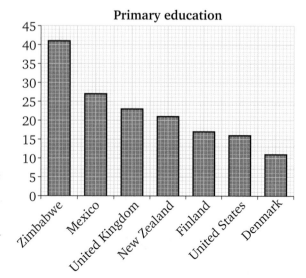
Primary education

Assess

1 **a** Write each of the following ratios in its simplest form.

  i   6 : 8

  ii   27 : 81

  iii   1000 : 10

  iv $\frac{1}{4}$: 2

  v $2\frac{1}{2}$: $3\frac{1}{2}$

 b **i**   In a choir there are 12 boys and 18 girls.
         Express this as a ratio in its simplest form.

  ii   Two more boys and two more girls join the choir.
        Express the new ratio in its simplest form.

2 A school has 45 teachers and 810 students. Express the ratio of teachers to students in its simplest form.

3 In a dance class, 30% of the dancers are male. What is the ratio of male dancers to female dancers? Give your answer in its simplest form.

4 To make sugar syrup, 100 grams of sugar is mixed with 250 ml of water.

 a How many grams of sugar are mixed with 1000 ml (one litre) of water?

 b How much water is mixed with 150 grams of sugar?

5 Darren gets 16 out of 20 in Test A and 20 out of 25 in Test B.

 a In which test did he do better?

 b The next test is marked out of 30. How many marks will Darren need in order to do as well as he did on Test A?

6 A litre of paint covers 15 m² of woodwork.

 a How much paint is needed for 50 m² of woodwork?

 b Draw a graph to show the amounts of woodwork covered by amounts of paint up to 6 litres.

7 Divide £12 in the ratio 1 : 5

8 40% of the pupils in a Year 5 class are girls. What is the girl to boy ratio in this class?
There are 14 girls in the class. How many boys are there?

9 To make sugar syrup, 100 grams of sugar is mixed with 250 ml of water.

 a How many grams of sugar are mixed with 1000 ml (one litre) of water?

 b How much water is mixed with 150 grams of sugar?

10 18 carat gold is gold mixed with other metals in the ratio 3 : 1.
How much gold is there in an 18 carat gold bracelet weighing 30 g?

11 The table shows the ratio of teachers of different ages in the UK.*

Under 30		30–39		40–49		50 and over
4	:	4	:	7	:	5

Numbers rounded to nearest integer

a What is the ratio
teachers under 30 : teachers aged 30 or over?

b There are approximately 500 000 teachers in the UK. How many of them are under 30?

12 It takes Kelly 25 seconds to run 200 m. At the same pace, how long will it take her to run these distances?

a 56 m **b** 128 m

13 The table shows the approximate population and the number of doctors in some countries of the world.

Country	Population (millions)	Number of doctors
Cuba	10.9	64 300
Israel	5.4	20 600
Italy	57.2	240 000
Nigeria	108.4	30 400
Tanzania	29.7	594
Thailand	58.4	21 600
UK	58.3	128 000
USA	263.6	606 000

a In which country is the ratio of doctors : population the greatest?

b Work out the number of doctors in each country if the doctors are shared out equally among the total population.

14 Tom has a total of 100 5p and 10p coins in the ratio 1 : 4

Jess has a total of 70 10p and 20p coins in the ratio 5 : 2

Who has the most money?

You **must** show your working.

Practice questions 🄚

1 Year 10 and Year 11 students are in an assembly.
Here are some facts about the students in the assembly.

Year	Boys : Girls	Student data
10	4 : 5	84 boys
11	2 : 3	150 students

Work out the total number of girls in the assembly.
You **must** show your working. *(5 marks)*

AQA 2008

2 A short necklace has 24 gold beads and 16 black beads.
A long necklace has a total of 60 beads.
Both necklaces have the same ratio of gold beads to black beads.
How many black beads are on the long necklace? *(3 marks)*

AQA 2004

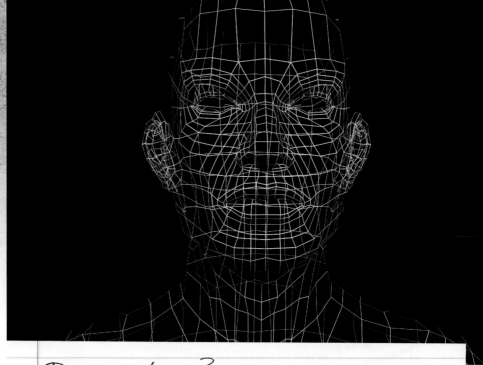

Objectives

Examiners would normally expect students who get these grades to be able to:

G

recognise and name shapes such as parallelogram, rhombus, trapezium

E

calculate interior and exterior angles of a quadrilateral

D

classify a quadrilateral using geometric properties

C

calculate exterior and interior angles of a regular polygon.

Did you know?

Polygons and video games

Objects in video games are made up of lots of polygons. Pictures are made up of a series of polygons such as triangles, squares, rectangles, parallelograms and rhombuses. The more polygons there are, then the better the picture looks.

The polygons are all given coordinates. The computer changes and rotates the coordinates to match your position in the game. This gives the impression of movement.

For example, if you are far away, the computer shrinks all the coordinates of the polygons. This makes the polygons appear smaller on the screen so they look further away.

Key terms

quadrilateral
polygon
exterior angle
interior angle
diagonal
bisect
perpendicular
pentagon
hexagon
regular
octagon
decagon
nonagon

You should already know:

✓ how to use properties of angles at a point, angles on a straight line, perpendicular lines, and opposite angles at a vertex

✓ the differences between acute, obtuse, reflex and right angles

✓ how to use parallel lines, alternate angles and corresponding angles

✓ how to prove that the angle sum of a triangle is 180°

✓ how to prove that the exterior angle of a triangle is equal to the sum of the interior opposite angles

✓ angle properties of equilateral, isosceles and right-angled triangles.

Learn... 14.1 Properties of quadrilaterals

A **quadrilateral** is a **polygon** with four sides.

You need to know the names and properties of the following special quadrilaterals.

Square – a quadrilateral with four equal sides and four right angles

Trapezium – a quadrilateral with one pair of parallel sides

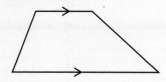

Rectangle – a quadrilateral with four right angles, and opposite sides equal in length

Parallelogram – a quadrilateral with opposite sides equal and parallel

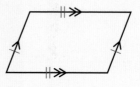

Kite – a quadrilateral with two pairs of equal adjacent sides

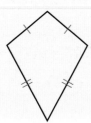

Rhombus – a quadrilateral with four equal sides and opposite sides parallel

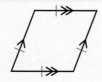

Isosceles trapezium – a trapezium where the non-parallel sides are equal in length

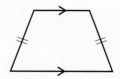

All quadrilaterals have four sides and four angles.

A quadrilateral can be split into two triangles.

The angles in a triangle add up to 180°.

The quadrilateral is made up of two triangles.

The angles in a quadrilateral add up to 2 × 180° = 360°

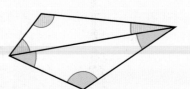

Example: Calculate the angles marked with letters in this shape.

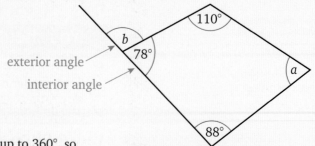

exterior angle
interior angle

Solution: The angles in the quadrilateral add up to 360°, so

$a = 360° − (78° + 88° + 110°)$

$= 360° − 276°$

$= 84°$

The **exterior** and **interior angles** add up to 180°, so

$b = 180° − 78°$

$= 102°$

Study tip

Always make sure that your answer is reasonable. Angle b is an obtuse angle so that answer is reasonable.

Practise...

14.1 Properties of quadrilaterals

G F E D C

1 Write down the mathematical name of these quadrilaterals.

a

b

c

d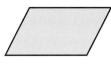

e

f

G

2 Small metal rods can be joined at the ends to make shapes.
The rods are all the same length.
Three rods can be used to make an equilateral triangle like this.

Alan uses four rods.
Write down the names of the shapes that he can make.

F

3 Calculate the angles marked with letters.

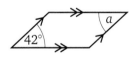

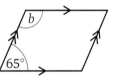

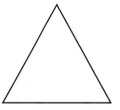

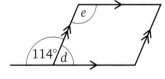

Not drawn
accurately

E

4 **a** Three angles of a quadrilateral are 60°, 65° and 113°.
Work out the size of the fourth angle.

b Two angles of a quadrilateral are 74° and 116° and the other
two angles are equal.
Work out the size of the other two angles.

c **i** If all four angles of a quadrilateral are equal, what size are they?

ii What sorts of quadrilateral have four equal angles?

E
D

5 Calculate the angles a, b, c, d and e in these quadrilaterals.

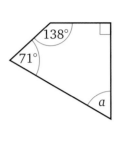

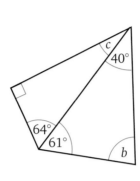

Not drawn
accurately

D

6 square   rectangle   parallelogram   rhombus   kite   trapezium

   a   Which of these quadrilaterals have all four sides equal?

   b   Which of these quadrilaterals have opposite sides which are parallel?

   c   Which of these quadrilaterals have adjacent sides which are equal?

   d   Which of these quadrilaterals has only one pair of parallel sides?

7 Barry measures the angles of a quadrilateral. He says that three of the angles are 82° and the other one is 124°. Is he right?
Give a reason for your answer.

C

8 Harry measures the angles of a quadrilateral. He says that the angles are 72°, 66°, 114° and 108°. He says the shape is a trapezium. Is he right?
Give a reason for your answer.

9 A cyclic quadrilateral is a quadrilateral where all four vertices (corners) can be drawn on the circumference of a circle.

Which of the following are cyclic quadrilaterals?

square   rectangle   parallelogram   rhombus   kite

10 Tracey says that it is possible for a trapezium to be a cyclic quadrilateral.

Is she correct?

Give a reason for your answer.

11 One angle of a quadrilateral is 150° and the other three angles are equal.

Write down and solve an equation in x.

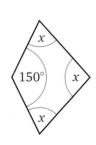

12 EDC is a straight line and angle DAB = angle ABC
Work out angle ABC.

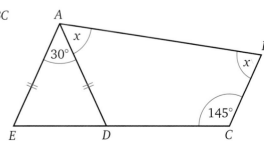

13   Charlie has two pieces of card in the shape of
equilateral triangles. Each side is 4 cm long.

He cuts each piece of card in half along the
dotted lines as shown.

He now has four right-angled triangles.

Each triangle is exactly the same.

    a   Use the four triangles to make:

        i   a rectangle   **iii**   a parallelogram

        ii   a trapezium   **iv**   a rhombus.

        Draw a diagram to show each of your answers.

    b   Work out the size of the angles in each of the shapes you made in part **a**.

14   **a**   A kite always has an obtuse angle. True or false?
Give a reason for your answer.

    b   Can a kite have two obtuse angles?
Give a reason for your answers.

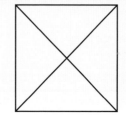

Learn...   14.2 Diagonal properties of quadrilaterals

A **diagonal** is a line joining one vertex (corner) of a quadrilateral
to another.

    Each quadrilateral has two diagonals.

    The square has two diagonals.

    The diagonals are the same length.

    The diagonals **bisect** one another.   Bisect means they cut one another in half.

    The diagonals are **perpendicular**.   Perpendicular means at right angles.

Example: What is the mathematical name of this quadrilateral?

• The diagonals are different lengths.

• The diagonals are at right angles to each other.

• Only one diagonal is bisected by the other.

Solution:

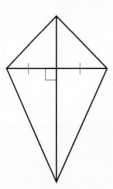

Drawing the diagonals using the
information given, you can see
what the shape is.

The quadrilateral is a kite.

Practise...

14.2 Diagonal properties of quadrilaterals

1 **a** Copy each of these shapes and draw their diagonals.

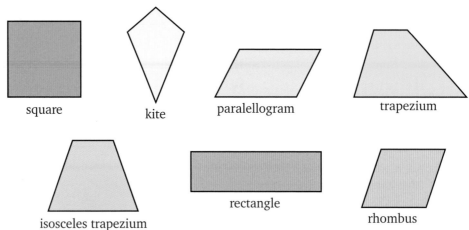

square   kite   paralellogram   trapezium

isosceles trapezium   rectangle   rhombus

b Copy and complete this table.

Shape	Are the diagonals equal? (Yes/No)	Do the diagonals bisect each other? (Yes/No/Sometimes)	Do the diagonals cross at right angles? (Yes/No)	Do the diagonals bisect the angles of the quadrilateral? (Yes/No/Sometimes)
Square				
Kite				
Parallelogram				
Trapezium				
Isosceles trapezium				
Rectangle				
Rhombus				

2 Rajesh has drawn a quadrilateral. Its diagonals are equal.

What shapes might he have drawn?
(Use the table from Question 1 to help you.)

3 Michelle says that the diagonals of a rectangle bisect the angles.

So angles *a* and *c* are both 45°, and angle *b* must be 90°.

Is she right? Give a reason for your answer.

Not drawn accurately

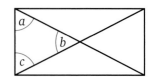

4 The diagram shows a rhombus *ABCD*. *AC* and *BD* are the diagonals. Angle *ADB* = 32°

Calculate angle *DAC*.

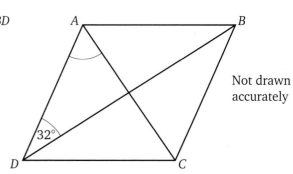

Not drawn accurately

5   square   rectangle   parallelogram   rhombus   kite   trapezium

a   Which of these quadrilaterals have diagonals of different lengths?

b   Which of these quadrilaterals have diagonals that cross at right angles?

c   Which of these quadrilaterals have all four sides equal and diagonals that bisect at right angles?

d   Which of these quadrilaterals have opposite sides which are parallel and diagonals of different lengths?

6   Calculate the angles *a–f* in the diagrams.

Give a reason for each answer.

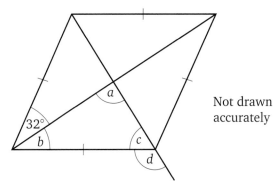

Not drawn accurately

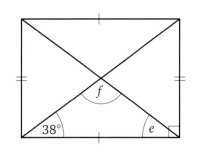

7   Copy and complete this table. The first row has been done for you.

Shape	Number of different length sides (at most)	Number of right angles (at least)	Pairs of opposite sides parallel	Diagonals must be equal	Diagonals bisect each other	Diagonals cross at right angles
Square	1	4	Both	Yes	Yes	Yes
Rectangle						
Trapezium						
Rhombus						
Parallelogram						
Kite						
Isosceles trapezium						

Learn...   14.3 Angle properties of polygons (k)

The interior angles of a triangle add up to 180°.

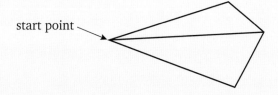

start point

A quadrilateral has four sides and can be split into two triangles by drawing diagonals from a point.

The sum of the angles is $2 \times 180° = 360°$

A **pentagon** has five sides and can be split into three triangles by drawing diagonals from a point.

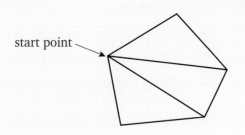

start point

The sum of the angles is $3 \times 180° = 540°$

A **hexagon** has six sides and can be split into four triangles by drawing diagonals from a point.

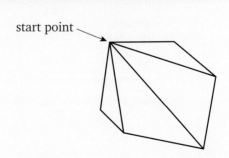

start point

The sum of the angles is $4 \times 180° = 720°$

In general a polygon with n sides can be split into $(n - 2)$ triangles.

The sum of the angles is $(n - 2) \times 180°$.

The **interior angles** of a polygon are the angles inside the polygon.

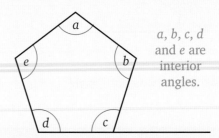

a, b, c, d and e are interior angles.

The **exterior angles** of a polygon are the angles between one side and the extension of the side.

The exterior angles of a polygon add up to $360°$.

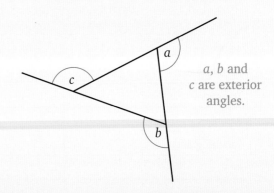

a, b and c are exterior angles.

Example: Find the interior angle of a **regular octagon**.

Solution: **Either:**

An octagon has eight sides.

So the sum of the angles is $(8 - 2) \times 180° = 1080°$

A regular octagon has all angles equal, so each angle is $1080° \div 8 = 135°$

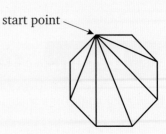

start point

Or:

A regular octagon has eight equal exterior angles.

So each exterior angle is $360° \div 8 = 45°$

So each interior angle is $180° - 45° = 135°$

Example: A regular polygon has interior angles of 144°. How many sides does it have?

Solution:

interior angle
exterior angle
144°

Each exterior angle must be 180° − 144° = 36°

The exterior angles of a convex polygon add up to 360°.

A regular polygon has all sides equal and all angles equal.

So there must be 360° ÷ 36° = 10 exterior angles

The polygon has 10 sides.

Study tip

Always draw a diagram to help answer the questions.

You can then label the diagram to keep track of what you know.

14.3 Angle properties of polygons

Practise...

G F E D C

C

1   Four of the angles of a pentagon are 110°, 130°, 102° and 97°.

Calculate the fifth angle.

2   Calculate the angles marked *a* and *b* in the diagram.

Explain how you worked them out.

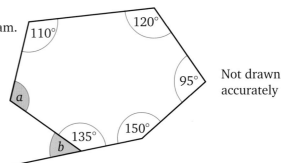

110°
120°
95°
Not drawn accurately
a
135°
150°
b

3   A regular polygon has an exterior angle of 60°.

How many sides does it have?

4   Calculate the difference between the interior angle of a regular **decagon** (ten-sided shape) and the interior angle of a regular **nonagon** (nine-sided shape).

5   James divides a regular hexagon into six triangles as shown.

He says the angle sum of a regular hexagon is 6 × 180°.

Is he correct?

Give a reason for your answer.

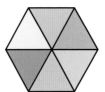

6   Lisa says that a regular octagon can be split into two trapeziums and a rectangle as shown.

She says the angle sum of the octagon is 3 × 360°.

Show that Lisa is correct.

7 The diagrams show how you draw an equilateral triangle and a regular pentagon inside a circle.

You do this by dividing the angle at the centre equally.

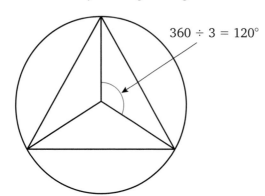
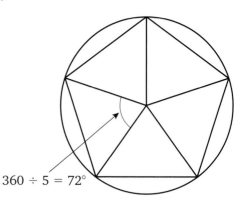

$360 \div 3 = 120°$

$360 \div 5 = 72°$

Use the same method to draw a regular hexagon and a regular nonagon (nine-sided shape) inside a circle.

8 The diagram shows a regular pentagon *ABCDE* and a regular hexagon *DEFGHI*.

Calculate:

a angle *EDC*   **e** angle *CAE*

b angle *EDI*   **f** angle *HIG*

c obtuse angle *CDI*   **g** angle *DIG*.

d angle *BAC*

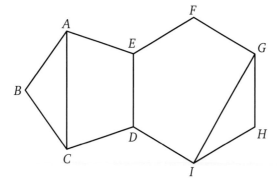

9 A badge is in the shape of a regular pentagon.

The letter V is written on the badge.

What is the size of the angle marked *x*?

10 A company makes containers as shown.

The top is in the shape of a regular octagon.

a What is the size of each interior angle?

b When the company packs them into a box, will they tessellate (fit together exactly)? If not, what shape will be left between them?

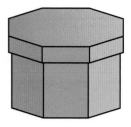

14

Assess (k)

1 Write down the mathematical name of each of these shapes.

a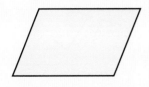

c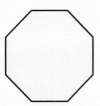

e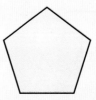

b

d

f

2 Write down the letters of the shapes in Question 1 that have:

a some sides equal (but not all)

b all sides equal

c any acute angles

d any obtuse angles

e some equal angles

f any adjacent sides equal

g all diagonals equal

h diagonals perpendicular to each other

i diagonals of different lengths

j any adjacent angles equal.

3 Calculate the angles marked *a*, *b* and *c* in this parallelogram.

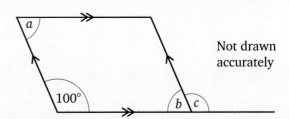

Not drawn accurately

4 Which of the following polygons are possible and which ones are not possible?

Make an accurate drawing of each one that is possible.

a A kite with a right angle

b A kite with two right angles

c A trapezium with two right angles

d A trapezium with only one right angle

e A triangle with a right angle

f A triangle with two right angles

g A pentagon with one right angle

h A pentagon with two right angles

i A pentagon with three right angles

j A pentagon with four right angles.

G

F

E

D

D
C

5 Find the value of the angles marked in these diagrams.

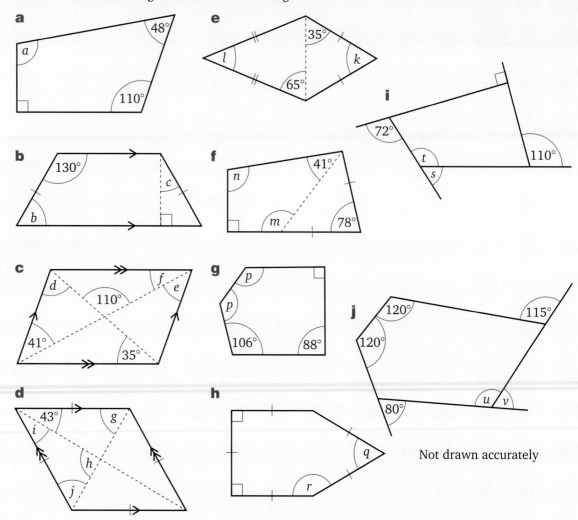

6 Sophie says her regular polygon has an exterior angle of 40°.

Adam says that is not possible.

Who is correct?

Give a reason for your answer.

7 The exterior angle of a regular polygon is 4°.

a How many sides does the polygon have?

b What is the size of each interior angle in the polygon?

c What is the sum of the interior angles of the polygon?

8 ABCDE is a regular pentagon.

DEG, DCF and GABF are straight lines.

Work out the size of angle x.

Not drawn accurately

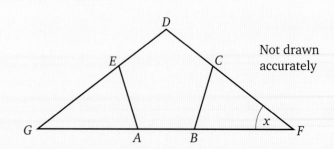

Practice questions

1   **a**   The diagrams show the diagonals of two different quadrilaterals.

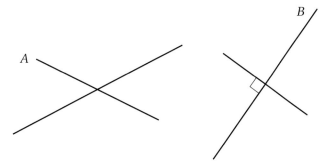

Write down the names of these quadrilaterals.   *(3 marks)*

   b **i**   Draw a quadrilateral that has only one pair of parallel lines and exactly two
           right angles.   *(2 marks)*
       ii   Write down the name of this quadrilateral.   *(1 mark)*

AQA 2004

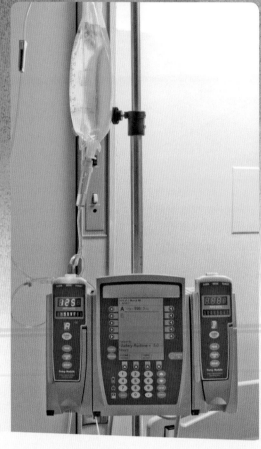

Objectives

Examiners would normally expect students who get these grades to be able to:

F

set up and solve a simple equation such as $5x = 10$ or $x + 4 = 7$

E

set up and solve an equation involving fractions such as $\dfrac{x}{3} = 4$ or $2x - 3 = 8$

D

set up and solve more complicated equations such as $3x + 2 = 6 - x$ or $4(2x - 1) = 20$

C

set up and solve an equation such as $4x + 5 = 3(x + 4)$ or $\dfrac{2x - 7}{4} = 1$

Did you know?

Nurses use algebra

Students often ask, 'Why do we have to do algebra at school when we are never going to use it again?'

This is not true. There are many jobs that involve algebra.

Nurses, for example, use algebra every day in their administration of medicines and drips.

Here is an equation that they would use to control an electronic drip for a patient.

$$\text{rate of drip (drops per min)} = \frac{\text{volume of infusion (ml)}}{\text{time (min)}}$$

Key terms

unknown
solution
operation
brackets
expanding
denominator
lowest common denominator

You should already know:

✔ the inverse operations of $+$, $-$, $\times$ and $\div$

✔ how to collect like terms

✔ how to use substitution

✔ how to multiply out brackets by a positive or negative number

✔ how to find the lowest common denominator for two fractions.

Learn... **15.1 Simple equations**

When you find the value for an **unknown**, you have found the **solution** to an equation.

Equations can involve any of the **operations** $+, -, \times, \div$.

Many equations involve more than one operation, e.g.

$2x + 3$ means 2 lots of x add 3.

$$x \longrightarrow \boxed{\times 2} \xrightarrow{2x} \boxed{+ 3} \longrightarrow 2x + 3$$

When solving the equation you would use the inverse of each operation.

You would also perform them in the reverse order.

$$x \longleftarrow \boxed{\div 2} \xleftarrow{2x} \boxed{- 3} \longleftarrow 2x + 3$$

Example: Solve the equation $6x = 24$

> **Hint**
> Remember that $6x$ means $6 \times x$

Solution: $6x = 24$

$\dfrac{6x}{6} = \dfrac{24}{6}$ Divide both sides by 6.
       The inverse (opposite) of multiplying by 6 is dividing by 6.

$x = 4$

Check
$6 \times 4 = 24$ ✓

> **Study tip**
> Always check your answer by substituting its value back into the original equation.

Example: Solve the equation $x - 2 = 7$

Solution: $x - 2 = 7$

$x - 2 + 2 = 7 + 2$ Add 2 to both sides. The inverse of subtracting 2 is adding 2.

$x = 9$

Check
$9 - 2 = 7$ ✓

Example: Solve the equation $4x + 3 = 17$

Solution: This is an equation with two operations: $\times$ and $+$

The expression $4x + 3$ was formed by multiplying by 4, then adding 3.

The inverse of adding 3 is subtracting 3. So to solve the equation you need to begin by subtracting 3 from both sides.

$4x + 3 - 3 = 17 - 3$ Subtract 3 from both sides.

$4x = 14$

$\dfrac{4x}{4} = \dfrac{14}{4}$ Divide both sides by 4.
       (Dividing by 4 is the inverse of multiplying by 4.)

$x = 3\frac{2}{4}$ Change all improper fractions to mixed numbers.

$x = 3\frac{1}{2}$ Simplify any fractions.

Check
$(4 \times 3\frac{1}{2}) + 3 = 17$ ✓

Example: The smallest angle of a triangle is $x°$.

The middle-sized angle is double the smallest angle plus $10°$.

The largest angle is double the middle-sized angle plus $10°$.

Calculate x.

Solution: The smallest angle $= x°$

The middle angle $= (2x + 10)°$

The largest angle $= 2(2x + 10)° + 10° = (4x + 20 + 10)°$

$x + (2x + 10) + (4x + 20 + 10) = 180$ The angles in a triangle add up to $180°$.

$7x + 40 = 180$ Collect like terms.

$7x + 40 - 40 = 180 - 40$ Subtract 40 from both sides.

$7x = 140$

$\dfrac{7x}{7} = \dfrac{140}{7}$ Divide both sides by 7.

$x = 20°$

Check

$20 + 2(20) + 10 + 4(20) + 20 + 10 = 20 + 40 + 10 + 80 + 20 + 10 = 180$ ✓

Practise... 15.1 Simple equations ⓚ

G F E D C

1 Solve these equations.

a $5x = 35$

b $6b = 3.6$

c $x - 3 = 8$

d $y + 3 = 17$

e $c + 9.9 = 2.7$

f $6 = 8 - 3t$

Hint

If the unknown is on the right-hand side of the equation, turn it round completely before you start to solve it, e.g.

$4 = 13 - 6z$ becomes $13 - 6z = 4$

2 Set up and solve an equation to find the value of x in the diagram.

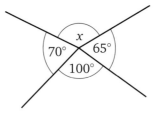

3 Two angles of a parallelogram are $2x + 40°$ and $3x$.

Find the value of x if:

a the angles are opposite each other

b the angles are next to each other.

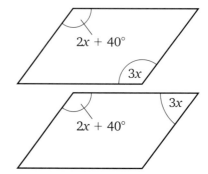

4 The diagram shows the position of two ships A and B.

The bearing of B from A is 110°.

Find the value of x.

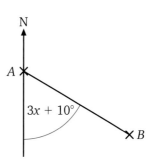

5 Nicole was given £2.00 to go to the shop and buy some cans of drink.

She bought two cans and was given 86p change.

   a   Write down an equation to represent this situation.

   b   Solve your equation to work out the cost of a can.

6 Simone thinks of a number, doubles it and subtracts 3. The answer is 7.

Use x to represent the number Simone thought of.

   a   Write down an equation in x using the information given.

   b   Solve your equation to find Simone's number.

7 The diagram shows three angles on a straight line.

   a   Write down an equation in x.

   b   Solve your equation to find the value of x.

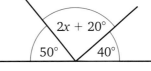

8   **a**   Use the diagram to write down an equation in z.

   b   Solve your equation to find the value of z.

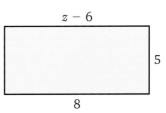

Learn... 15.2 Harder equations

Some equations have x terms on both sides.

Follow these steps to solve the equation.

- Collect together, on one side, all the terms that contain x.
- Collect together, on the other side, all the terms that do not contain x.
- Solve by doing the same to both sides of the equation, as in Learn 6.1.
- Check your answer by substituting it back into the equation.

Remember that a sign belongs to the term **after** it.

Take one step at a time. Do not try to do two steps at once.

Collect the terms in x on the side that has the largest number of them already.

Be extra careful if the equation involves negative amounts of the letter,
e.g. in an equation containing both $-4x$ and $2x$, you would collect the terms on the side where $2x$ is.

$2x$ is larger than $-4x$.

It helps to think of the number line. Which of the numbers is further to the right?

Example: Solve the equation $9 - 4y = -2y + 7$

Hint

$-2y$ is larger than $-4y$ so collect the y terms on the right-hand side.

Solution:

$9 - 4y + 4y = -2y + 7 + 4y$ Add $4y$ to both sides.

$9 = 2y + 7$ (This collects all the y terms on the right-hand side.)

$9 - 7 = 2y + 7 - 7$ Take 7 from both sides.

$2 = 2y$

$1 = y$

$y = 1$ Write the equation with y on the left-hand side.

Check

LHS: $9 - 4 \times 1 = 5$

RHS: $-2 \times 1 + 7 = 5$ left-hand side = right-hand side

LHS $=$ RHS $\checkmark$ They both have a value of 5.

Example: Find:

a the width

b the length of this rectangle.

All dimensions are in centimetres.

$6b - 2.5$

$b \quad\boxed{}\quad b$

$3.5 + b$

Solution:

a The opposite sides of a rectangle are equal in length.

So $\quad 6b - 2.5 = 3.5 + b$ Collect the b terms on the left-hand side.

$6b - 2.5 - b = 3.5 + b - b$ Take b from both sides.

$5b - 2.5 = 3.5$

$5b - 2.5 + 2.5 = 3.5 + 2.5$ Add 2.5 to both sides.

$5b = 6$

$\dfrac{5b}{5} = \dfrac{6}{5}$ Divide both sides by 5.

$b = 1.2 \, \text{cm}$ This is the width of the rectangle as shown on the diagram.

The width of the rectangle is 1.2 cm.

b Length $= 3.5 + b$ Substitute for b in one of the expressions for the length shown on the diagram.

$= 3.5 + 1.2$

$= 4.7$

The length of the rectangle is 4.7 cm.

Hint

When finding the width, you could use the other expression, $6b - 2.5$

This is more complicated so choose the easier one.

The harder expression can be used as a check.

Check

$6b - 2.5 = 6 \times 1.2 - 2.5 = 7.2 - 2.5 = 4.7 \checkmark$

Study tip

It is good practice to do a check whenever you solve an equation.

Practise... 15.2 Harder equations G F E D C

1 Solve these equations.

a $3x + 1 = x + 13$ **e** $2 + 2p = 4p - 1$

b $6y + 4 = -24 - y$ **f** $5b + 16 = 8b + 10$

c $4z + 1.5 = 2z - 3$ **g** $-7c - 3 = 30 - 4c$

d $8t - \frac{1}{2} = 4t + \frac{1}{2}$ **h** $10d - 0.6 = 0.9 - 5d$

D

2 Jared solves the equation $9x + 7 = 9 - x$

His first step is $8x + 7 = 9$

What mistake has Jared made?

3 Helen solves the equation $3y - 4 = 6 + 2y$

She gets the answer $y = 2$

Can you find Helen's mistake?

4 Work out the value of x.

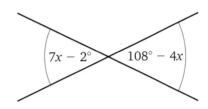

$7x - 2°$ $108° - 4x$

5 The perimeters of the equilateral triangle and the rectangle are equal.

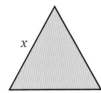 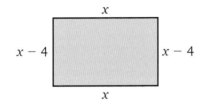

x

x $x - 4$ $x - 4$

x

Work out the value of x.

6 The perimeters of the regular hexagon and the equilateral triangle are equal.

a Use this information to write down an equation in y.

b Solve your equation to find the value of y.

c What is the actual perimeter of each of the shapes?

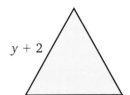

y

$y + 2$

7 The perimeters of each of these shapes are equal.

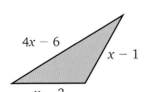 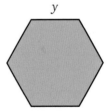 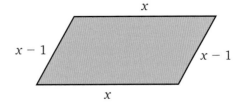

x

$4x - 6$ $x - 1$ $x - 1$ $x - 1$

$x - 3$ x

a Use this information to write down an equation in x.

b Solve your equation to find the value of x.

c What is the actual perimeter of each of the shapes?

D

8 Work out the value of x.

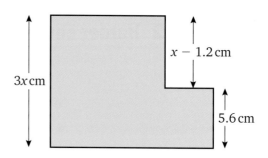

9 The diagram shows a rectangular lawn. The gardener has dug up a rectangular area. He is going to use this as a vegetable patch.

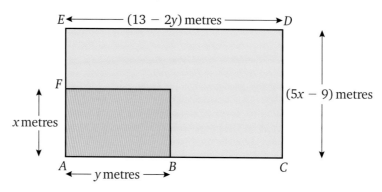

B and F are the midpoints of the sides AC and AE respectively.

a Form two equations, one in x and one in y.

b Solve your equations to find the values of x and y.

c What are the dimensions of the vegetable patch?

d What are the dimensions of the outer rectangle, the whole garden?

10 The line EF intersects the lines AB and CD.
The angles are as shown on the diagram.
Is AB parallel to CD?
Show working to justify your answer.

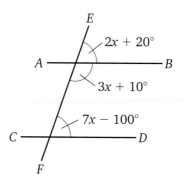

Learn... 15.3 Equations with brackets

Whenever you are asked to solve equations with **brackets**, you will usually begin by removing the brackets. Usually they are removed by **expanding** the brackets.

×	x	$+4$
2	$2x$	$+8$

or $2(x + 4) = 2x + 8$

Multiply everything inside the bracket by the number outside the bracket.

For example, $2(x + 4)$ becomes $2x + 8$

and $-6(3x - 1)$ becomes $-18x + 6$.

Sometimes you can remove brackets by dividing the equation by a number. (See the alternative method in the first example overleaf.)

Example: Solve the equation $5(2x - 3) = 25$

Solution:

$$5(2x - 3) = 25$$ Expand the brackets first, then follow the rules for solving equations.

$$10x - 15 = 25$$ Remember to multiply both terms in the bracket by 5.

$$10x - 15 + 15 = 25 + 15$$ Add 15 to both sides.

$$10x = 40$$

$$\frac{10x}{10} = \frac{40}{10}$$ Divide both sides by 10.

$$x = 4$$

Check

$$5(2 \times 4 - 3) = 5(8 - 3) = 5 \times 5 = 25 \checkmark$$

Alternative method:

$$5(2x - 3) = 25$$

$$\frac{5(2x - 3)}{5} = \frac{25}{5}$$ Divide both sides by 5.

$$2x - 3 = 5$$

$$2x - 3 + 3 = 5 + 3$$ Add 3 to both sides.

$$2x = 8$$

$$\frac{2x}{2} = \frac{8}{2}$$ Divide both sides by 2.

$$x = 4$$

Check

$$5(2 \times 4 - 3) = 5(8 - 3) = 5 \times 5 = 25 \checkmark$$

This alternative method is only worth using here because 25 is divisible by 5.

Example: Solve the equation $2(y - 4) - 1 = 12 - 5y$

Solution:

$$2y - 8 - 1 = 12 - 5y$$ Expand the brackets first. $2 \times -4 = -8$

$$2y - 9 = 12 - 5y$$ Simplify any like terms.

$$2y - 9 + 9 = 12 - 5y + 9$$ Add 9 to both sides.

$$2y = 21 - 5y$$

$$2y + 5y = 21 - 5y + 5y$$ Add 5y to both sides.

$$7y = 21$$

$$\frac{7y}{7} = \frac{21}{7}$$ Divide both sides by 7.

$$y = 3$$

Check

LHS: $2(3 - 4) - 1 = 2 \times (-1) - 1 = -2 - 1 = -3$

RHS: $12 - 5 \times 3 = 12 - 15 = -3$

LHS = RHS $\checkmark$

Example: This shape is made up of two rectangles A and B. The total area of the shape is 18 cm^2.

a Write down an equation for the area of the shape in terms of x.

b Solve your equation to find the value of x.

c Redraw your shape replacing all measurements with numbers.

This does not have to be to scale.

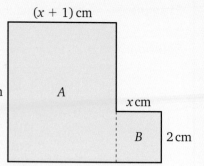

$(x + 1)$ cm

6 cm A

x cm

B 2 cm

Solution: a The area consists of two rectangles.
Begin by writing down the area for each of them separately.

$$\text{Area of } A = 6(x + 1) \quad \text{Area of } B = 2x$$

$$\text{Area of } A + \text{Area of } B = \text{Total area}$$

$$6(x + 1) + 2x = 18$$

b $6x + 6 + 2x = 18$ Expand the brackets.

$8x + 6 = 18$ Simplify by collecting x terms.

$8x + 6 - 6 = 18 - 6$ Take 6 from both sides.

$8x = 12$

$\dfrac{8x}{8} = \dfrac{12}{8}$ Divide both sides by 8.

$x = 1\frac{4}{8} \text{ or } 1\frac{1}{2}$

c Width of $A = x + 1 = 2\frac{1}{2}$ cm

Width of $B = x = 1\frac{1}{2}$ cm

$2\frac{1}{2}$ cm

6 cm A

$1\frac{1}{2}$ cm

B 2 cm

Study tip

Don't try to do two steps at once. Most students make mistakes if they rush their working.

Practise... 15.3 Equations with brackets

D

1 Solve these equations.

a $4(2x + 1) = 44$

b $2(y - 3) = 32$

c $35 = 7(3z - 1)$

d $-15 = 3(6a + 4)$

e $11(3b + 1) = 44$

f $45 = 5(c + 1.5)$

C

2 Solve these equations.

a $8b + 7 = 3(3b - 1)$

b $12 + 3c = 8(c - 1)$

c $3 - 2d = 4(2d - 7)$

d $0.1f - 6.5 = 2(0.8f - 1)$

e $4(3y - 2) = 3(3y + 1)$

f $8(j - 1) = 5(j - 2)$

g $5(t + 1) = 3(t - 3)$

3   Emma thinks of a number, x, adds 5 and then doubles the result.

Her answer is 40.

Write down and solve an equation in x to work out Emma's number.

4   Dan thinks of a number, x, subtracts 2 and then multiplies the result by 5.

His answer is 30.

Write down and solve an equation in x to work out Dan's number.

5   These rectangles have the same area.

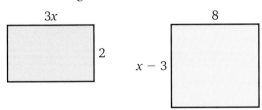

Work out the value of x.

6   The diagram shows a garden. A section of the lawn has been removed to make a pond.

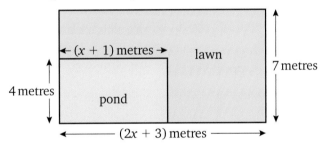

The area of the lawn is $35\,\text{m}^2$.

a   Write down an equation for the area of the lawn.

b   Solve your equation to find the value of x.

c   Find the dimensions of the pond and the whole garden.

d   How can you check this? Were you correct?

7   The area of this triangle is $64\,\text{cm}^2$.

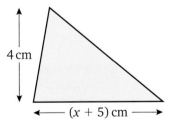

a   Write down an equation, in x, for the area of the triangle.

b   Solve your equation to find the value of x.

c   Find the length of the base of the triangle.

8   The following shape is made from equilateral triangles of sides $(x - 2)$ cm.

The perimeter is 42 cm.

a   Write down an equation in x.

b   Work out the value of x.

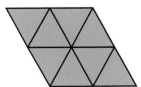

Learn...   15.4 Equations with fractions

Fractions are removed by multiplying both sides by the **denominator**.

For example, if the equation contains $\frac{x}{4}$, you would multiply by 4.

If there is more than one fraction, say $\frac{3x}{5}$ and $\frac{x}{2}$, you would multiply everything by 5 throughout and then by 2.

An alternative method would be to multiply, just the once, by the **lowest common denominator**.

The lowest common denominator for these two fractions is 10. This is because 10 is the smallest number which both 5 and 2 divide into exactly.

Harder equations have numerators with more than one term on the top of the fraction, e.g. $\frac{3x - 2}{4}$

There are 'invisible brackets' around the terms on top of an algebraic fraction.

To make this clear, you should put them in: $\frac{(3x - 2)}{4}$. Then you are less likely to make a mistake.

Example: Solve the equation $\frac{x}{4} + 3 = 5$

Solution: This is an example of the simplest type of equation with a fraction.

With only one fraction in the equation, you should first get the fraction on its own on one side of the equation and then multiply by 4.

You are working towards finding $x = ...$, so $+ 3$ is the first term to go from the left-hand side of the equation.

$\frac{x}{4} + 3 - 3 = 5 - 3$ Take 3 from both sides.

$\frac{x}{4} = 2$ Now the fraction term is on its own.

$\frac{x}{4} \times 4 = 2 \times 4$ Multiply both sides by 4 (the denominator).

$x = 8$

Check

$$\text{LHS} = \frac{8}{4} + 3 = 2 + 3 = 5 = \text{RHS} \checkmark$$

> **Hint**
>
> To remove the denominator of the fraction, multiply both sides by 4.

Example: Solve the equation $\frac{3x - 2}{2} = 5$

Solution: This is an example of an equation with more than one term on the top of the fraction.

The whole of $3x - 2$ is divided by 2.

$\frac{(3x - 2)}{2}$ is the same as one half of $3x - 2$.

$2 \times \frac{(3x - 2)}{2} = 2 \times 5$ Multiply both sides by 2.

$3x - 2 = 10$

$3x - 2 + 2 = 10 + 2$ Add 2 to both sides.

$3x = 12$

$\frac{3x}{3} = \frac{12}{3}$ Divide both sides by 3.

$x = 4$

> **Study tip**
>
> You can put in the invisible brackets before you start your working. Here the brackets have been put round $3x - 2$.

Check

$$\text{LHS} = \frac{(3 \times 4 - 2)}{2} = \frac{(12 - 2)}{2} = \frac{10}{2} = 5 = \text{RHS} \checkmark$$

Example: A stick is $2x + 15$ cm long.

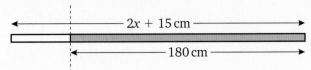

$$\longleftarrow \text{———} 2x + 15\,\text{cm} \text{———} \longrightarrow$$

$$\longleftarrow \text{———} 180\,\text{cm} \text{———} \longrightarrow$$

If one fifth of the stick is cut off, the stick will now be 180 cm long.

How long was the stick before the piece was cut off?

Solution: One fifth of the stick was cut off so four fifths remains. This remaining part is 180 cm.

This can be turned into an equation.

$$\frac{4(2x + 15)}{5} = 180$$

$$\frac{(8x + 60)}{5} = 180 \qquad \text{Multiply out the brackets.}$$

$$\frac{5 \times (8x + 60)}{5} = 5 \times 180 \qquad \text{Multiply both sides by 5.}$$

$$8x + 60 = 900$$

$$8x + 60 - 60 = 900 - 60 \qquad \text{Take 60 from both sides.}$$

$$8x = 840$$

$$\frac{8x}{8} = \frac{840}{8} \qquad \text{Divide both sides by 8.}$$

$$x = 105\,\text{cm}$$

This means that the stick was originally $2 \times 105 + 15 = 210 + 15 = 225$ cm long.

Check

$$\text{LHS} = \frac{4(2 \times 105 + 15)}{5} = \frac{4(225)}{5} = 4 \times 45 = 180 = \text{RHS} \checkmark$$

Practise... **15.4 Equations with fractions** (k)   G F E D C

1 Solve these equations.

a $\dfrac{x}{3} - 1 = 5$

b $\dfrac{y}{9} + 4 = 9$

c $\dfrac{f}{2} + 5 = -3$

d $\dfrac{5x + 1}{3} = 12$

e $\dfrac{2y - 3}{4} = 6$

f $7 = \dfrac{11 - z}{5}$

g $\dfrac{x}{4} + \dfrac{x}{3} = 7$

h $\dfrac{y}{3} - \dfrac{y}{5} = 4$

i $\dfrac{5z}{9} + \dfrac{z}{3} = 8$

2

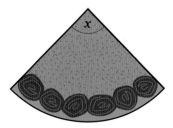

Ravi decides to share his piece of cake with his friends.

The original piece made an angle of x at the centre.

He took one-third of this slice. The angle at the centre of his slice was 25°.

a Use this information to write down an equation in x.

b Solve this equation to find the angle at the centre of Ravi's original piece of cake.

C

3 David has a large piece of cake.

He helps himself to one-quarter of it. Once he has taken this, the angle at the centre is reduced to 207°.

Work out the value of x.

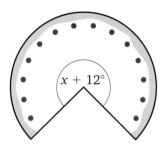

4 A farmer is building somewhere for his prize pig to live.

The area consists of a pig sty for the pig to shelter in, and a run.

All measurements are in metres.

One-quarter of the pig's accommodation is taken up by the pig sty.

The run has an area of 13.5 m².

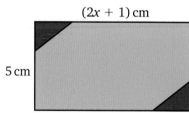

a Write down an expression for the total area.

b Write down an expression for the area of the run.

c Using the information given, form an equation in x and solve it to find the value of x.

d Find the total area of the pig sty and the run.

⚠ 5 The red areas make up one-sixth of the total area of the rectangle.

Each of the red parts has an area of 7 cm².

Work out the perimeter of the rectangle.

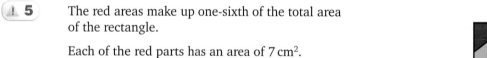

⚠ 6 A factory is making metal brackets.

It cuts them from a sheet of material $2x$ cm by $3x$ cm.

The remaining material, shown in purple, is the metal that is wasted.

The factory wastes one-third of the material every time they cut out a bracket.

The area of the wasted material is 450 cm².

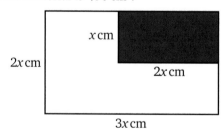

a Use the information to write down an equation for the wasted material.

b Work out the dimensions of the metal sheet.

❓ 7 There are two bags containing sweets.

One contains $x - 1$ sweets and the other contains $2x + 4$ sweets.

Hannah takes half of the sweets in the first bag and a third of the sweets in the second bag.

She takes nine sweets altogether.

$x - 1$ sweets $2x + 4$ sweets

a Find the value of x.

b Find out how many sweets there were in each bag to start with.

15 **Assess** (k)

1 Solve these equations.

a $3x = 24$ **b** $y - 8 = 3$ **c** $2z = 5$

2 Solve these equations.

a $\dfrac{a}{5} = 2$ **c** $6c - 5 = 13$ **e** $4 = 7 - 2e$

b $\dfrac{b}{6} = -5$ **d** $3 + 2d = 1$

3 Solve these equations.

a $7q - 2 = 4q + 7$ **d** $5(p + 3) = 35$

b $9m + 7 = 4m - 3$ **e** $24 = 3(2t - 3)$

c $4n - 9 = 2 - 7n$ **f** $4(2v + 1) = 3(5v - 8)$

4 The diagram contains two parallel lines.

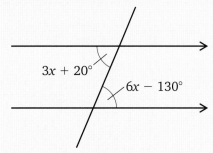

$3x + 20°$

$6x - 130°$

Write down and solve an equation in x.

5 Solve these equations.

a $4(x + 3) + 3(2x - 1) = 39$ **d** $3 - \dfrac{z}{2} = 7$

b $5(2y - 1) = 1 + 2(y + 3)$ **e** $\dfrac{5d - 4}{3} = 1$

c $\dfrac{t}{6} + 3 = 8$

6 The diagram shows a rectangular garden.

There is a rectangular vegetable patch in the garden.
The rest of the garden is lawn.

The area of the lawn is 9.5 m^2.

Work out the area of the vegetable patch.

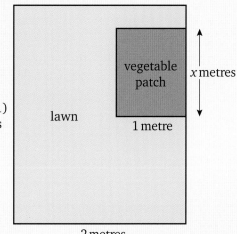

$(3x + 1)$ metres

lawn

vegetable patch

x metres

1 metre

2 metres

F

E

D

C

Practice questions (k)

1   The total of each row is given at the side of the table.

$4x + 1$	$2(x + 5)$	20
$2x$	4	A

Find the values of x and A.   *(3 marks)*

AQA 2007

2   Dean picks three numbers, which total 77.
His first number is y. His second number is five more than his first number. His third number is double his first number.
Work out his three numbers.   *(3 marks)*

AQA 2007

16 Indices

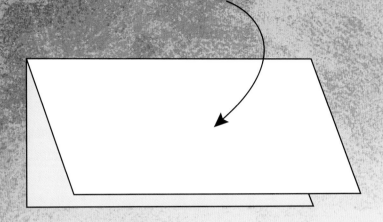

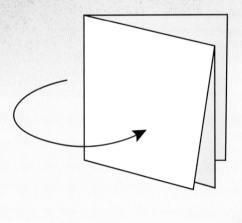

Objectives

Examiners would normally expect students who get these grades to be able to:

F

work out or know simple squares and square roots

E

work out or know simple cubes and cube roots

D

use the terms square, positive square root, negative square root, cube and cube root

recall integer squares from 2×2 to 15×15 and the corresponding square roots

recall the cubes of 1, 2, 3, 4, 5 and 10 and the corresponding cube roots

C

use index notation and index laws for multiplication and division for positive integer powers.

Did you know?

Folding paper

Did you know that it is impossible to fold a piece of paper more than 12 times?

If you fold the paper in half your paper is two sheets thick.

If you fold it in half again your paper is four sheets thick.

If you fold it in half again your paper is eight sheets thick.

How thick would your paper be after 12 folds?

Use the fact that paper is 0.1 millimetre thick.

Key terms

square number
cube number
square root
cube root
index
power
indices

You should already know:

✔ how to add, subtract, multiply and divide whole numbers

✔ how to use negative numbers

✔ how to use algebra.

Learn... 16.1 Powers and roots

Square numbers
A **square number** is the outcome when a number is multiplied by itself.

16 is a square number because $4 \times 4 = 16$ ← 4 squared

-4 squared is $-4 \times -4 = 16$

> **Hint**
> A negative number times a negative number is always a positive number.

A square number is a number 'to the power of 2' so 4 squared is also 4 to the power 2, which is written as 4^2.

Cube numbers
A **cube number** is the outcome when a number is multiplied by itself then multiplied by itself again.

125 is a cube number because $5 \times 5 \times 5 = 125$ ← 5 cubed

-5 cubed is $-5 \times -5 \times -5 = -125$

A cube number is a number 'to the power of 3' so 5 cubed is also 5 to the power 3, which is written as 5^3.

Square roots
The **square root** of a number, such as 16, is the number that gives 16 when multiplied by itself.

The square root of 16 is 4 because $4 \times 4 = 16$

However, the square root of 16 is also -4 because $-4 \times -4 = 16$

The square root of 16 is written as $\sqrt{16}$ or $\sqrt[2]{16}$, so $\sqrt{16} = 4$ (or -4)

Cube root
The **cube root** of a number, such as 125, is the number that gives 125 when multiplied by itself then multiplied again.

The cube root of 125 is 5 because $5 \times 5 \times 5 = 125$

The cube root of 125 is written as $\sqrt[3]{125}$, so $\sqrt[3]{125} = 5$

> **Study tip**
> Do not confuse cube roots with square roots where you have two answers. The $\sqrt[3]{125}$ is not -5 because $-5 \times -5 \times -5 = -125$

Practise... 16.1 Powers and roots 　

F

1 Write down the value of:

a 6^2　　c 13^2　　e $\sqrt{121}$　　g 1^2　　i $\sqrt{225}$

b 9^2　　d $\sqrt{25}$　　f $\sqrt{64}$　　h $\sqrt{81}$

F E

2　3　5　8　12　15　20　25

From the list of numbers above, write down:

a　a square number　　　　　c　the square root of 144

b　a cube number　　　　　　d　the cube root of 512.

E

3 Write down the value of:

a 2^3　　b 4^3　　c 10^3　　d $\sqrt[3]{216}$　　e $\sqrt[3]{1}$　　f $\sqrt[3]{27}$

4 Work out:

a $1^3 + 4^2$　　　　d $\sqrt[3]{8} + 4^2$　　　　g $\sqrt[3]{1\,000\,000} - \sqrt{10\,000}$

b $6^2 - 3^2$　　　　e $\sqrt[3]{1000} - \sqrt{81}$

c $\sqrt{144} - \sqrt{100}$　　f $\sqrt{169} - 3^2$

5 Neil says -5^2 is 25

Andrea says -5^2 is -25

Who is correct?

Give a reason for your answer.

6 Which is the higher number?

a 2^3 or 3^2 **b** $\sqrt{64}$ or $\sqrt[3]{125}$ **c** $\sqrt[3]{-8}$ or $-\sqrt{9}$?

7 Write down an approximate answer to the following.

a 4.99^2 **b** $\sqrt{50}$ **c** $\sqrt[3]{999}$

8 Vivek says that $-11^2 = 121$

Is this correct?

Give a reason for your answer.

9 Write down the square roots of 0.01

10 Write down the cube root of -0.027

11 The number 50 can be written as $5^2 + 5^2$ or as $1^2 + 7^2$

a Write 100 as the sum of square numbers in as many different ways as you can.

b Can you write the number 100 as the sum of cube numbers?

12 Jenny investigates the sum of the cubes of the first two integers.

She notices that the sum gives a square number:

$1^3 + 2^3 = 9 \ (= 3^2)$

Jenny now investigates the sum of the cubes of the first three integers.

She notices, again, that the sum gives a square number:

$1^3 + 2^3 + 3^3 = 36 \ (= 6^2)$

Does this work for the sum of the cubes of the first four integers?

Give a reason for your answer.

What about the other sums of consecutive cubes?

Learn... 16.2 Rules of indices k

The **index** (or **power**) tells you how many times the base number is to be multiplied by itself.
This means that 10^3 tells you that 10 (the base number) is to be multiplied by itself three times (the index or power).

$$10^3$$

index (or power)

base

So $10^3 = 10 \times 10 \times 10 = 1000$

Rules of indices

$a^3 \times a^5 = (a \times a \times a) \times (a \times a \times a \times a \times a)$ $\quad = a \times a \times a \times a \times a \times a \times a \times a$ $\quad = a^8$	So $\quad a^3 \times a^5 = a^8$ In general $a^m \times a^n = a^{m+n}$
$a^7 \div a^3 = \dfrac{a^7}{a^3}$ $\quad = \dfrac{a \times a \times a \times a \times a \times a \times a}{a \times a \times a}$ $\quad = \dfrac{\cancel{a} \times \cancel{a} \times \cancel{a} \times a \times a \times a \times a}{\cancel{a} \times \cancel{a} \times \cancel{a}}$ $\quad = a \times a \times a \times a$ $\quad = a^4$	So $\quad a^7 \div a^3 = a^4$ In general $a^m \div a^n = a^{m-n}$
$(a^2)^3 = a^2 \times a^2 \times a^2$ $\quad = (a \times a) \times (a \times a) \times (a \times a)$ $\quad = a \times a \times a \times a \times a \times a$ $\quad = a^6$	So $\quad (a^2)^3 = a^6$ In general $(a^m)^n = a^{m \times n}$

Example: Simplify:

	Number	*Algebra*
a	$6^3 \times 6^2$	$a^3 \times a^2$
b	$\dfrac{2^5}{2^2}$	$\dfrac{a^5}{a^2}$
c	$(3^5)^2$	$(a^5)^2$

Solution:

	Number	*Algebra*
a	$6^3 \times 6^2$	$a^3 \times a^2$
	$= 6^{(3+2)}$	$= a^{(3+2)}$
	$= 6^5$	$= a^5$
b	$\dfrac{2^5}{2^2}$	$\dfrac{a^5}{a^2}$
	$= 2^5 \div 2^2$	$= a^5 \div a^2$
	$= 2^{(5-2)}$	$= a^{(5-2)}$
	$= 2^3$	$= a^3$
c	$(3^5)^2$	$(a^5)^2$
	$= 3^{5 \times 2}$	$= a^{5 \times 2}$
	$= 3^{10}$	$= a^{10}$

Practise... 16.2 Rules of indices

1 Write in index notation:

    a $5 \times 5 \times 5 \times 5$

    b $10 \times 10 \times 10 \times 10 \times 10 \times 10 \times 10$

    c $6 \times 6 \times 6 \times 6 \times 6 \times 6 \times 6 \times 6 \times 6 \times 6 \times 6 \times 6$

    d 13×13

    e $2 \times 2 \times 2 \times 2 \times 2 \times 2 \times 2 \times 2 \times 2 \times 2 \times 2 \times 2 \times 2 \times 2 \times 2 \times 2 \times 2 \times 2 \times 2$

    f $12 \times 12 \times 12 \times 12$

    g $p \times p \times p \times p$

    h $s \times s \times s \times s \times s \times s \times s \times s \times s \times s$

2 Work out the value of each of the following.

    a 7^2 **c** 11^2 **e** 2^3 **g** 1^5 **i** 4^3

    b 4^2 **d** $(-3)^2$ **f** 10^4 **h** 3^4 **j** $(-10)^6$

3 Use the rules of **indices** to simplify the following. Give your answers in index form.

    a $5^6 \times 5^2$ **e** $10^6 \times 10^{12}$ **i** $\dfrac{9^{12}}{9^{11}}$

    b $12^8 \times 12^3$ **f** $7^{11} \div 7^6$ **j** $(6^2)^5$

    c $3^5 \div 3^2$ **g** $6^5 \div 6^3$ **k** $(11^5)^4$

    d $4^3 \times 4^8$ **h** $\dfrac{4^7}{4^3}$ **l** $(10^{10})^{10}$

4 Are the following statements true or false? Give a reason for your answer.

    a $6^2 = 12$ **b** $1^3 = 1$ **c** $\dfrac{2^{10}}{4^5} = 1$ **d** $3^2 + 3^3 = 3^5$

5 Simplify the following.

    a $x^6 \times x^2$ **c** $\dfrac{a^7}{a^3}$ **e** $q^7 \div q^7$

    b $e^8 \times e^3$ **d** $p^{10} \div p^5$ **f** $(b^2)^5$

6 Adnan writes: $a^2 \div a^2 = \dfrac{a \times a}{a \times a}$

$$= \dfrac{\not a \times \not a}{\not a \times \not a} = \dfrac{1}{1} = 1$$

He says that $a^0 = 1$

Is he correct?

Give a reason for your answer.

7 The number one million $= 10^6$ which is $10 \times 10 \times 10 \times 10 \times 10 \times 10 = 1\,000\,000$

Write down the value of: **a**   one billion $= 10^9$

                                b   one trillion $= 10^{12}$

8 The number 64 can be written as 8^2 in index form.

Write down three other ways of writing 64 in index form.

9 Sue says the sum of the squares of two odd numbers is always odd.

Ravi says the sum of the squares of two odd numbers is always even.

Keith says the sum of the squares of two odd numbers could be odd or even.

Who is correct? Give a reason for your answer.

16 Assess (k)

1 Evaluate the following.

a 4^2 b 11^2 c $\sqrt{36}$ d $\sqrt{196}$ e 0^2 f $(-3)^2$

2 Evaluate the following.

a 5^3 b 10^3 c $\sqrt[3]{27}$ d $\sqrt[3]{64}$ e $\sqrt[3]{0}$ f $\sqrt[3]{-8}$

3 Write down an approximate answer to the following.

a 9.99^2 b $\sqrt{102}$ c $\sqrt[3]{-126}$

4 a Sam says all numbers have two square roots. Gareth says some numbers have no square roots. Who is right?

Give a reason for your answer.

b Livia joins in the conversation and says that all numbers have two cube roots. Is she right?

Give a reason for your answer.

5 Simplify the following, leaving your answers as single powers.

a $4^6 \times 4^2$ d $7^5 \times 7$ g $21^7 \div 21^5$ j $2^3 \div 2^3$

b $11^5 \times 11^3$ e $6^4 \times 6^2 \times 6^3$ h $16^{10} \div 16^9$

c $(5^3)^2$ f $10^4 \div 10^2$ i $5^8 \div 5^7$

6 Find the value of:

a $3^2 \times 4^2$ b $5^3 \div 5^2$ c $6^5 \times 6^3 \div 6^4$ d $\dfrac{10^8 \times 10^7}{10^7 \times 10^6}$

7 Which is greater:

a 3^5 or 5^3 b 11^2 or 2^{11} c 2^4 or 4^2 ?

8 Alex says the sum of two consecutive squares is always odd.

Kate says the sum of two consecutive squares is always even.

Dan says the sum of two consecutive squares could be odd or even.

Who is correct? Give a reason for your answer.

Practice questions (k)

1 a Simplify $t^4 \times t^5$ (1 mark)

  b Simplify $p^6 \div p^2$ (1 mark)

  c i Chris simplifies 2×2^5
      His answer is 2^5
      Explain the mistake he has made. (1 mark)

    ii Simplify $3^6 \div 3$
        Write your answer as a power of 3. (1 mark)

AQA 2008

17 Graphs of linear functions

Examiners would normally expect students who get these grades to be able to:

E

produce a table of values for equations such as $y = 3x - 5$ or $x + y = 7$ and draw their graphs

D

solve problems such as finding where the line $y = 3x - 5$ crosses the line $y = 4$

C

find the gradients of straight-line graphs.

Did you know? k

Rollercoaster

The design of a rollercoaster has to have a long slope with a chain lift to drag the rollercoaster car to the top. This gives it enough energy to reach the end of the track. The slope needs to be high enough so that the car will roll along to the end of the track. The designer has to choose a gradient for the first slope. If it is too steep, it could be unsafe. If it is too shallow, the rollercoaster ride would take up too much space in the theme park. Choosing the proper gradient is very important.

Key terms

linear
gradient
variable
coefficient

You should already know:

✔ how to plot points in all four quadrants

✔ how to recognise lines such as $y = 4$ or $x = -3$

Learn... **17.1 Drawing straight-line graphs**

An equation such as $y = 3x - 5$ can be shown on a graph.

The graph will be a straight line and $y = 3x - 5$ is called a **linear** equation.

A linear equation does not contain any powers of x or y.

To draw the graph, you need to work out the coordinates of three points on the line.

You may be given a table of values to use.

If not, choose any three values of x that lie within the range you have been given.

Work out the corresponding y values, using the linear equation.

Plot the points. Draw the line through the points.
The line must go across the full range of values for x.

> **Study tip**
>
> It is a good idea to use zero as one of your x-values, as it is easy to substitute.

Example: Draw the graph of $y = 3x - 5$ for values of x from -2 to 4.

Solution: Choose three values, for example $x = 0$ and $x = -2$ and $x = 4$, the end values.

Work out the y values and put them in a table.

> **Study tip**
>
> Always use three points, not just two. They should be in a straight line. If they are not, you have made a mistake in working out one of the y-values, so check and correct the values.

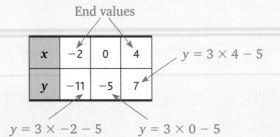

End values

x	-2	0	4
y	-11	-5	7

$y = 3 \times 4 - 5$

$y = 3 \times -2 - 5$ $y = 3 \times 0 - 5$

Plot the points.

(In the exam the axes will be drawn for you.)

Draw the line through the plotted points, making sure it goes from $x = -2$ to $x = -4$

This straight-line graph has been drawn using the same scale on both axes.

This makes it easy to plot the points.

The range of y-values is large, so the graph is tall and narrow.

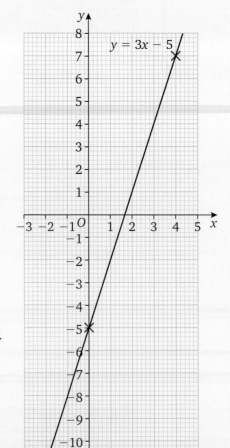

This straight-line graph plots the same points, but uses a different scale on the y-axis.

This makes it a little harder to plot the points, but the graph is not so tall.

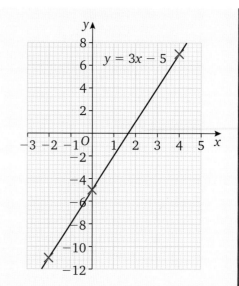

Study tip

Make sure you can plot points on axes with different scales. You may be asked to do this in the exam.

Example: Draw the graph of $x + y = 6$ for values of x from -1 to 6.

Solution: Choose three values that are easy to substitute, for example $x = 0$, $y = 0$, and one other value.

Easy to substitute

Work out the corresponding values and put them in a table.

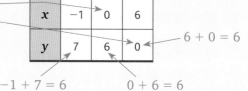

x	-1	0	6
y	7	6	0

$-1 + 7 = 6$ $0 + 6 = 6$ $6 + 0 = 6$

Plot the points.

Draw the line through the plotted points, making sure it goes from $x = -1$ to $x = 6$

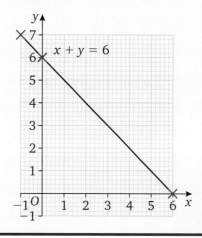

Practise... 17.1 Drawing straight-line graphs 🅚 G F E D C

Next to each of the first three questions there is a sketch to show you the range you will need on your axes.
The sketch is not drawn to scale.

1 **a** Draw the graph of $y = x + 2$ for values of x from -3 to 4.

  b Write down the coordinates of the point where this graph crosses the y-axis.

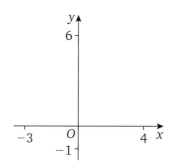

E
D

2

a Draw the graph of $y = 3x - 1$ for values of x from -3 to 3.

b Write down the coordinates of the point where this graph crosses the line $y = -3$.

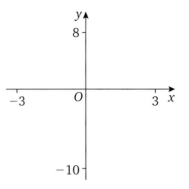

3

a Draw the graph of $y = \frac{1}{2}x$ for values of x from -4 to 4.

b If this line were extended, would it go through the point $(7, 4)$?

Explain your answer.

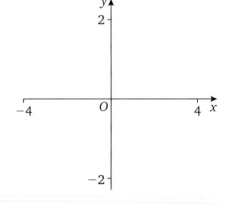

4

a Draw the graph of $y = 2x$ for values of x from -3 to 3.

b On the same axes, draw the graph of $y = x$ for values of x from -3 to 3.

c The two lines go through the same point.
What is this point?

5

a Draw the graph of $y = 2x + 1$ for values of x from -3 to 3.

b On the same axes, draw the graph of $y = 1 - 3x$ for values of x from -3 to 3.

c Write down the coordinates of the point where these two lines cross.

6

a Complete this table of values for $x + 2y = 9$.

x	0	1	
y			0

b Draw the graph of $x + 2y = 9$ for values of x from 0 to 9.

c Write down the coordinates of the point where your graph crosses the line $x = 4$.

7

a Complete this table of values for $x - 2y = 1$.

x	0		3
y		0	

b Draw the graph of $x - 2y = 1$ for values of x from -3 to 3.

c Write down the coordinates of the point where your graph crosses the line $y = \frac{1}{2}$.

8 Which of these equations represent straight-line graphs?

    A $y = 1 - 8x$ **B** $2y = 5x + 4$ **C** $y = x^2 + 7$ **D** $4x + 3y = 8$

9   Which of these points lies on the line $3x + 2y = 12$? Show how you found your answers.

A $(0, 4)$ D $(1, 4\frac{1}{2})$

B $(2, 3)$ E $(6, -3)$

C $(3, 2)$ F $(-2, 8)$

10 $P(-3, 6)$, $Q(0, 0)$ and $R(2, -4)$ are three points on a straight line.

Which of the following is the equation of the line?

A $y = x + 9$ B $x + y = 3$ C $y + 2x = 0$

Show how you found your answer.

11   Each of the following points lies on one or more of the given lines.

Match the points to their lines.

Points: $A(-2, 7)$ $B(0, 0)$ $C(1, 4)$ $D(2, 5)$ $E(3, 3)$ $F(4, 1)$

Lines: $y = 4x$ $2x + y = 9$ $x + y = 5$ $y = 6x - 7$

Learn...   17.2 Gradients of straight-line graphs   k

The **gradient** of a straight-line graph is a measure of how steep it is.

A line that slopes from top right to bottom left has a positive gradient, because y increases as x increases.

The gradient can be found from the graph of the line.

$$\text{Gradient} = \frac{\text{change in vertical distance}}{\text{change in horizontal distance}} = \frac{y}{x}$$

To find the gradient, draw a line parallel to the x-axis and a line parallel to the y-axis to make a right-angled triangle on the graph.

The triangle can be anywhere on the graph.

Example: Find the gradient of the graph below.

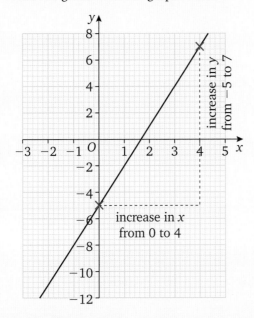

increase in y from -5 to 7

increase in x from 0 to 4

Study tip

Take a careful note of the scales on the graph. They might be different on the x- and the y-axes.

Change in $y = 12$

Change in $x = 4$

Gradient $= \dfrac{12}{4} = 3$

Make the graph as big and convenient as possible.

A line that slopes from top left to bottom right has a negative gradient because y decreases as x increases.

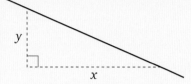

Gradient $= -\dfrac{y}{x}$

The gradient can also be found from the equation of the line.

To find the gradient, write the equation of the line in the form: $y = mx + c$

y and x are the **variables** in the equation.

m (the **coefficient** of x) is the gradient of the line.

Example: What is the gradient of $y = 5x + 2$?

Solution: The coefficient of x is 5, so the gradient is 5.

Example: What is the gradient of $y = 3 - 2x$?

Solution: The coefficient of x is -2, so the gradient is -2.

Example: What is the gradient of $x + y = 5$?

Solution: Make sure the equation is in the form $y = mx + c$

$$x + y = 5$$
$$x + y - x = 5 - x \qquad \text{Subtract } x \text{ from both sides.}$$
$$y = 5 - x$$

The coefficient of x is -1 so the gradient is -1.

Practise...   **17.2 Gradients of straight-line graphs**   ⓚ   G F E D C

C

1   Work out the gradient of each line.

a

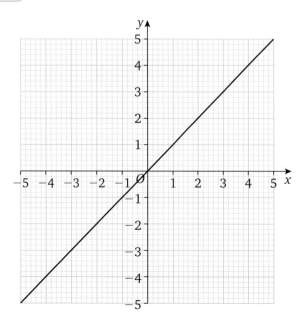

b

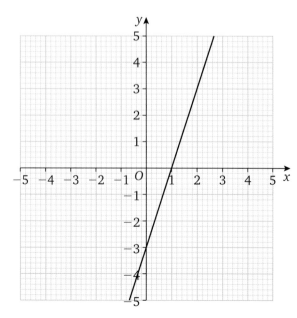

c

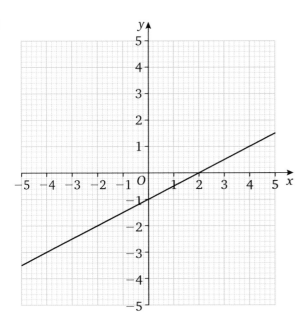

d

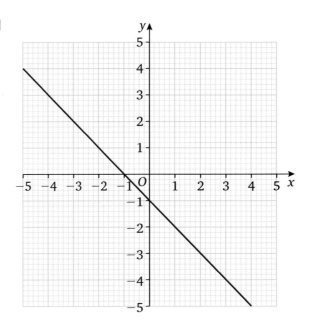

2   Work out the gradient of each of these straight lines.

a $y = 5x + 4$ **d** $y + 5 = 3x$

b $y = 2 + x$ **e** $2y = 6x - 7$

c $y = 3 - 2x$ **f** $4x + y = 9$

3   Jo says that the lines whose equations are $y = 5 - 2x$ and $y = 5 - 4x$ have the same gradient.
Explain why Jo is wrong.

4   The diagram opposite shows four lines
labelled A, B, C, D.

a   Which line has a gradient of 2?

How do you know?

b   Which line has a gradient of 1?

How do you know?

c   Which line or lines have a negative gradient?

How do you know?

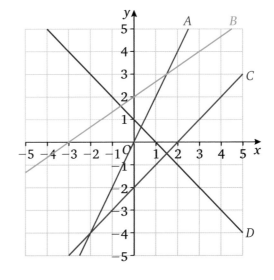

5   The diagram opposite shows the line $y = 3x - 5$

$RQ = 3$ units.

What is the length of PQ?

Show your working.

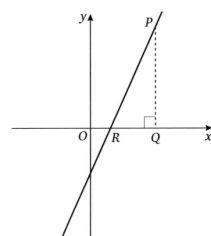

C

6 On the same axes, draw the graphs of $y = 2x$, $y = 2x + 4$ and $y = 2x - 5$ for values of x from -4 to 4.

What do you notice?
How does this relate to the equations?

7 Use your knowledge of gradients to match the equations to the sketch graphs.

$y = 3x$ $y = -2x$ $y = 4 - x$ $y = 3x + 8$

a
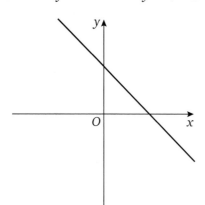

c
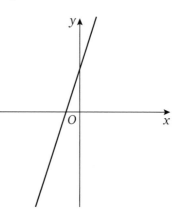

> **Hint**
> Think about which equations would give a line through $(0, 0)$.

b
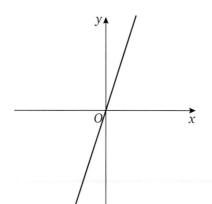

d
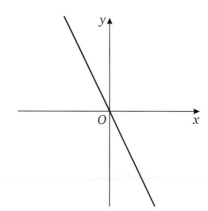

Assess

1 **a** Draw the graph of $y = x - 3$ for values of x from -3 to 4.

b Write down the coordinates of the point where this graph crosses the y-axis.

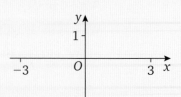

2   **a**   Draw the graph of $y = 5 - 4x$ for values of x from -2 to 3.

b   Write down the coordinates of the point where this graph crosses the line $y = 2$

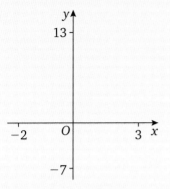

3   **a**   Complete this table of values for $2x + y = 8$

x	-1	0	5
y			-2

b   Draw the graph of $2x + y = 8$ for values of x from -1 to 5.

c   Write down the coordinates of the point where this graph crosses the line $y = 3$

4   **a**   Complete this table of values for $y = 3 + \frac{1}{2}x$

x	-2	0	4
y			5

b   Draw the graph of $y = 3 + \frac{1}{2}x$ for values of x from -2 to 4.

c   If this graph were extended, would it go through the point $(6, 6)$?
Explain your answer.

5   Which of these points lie on the line $4x - 3y = 4$?

A $(0, 1)$ C $(3, 4)$ E $(7, 8)$

B $(1, 0)$ D $(4, 4)$ F $(8, 7)$

Show how you found your answers.

6   Work out the gradient of each of these lines.

a $y = 5x - 1$ **b** $y = 9 - 2x$ **c** $3x + y = 2$ **d** $y - x = 3$

7   Which of these equations does not represent a straight-line graph?

A $3x + 5y + 1 = 0$ B $y^2 = 2x - 5$ C $y = 12 - x$ D $4 = 4y + 3x$

8   The gradient of this line is -2.

$BC = 4$ units

What is the length of AB?

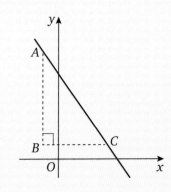

C

9 Jacqui says the equation of this graph is $y = 3x + 4$.

Explain how you can tell, by looking at the graph, that she is wrong.

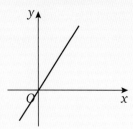

10 Rasheed says the equation of this graph is $y = x - 5$.

Ben says it is $y = 5 - x$.

Look at the graph to decide who is wrong and explain how you made your decision.

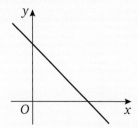

Practice questions ⓚ

1 The graph shows a sketch of the line $y = 3x + 1$

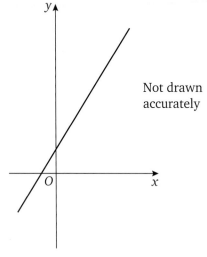

Not drawn accurately

a Does the point $(-2, -5)$ lie on the line? Explain your answer. *(2 marks)*

b Copy the graph and sketch the line $y = 3x + 4$ *(2 marks)*

AQA 2008

18 Reflections, rotations and translations

Objectives

Examiners would normally expect students who get these grades to be able to:

G

draw a line of symmetry on a 2-D shape

draw the reflection of a shape in a mirror line

F

draw all the lines of symmetry on a 2-D shape

give the order of rotational symmetry of a 2-D shape

name, draw or complete 2-D shapes from information about their symmetry

E

reflect shapes in the axes of a graph

D

reflect shapes in lines parallel to the axes, such as $x = 2$ and $y = -1$

rotate shapes about the origin

describe fully reflections in a line and rotations about the origin

translate a shape using a description such as 4 units right and 3 units down

C

reflect shapes in lines such as $y = x$ and $y = -x$

rotate shapes about any point

describe fully reflections in any line parallel to the axes, $y = x$ or $y = -x$ and rotations about any point

find the centre of a rotation and describe it fully

translate a shape by a vector such as $\begin{pmatrix} 4 \\ -3 \end{pmatrix}$.

Did you know?

Looking for symmetry

Everywhere you look you can see symmetry, both in nature and in man-made constructions. This is the Compact Muon Solenoid, one of the detectors in the Large Hadron Collider. This is the world's largest and highest-energy particle accelerator. It is a symmetrical construction being used to advance science. After being built by scientists and engineers from over 100 countries, it was in operation for the first time in September 2008.

Key terms

reflection	rotation
line of symmetry	order of rotation
mirror line	centre of rotation
object	clockwise
image	anticlockwise
congruent	angle of rotation
vertex, vertices	vector
coordinates	translation

You should already know:

✔ how to plot positive and negative coordinates

✔ equations of lines, such as $x = 3$, $y = -2$, $y = x$ and $y = -x$

✔ names of 2-D and 3-D shapes

✔ that angles in a full turn equal 360°.

Learn... **18.1 Reflection**

Reflectional symmetry

One half of this shape is a mirror **reflection** of the other. It has one **line of symmetry**. The **mirror line** is drawn so one side of the shape is a reflection of the other.

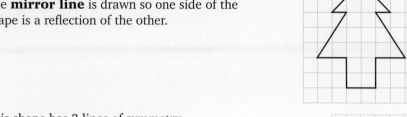

This shape has 3 lines of symmetry. One half of the shape can be reflected in three different ways.

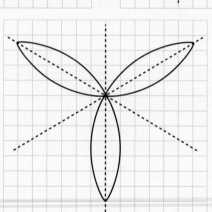

Example: How many lines of symmetry does each grid pattern have?

         Draw in the lines of symmetry that you find.

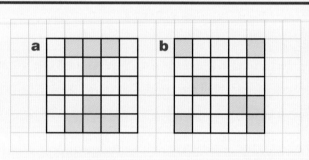

Solution: Grid pattern **a** has two lines of symmetry.
Grid pattern **b** has no lines of symmetry.

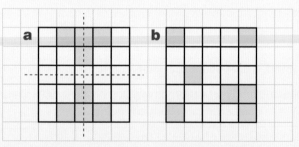

Reflecting a shape in a given line

Shapes can be reflected on grids, as shown in the previous examples, and on the axes on a graph.

The shape *T* has been reflected in the *x*-axis.

The equation of the *x*-axis is $y = 0$

The value of *y* is 0 for every point on the line.

The shape *T* is called the **object** and the reflection *T'* is called the **image**.

The object and the image are **congruent**. Two shapes are congruent if they are exactly the same size and shape.

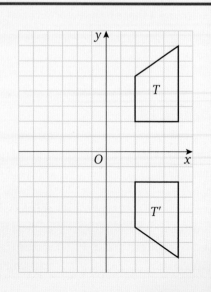

This shape, *P*, has been reflected in the line *x* = 2

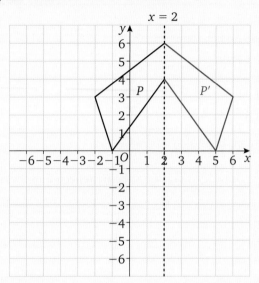

The reflection of *P* is *P′*.

The **vertices** or corners of *P′* can be written as **coordinates**.

P′ has coordinates (2, 4), (2, 6), (5, 0) and (6, 3).

Example: Step a: Draw a pair of *x*- and *y*-axes from −8 to 8.

Step b: Draw a polygon, *K*, by plotting and joining the points (−2, 1), (2, 1), (0, 4)

Step c: What is the name of this polygon?

Step d: Reflect the polygon in the line *y* = −2. Label your reflected shape *K′*.

Step e: Write down the coordinates of the vertices of the image, *K′*.

Solution:

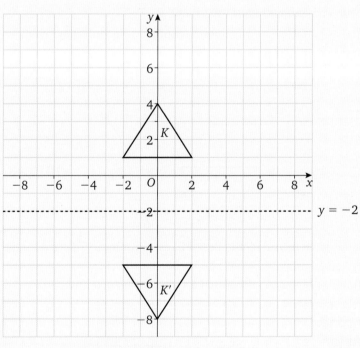

The polygon is an isosceles triangle.

K′ has coordinates (−2, −5), (2, −5), (0, −8).

Practise... 18.1 Reflection

G F E D C

1 **a** How many lines of symmetry does each letter have?
You can use tracing paper to help you.

i **M** iii **H** v **X**

ii **A** iv **B** vi **T**

b Write down six letters that have no lines of symmetry.

2 Copy each shape onto squared paper. Draw its image after being reflected in the mirror line.

a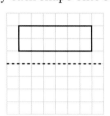

c 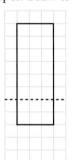 **d**  **f**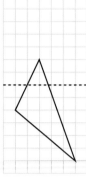

b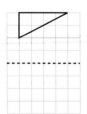

e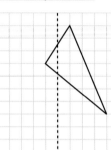

3 **a** All these shapes have reflectional symmetry.
How many lines of symmetry has each shape got?
Copy the shapes and draw all the lines of symmetry on your diagrams.
You can use tracing paper to help you.

i iii v vii ix

ii  iv  vi viii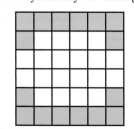

b Do all triangles have the same number of lines of symmetry? Give a reason for your answer.

4 **a** Give the number of lines of reflectional symmetry for each grid pattern.

i 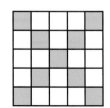 iii 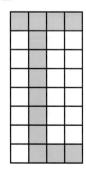 v

F

ii 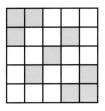 iv 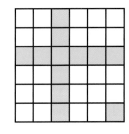 vi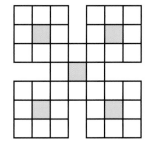

b On squared paper, draw your own grid diagram with 4 lines of symmetry.

5 Copy each diagram onto squared paper and complete it to give the required number of lines of symmetry.

a

4 lines of symmetry

b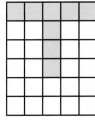

2 lines of symmetry

c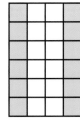

0 lines of symmetry

6 **a** **i** Copy each diagram onto axes on squared paper.

E

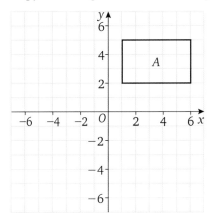

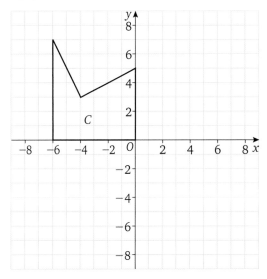

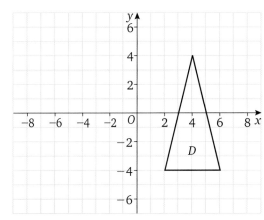

ii Reflect each shape in the *x*-axis. This will give you an image of the shape.

iii Write down the coordinates of the vertices of each shape.

iv Write down the coordinates of the vertices of each image.

E

v What is the relationship between the coordinates of the vertices of the shape and its image?

b **i** Copy each diagram in question part **a i** onto axes on squared paper.

ii Reflect each shape in the *y*-axis.

iii Write down the coordinates of the vertices of each shape.

iv Write down the coordinates of the vertices of each image.

v What is the relationship between the coordinates of the vertices of the shape and its image?

7 **a** **i** Draw a pair of *x*- and *y*-axes from −6 to 6.

ii Draw a polygon, *P*, by plotting and joining these points:

$(3, 3), (5, 1), (3, -4), (1, 1)$

iii What is the mathematical name of the polygon?

iv Reflect the polygon *P* in the *y*-axis and write down the coordinates of the vertices of the image, *P′*.

v Reflect the polygon *P* in the *x*-axis and write down the coordinates of the vertices of the image, *P″*.

b **i** Draw a pair of *x*- and *y*-axes from −6 to 6.

ii Draw a polygon, *Q*, by plotting and joining these points:

$(1, 2), (5, 2), (3, -1), (-1, -1)$

iii What is the name of the polygon?

iv Reflect the polygon *Q* in the *y*-axis and write down the coordinates of the vertices of the image, *Q′*.

v Reflect the polygon *Q* in the *x*-axis and write down the coordinates of the vertices of the image, *Q″*.

D

8 For each diagram **a–d**, write down the equation of the line of reflectional symmetry.

a

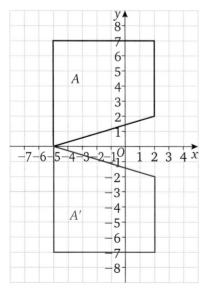

c

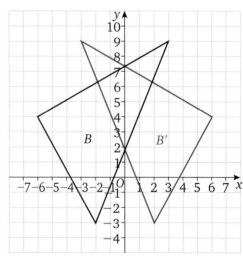

b

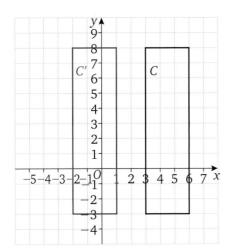

d

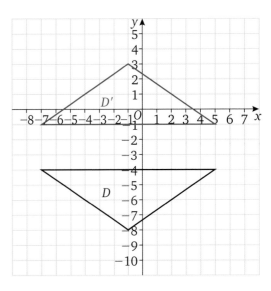

9

a Draw a pair of x- and y-axes from −6 to 6.

b Draw a polygon, R, by plotting and joining these points:
(1, −1), (3, −1), (3, −3), (1, −3)

c What is the name of the polygon?

d Reflect the polygon in the line x = y and write down the coordinates of the vertices of the image, R′.

e Reflect the polygon in the line x = −y and write down the coordinates of the vertices of the image, R″.

f Write down what you notice about the coordinates.

⚠ 10

a This diagram shows a shape, A, and its reflection, A′.
Describe the reflection that maps A onto A″.

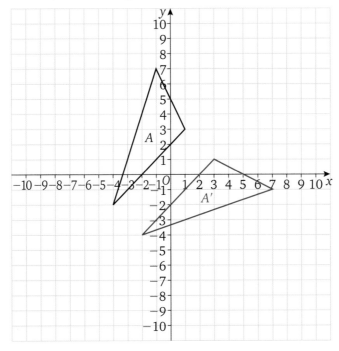

b Write down the coordinates of the vertices of both triangles.

c Find a rule that connects the coordinates before and after the reflection.

d Use your rule to work out the coordinates of the vertices of the image of the polygon which has the coordinates given below. Use the same line of reflection. Try and work it out by following your rule and not by drawing:
(2, 3), (−1, −2), (0, −4), (2, −2)

e Can you find a rule for each of these lines of symmetry without drawing them?
i x = 0   **ii** y = 3   **iii** x = −5

11   Alisha is investigating the reflectional symmetry of quadrilaterals. She has to find out which quadrilaterals have reflectional symmetry and whether all quadrilaterals have the same number of lines of symmetry.

a   Make a list of all the special quadrilaterals.

b   Draw each quadrilateral with the lines of symmetry.

c   Write an answer for Alisha's investigation.

12   This pattern is being created using repeated reflection.

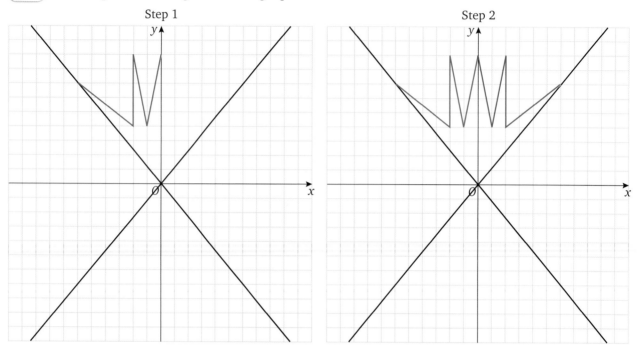

Step 1   Step 2

a   Write down the equations of all the lines of reflection.

b   Copy and complete the pattern.

c   Design your own pattern using the same lines of reflection.

Learn... 18.2 Rotation

Rotation means turning.

Rotational symmetry

How many ways does a shape look the same while it is being turned through 360°?

When turned around the point of rotation this shape looks the same in four positions.

When turned around the point of rotation this shape looks the same in one position.

It has **rotational symmetry of order 4 about the centre**.

It has **rotational symmetry of order 1 about the centre**.

You can always check your answer using tracing paper.

Trace the shape onto tracing paper.

Mark the centre of the shape.

Mark a small arrow or number one facing the top of the page.

This is the first position.

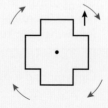

Hold your pencil on the centre point and turn your tracing clockwise.

As you turn the shape, count the number of times your traced image looks the same as the starting image before you get back to the starting point.

This is the **order of rotational symmetry** of the shape.

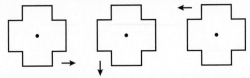

Example: Find the order of rotational symmetry of this shape.

Solution: When it is rotated around the centre this octagon looks the same in eight places.
The octagon has rotational symmetry of order 8.

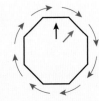

Rotating a shape about a given point

Shapes can be rotated on grids or axes.

The **centre of rotation** is the fixed point around which the object is rotated. It is given using coordinates.

The amount the shape turns is given as an angle or fraction of a complete turn, e.g. 270° or $\frac{3}{4}$ turn.

The direction of rotation is given as **clockwise** or **anticlockwise**.

This shape has a centre of rotation $(-1, 2)$.

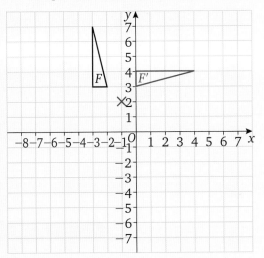

The **angle of rotation** is 90° clockwise.

The shape is called the **object** and the rotation is called the **image**.

The object and the image are **congruent**. If the object is F then the image is F'.

To describe a rotation fully, you must give:

* the centre of rotation
* the angle of rotation
* the direction of rotation.

> **Study tip**
>
> In your exam, you can ask for tracing paper to find the centre of rotation.

Example: In this diagram, the right-angled triangle, A, has been rotated anticlockwise by 90° about the origin.

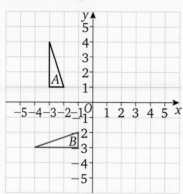

The image of A following this rotation is B.

a Write down the clockwise rotation that also maps A onto B.

b Draw a diagram showing the image of A after a rotation of 90° clockwise about the point (−1, 0). Label the image C.

c What are the three coordinates of the vertices of C?

Solution: **a** A clockwise rotation of 270° about the origin gives the same image as an anticlockwise rotation of 90° about the origin.

b

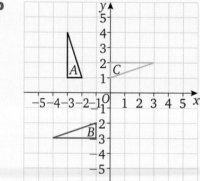

c The coordinates of the vertices of C are: (0, 1), (0, 2), (3, 2)

Practise... 18.2 Rotation

G F E D C

1 **a** Write down the order of rotational symmetry of each of these letters. You can use tracing paper to help you.

i H

iii N

v X

ii A

iv S

vi Z

b Harry says the order of rotational symmetry of the letter O is 8. Is Harry correct? Give a reason for your answer.

F

2   **a**   Write down the order of rotational symmetry of each of these shapes.

You can use tracing paper to help you.

i   iii   v 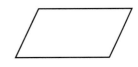   vii

ii   iv   vi   viii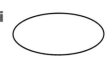

b   Is the order of rotational symmetry of a triangle always the same?
Draw a sketch of the special triangles and use these to explain your answer.

c   Is the order of rotational symmetry of a pentagon always the same?
Sketch some pentagons and use these to explain your answer.

Study tip

Make sure you use the word 'rotation' and not the word 'turn'.

3   What is the order of rotational symmetry for each of these grid shapes?

a 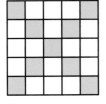   **c** 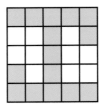   **e**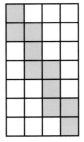

b 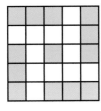   **d** 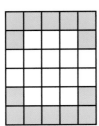   **f**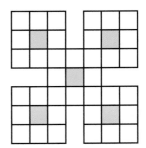

4   Copy and complete the grid diagrams so each one has the given order of rotational symmetry.

a   **b** 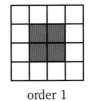   **c** 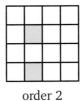   **d**

order 2   order 2   order 1   order 4

5   The hands of this clock each turn through 360° in one rotation.
The hour hand turns through an angle of 180° from 12.00 to 6.00.

Write down the angle the **hour** hand turns clockwise through from 12.00 for each of these times.

a   3.00   **c**   9.00   **e**   8.00

b   11.00   **d**   4.00

F

6 **a** For each question part, write down the order of rotational symmetry and the angle of rotation.

i 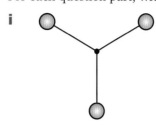 **ii** 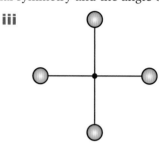 **iii**

b If a shape turns through 60° and looks the same as in its original position.
What is the order of rotational symmetry?

D

7 Draw *x*- and *y*-axes from −7 to 7 for each question part.

Copy each object *R* to *W* and rotate it by 180°.

Use the origin as the centre of rotation.

Label each image *R'* to *W'*.

a

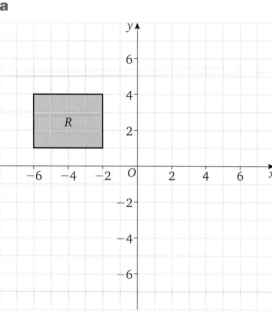

c

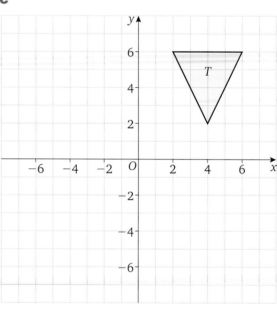

b

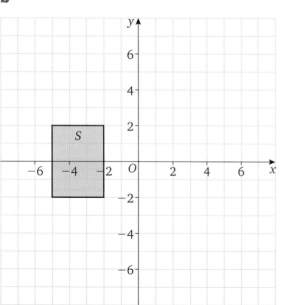

d

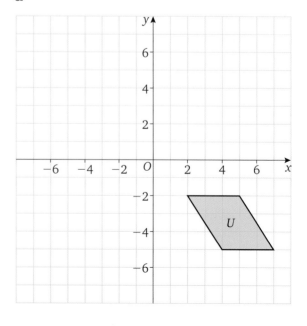

e

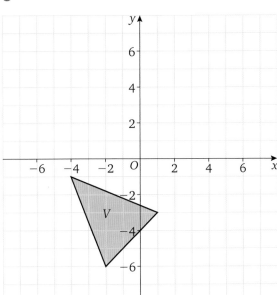

f

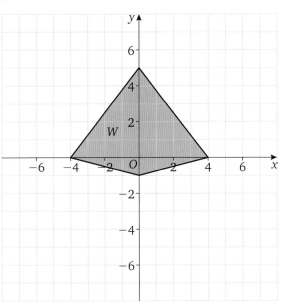

D

8   **a**   Draw a pair of x- and y-axes from −8 to 10 for each question part.

Copy each object A to F and rotate it by 90° clockwise.

Use the point (1, 2) as the centre of rotation.

Label each image A′ to F′.

b   Now rotate each image A′ to F′ by 270° clockwise.

Use the point (−1, −1) as the centre of rotation.

Label each image A′ to F″.

i

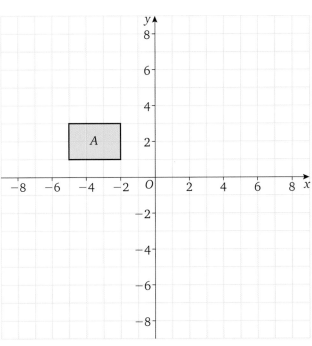

ii

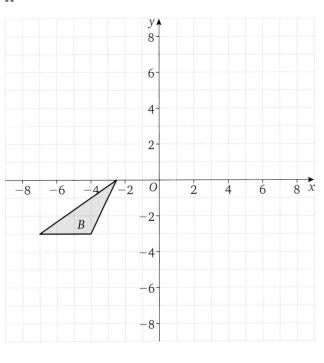

iii

v

iv

vi

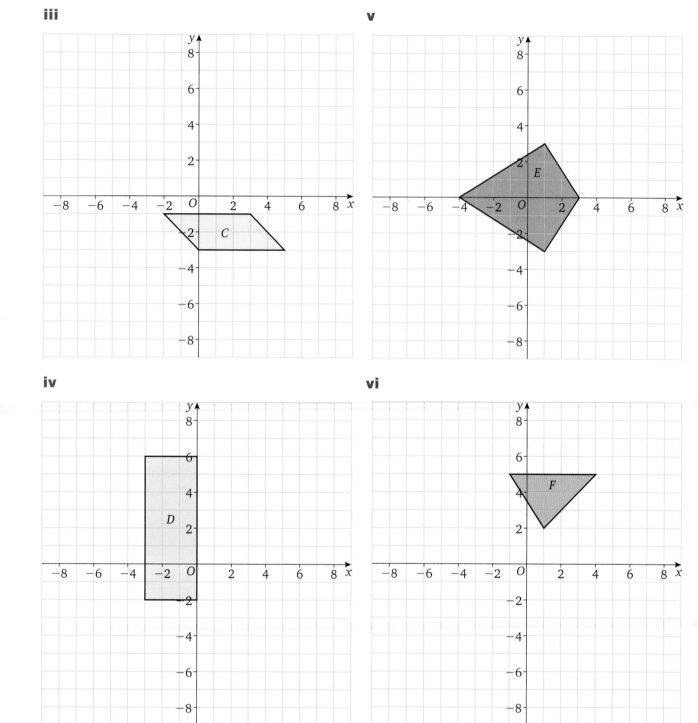

9

a   Draw a pair of x- and y-axes from -8 to 8 for each question.

Copy each object G to L and rotate it by 90° anticlockwise.

Use the point $(-1, -1)$ as the centre of rotation.

Label each image G' to L'.

b   Now rotate each image G' to L' by 270° anticlockwise.

Use the point $(0, -2)$ as the centre of rotation.

Label each image G'' to L''.

i

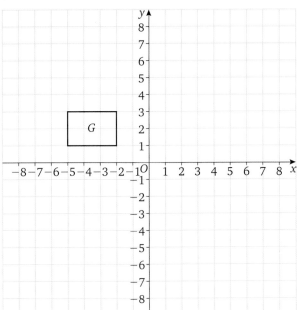

ii

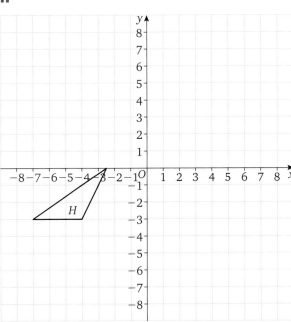

iii

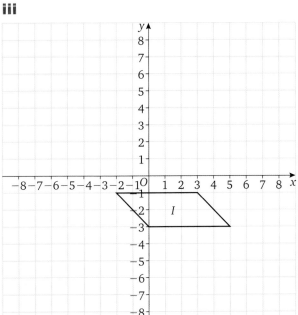

iv

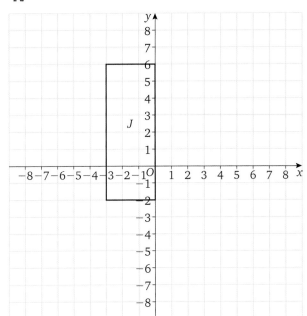

v

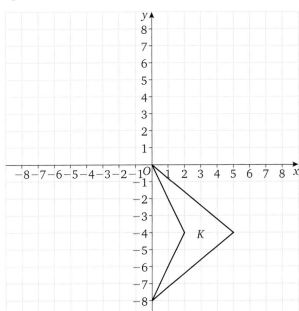

vi

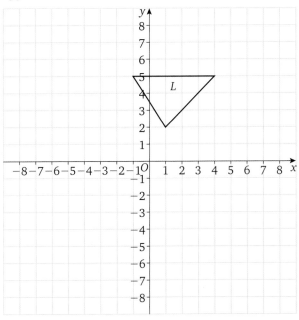

D

C

10 **a** Draw a pair of *x*- and *y*-axes from −7 to 7.

b Draw a triangle *T* by plotting and joining these points: (0, 0), (−2, −1), (−1, −2)

c Draw the image *V* by rotating *T* by 90° clockwise about (0, 0).

d Draw the image *W* by rotating *T* by 180° about (0, 0).

e Draw the image *X* by rotating *T* by 270° clockwise about (0, 0).

11 **a** Draw a pair of *x*- and *y*-axes from −7 to 7.

b Draw a polygon *Q* by plotting and joining these points: (4, 1), (6, 1), (4, −1), (3, −1)

c Draw the image *R'* by rotating *Q* by 90° clockwise about (2, 3).

12 For each diagram **a–f**, give the coordinates of the centre of rotation as *A* is mapped onto *B*.

a

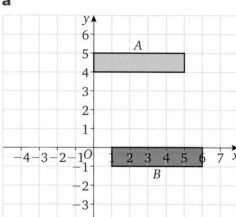

d

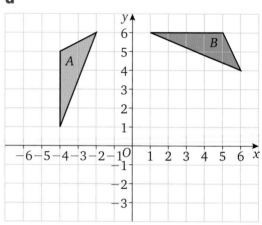

b

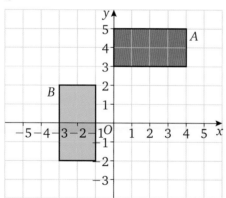

e

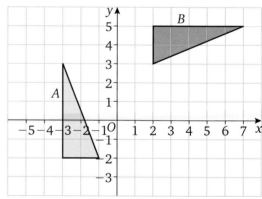

c

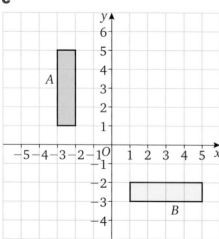

f

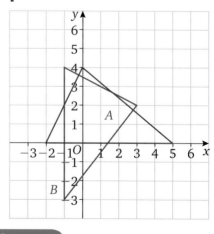

Hint

Use tracing paper to try different centres of rotation until you find the one that works for both images.

13   This diagram shows two different images
of a triangle A after two rotations by the
same angle.

B is the image of A after a rotation
clockwise about the point (0, 2).

C is the image of A after a rotation
anticlockwise about point (0, 2).

Find the position of triangle A.

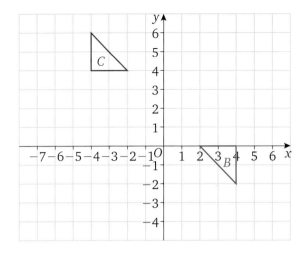

14   Rotational symmetry is often used in the design of company logos.

a   The arrows on this logo make it look like it has rotational
symmetry of order 2.

Explain why this logo does not have rotational symmetry of order 2.

b   This logo uses arrows too.

i   What is the order of rotational symmetry of this logo?

ii   Find the angle of rotation.

c   i   Design your own company logo with rotational symmetry.

ii   What is the order of rotational symmetry of your logo?

15   Use squared paper to draw your own grid shapes with the following
orders of rotational symmetry.

a   2   b   4   c   1

16   a   i   Draw a line 4 cm long. Mark one end of the line as the centre of rotation.

ii   Using a protractor, measure an angle of 45° from this centre of rotation
and draw another 4 cm line.

iii   Continue rotating the line and drawing a new line, always at 45° from
the previous line.

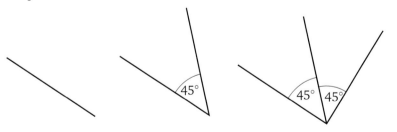

b   What is the order of rotational symmetry of your final pattern?

c   If you repeat this using a 30° angle instead of 45°, what is the order of
rotational symmetry?

d   Why is it impossible to draw a rotational symmetry pattern with 38° as the
angle of turn?

e   Is it possible to draw a rotational symmetry pattern with a 72° angle of turn?
Give a reason for your answer.

Learn... 18.3 Translation

This shape has been translated.

Every point moves the same distance in the same direction.

The **object** and the **image** are **congruent**.

The distance and direction can be written as a **vector**.

Shape A has been mapped onto shape B by a **translation** of 2 to the right and 3 units up.

Written as a vector, this is $\binom{2}{3}$ ←———— 2 to the right
←———— 3 up

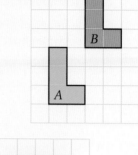

The vector that maps shape C onto shape D is $\binom{0}{-4}$

The top number is the horizontal move.

• If the number is positive the shape moves to the right.
• If the number is negative the shape moves to the left.

The bottom number is the vertical move.

• If the number is positive the shape moves up.
• If the number is negative the shape moves down.

Vectors can be used on any grid with or without a pair of axes.

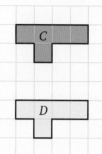

Example: Describe the translation that maps shape A onto shape B in each diagram.

a Diagram 1   **b** Diagram 2

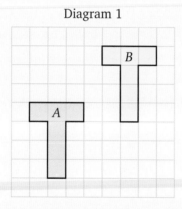 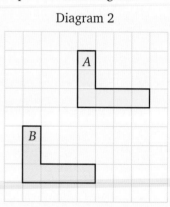

Use vectors in your answers.

Solution: **a** A has moved 4 to the right and 3 up so the vector translation is $\binom{4}{3}$

b A has moved 3 to the left and 4 down so the vector translation is $\binom{-3}{-4}$

Example: **a** Copy the diagram, drawing triangle T with the coordinates (2, 4), (4, 4) and (4, 1).

b Draw the image of T after the vector translation $\binom{-5}{-3}$. Label the image R.

c Write down the coordinates of the vertices of R.

d What is the relationship between the coordinates of the vertices of T and the coordinates of the vertices of R?

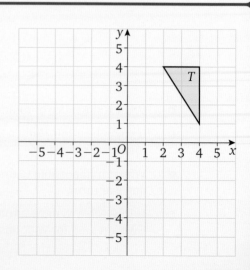

Solution: **a/b**

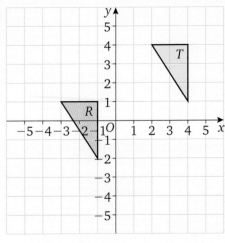

c (−3, 1), (−1, 1), (−1, −2)

d The x-coordinates of R are all 5 less than the x-coordinates of T.
The y-coordinates of R are all 3 less than the y-coordinates of T.

> **Study tip**
>
> Be careful not to mix up coordinates and vectors.
>
> (x, y) are coordinates. $\binom{x}{y}$ is a vector.

Practise... **18.3 Translation** (k)   G F E D C

1 Using squared paper, copy these shapes and translate each one by the given amount.   D

a 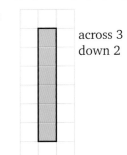 across 3
down 2

d 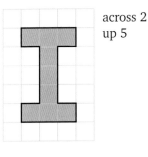 across 2
up 5

b 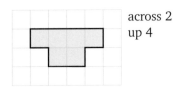 across 2
up 4

e 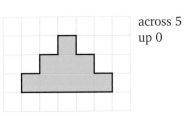 across 5
up 0

c 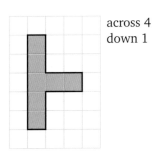 across 4
down 1

f 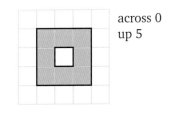 across 0
up 5

C

2 Describe the translation that maps shape *A* onto shape *B* in each diagram.

Give your answers as vectors.

a

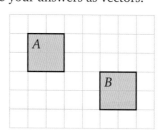

d

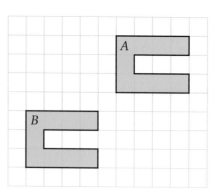

b

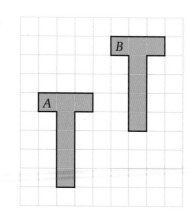

e

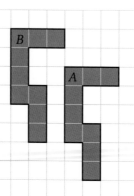

c

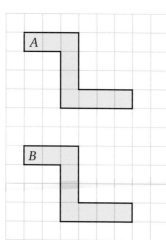

f

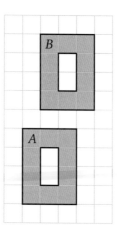

3 **a** Look at the diagram and then write down the vector translation that maps:

i *A* onto *B*

ii *A* onto *C*

iii *B* onto *C*

iv *C* onto *B*.

b Compare your answers for question parts **iii** and **iv**. Write down what you notice.

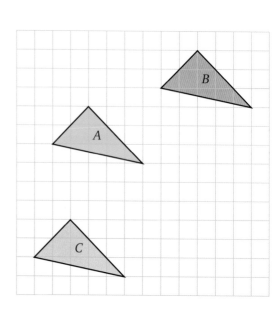

4   Look at the diagram and then write down the vector translation that maps:

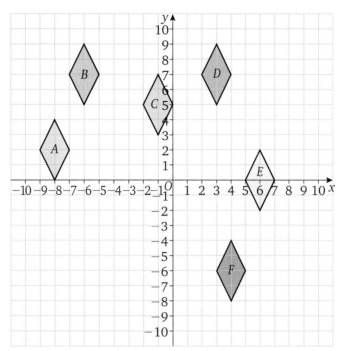

a   *A* onto *B*

b   *C* onto *F*

c   *E* onto *D*

d   *B* onto *E*.

5   **a**   **i**   Draw *x*- and *y*-axes from −5 to 5.

   ii   Plot and join the points (−4, −5), (−1, −5), (−4, 2). Label this shape *T*.

b   Translate *T* using the vector translation $\binom{4}{3}$ to give the image *U*.

c   Translate *U* using the vector translation $\binom{-5}{0}$ to give the image *V*.

d   Translate *V* using the vector translation $\binom{6}{-1}$ to give the image *W*.

e   Describe fully the single translation that maps *T* directly onto *W*.

6   **a**   Draw a pair of *x*- and *y*-axes from −5 to 5 onto squared paper.

b   Begin at the origin as a starting point. Translate this point using the vectors below. Each translation follows the previous one. After each translation, put a cross at the new point.

$$\binom{2}{1} \quad \binom{1}{1} \quad \binom{1}{0} \quad \binom{-1}{-1} \quad \binom{0}{-2} \quad \binom{-2}{-2} \quad \binom{-3}{-2}$$

c   Join the crosses you have drawn in the order in which you drew them.

d   Reflect the shape in the *y*-axis.

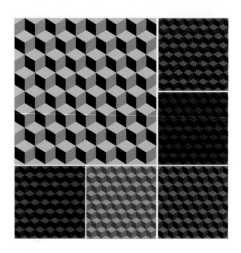

7 Some wallpaper designs use patterns that have been translated.
The design is made by repeatedly translating the feature design horizontally and vertically.

Emma is designing a wallpaper pattern on squared paper.

She translates her design by the vector $\begin{pmatrix} 4 \\ 3 \end{pmatrix}$

She then repeats the pattern in a different colour.

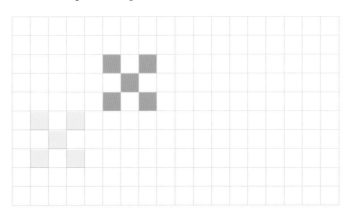

a On squared or isometric paper, create a simple design.

b Choose a translation vector. Repeat your pattern using your chosen translation vector to create your own wallpaper design.

8 Sam and Holly designed this board for a vector game.

A **vector route** starts at X and lands on each of the other squares before returning to X.

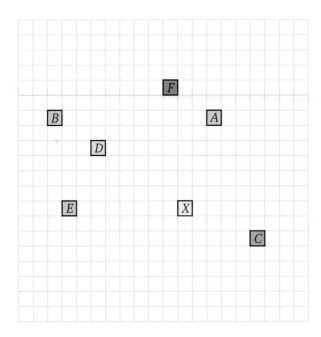

a Holly wrote down this vector route.
Write down the order in which she landed on the squares.

$$\begin{pmatrix} 5 \\ -2 \end{pmatrix} \quad \begin{pmatrix} -13 \\ 2 \end{pmatrix} \quad \begin{pmatrix} -1 \\ 6 \end{pmatrix} \quad \begin{pmatrix} 3 \\ -2 \end{pmatrix} \quad \begin{pmatrix} 5 \\ 4 \end{pmatrix} \quad \begin{pmatrix} -3 \\ -2 \end{pmatrix} \quad \begin{pmatrix} -2 \\ -6 \end{pmatrix}$$

b Sam chose to visit the squares in this order: X F D C B A E X
Write down Sam's vector route.

c Create a vector route of your own and test it on a friend.

Assess (k)

1   How many lines of symmetry does each letter have?

a **K**   b **G**   c **E**   d **T**   e **R**

G

2   Copy the diagrams and draw the image of each shape reflected in the mirror line.

a 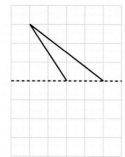   b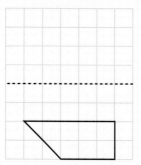

3   a   Copy this grid pattern and draw on the lines of symmetry.

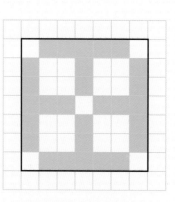

F

b   Copy this grid pattern and shade seven more squares so the grid has rotational symmetry of order 4 about its centre.

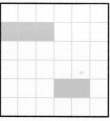

c   Copy this grid pattern and shade four more squares so the grid has 2 lines of reflectional symmetry.

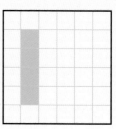

4   a   What is the order of rotational symmetry of this shape?

b   What is the angle of rotation?

E

5 **a** **i** Draw a pair of *x*- and *y*-axes from −6 to 6.

ii Draw the shape *A* by plotting and joining these points: (−1, 1), (−3, 1), (−4, 4), (−1, 3)

b What is the name of polygon *A*?

c Reflect *A* in the line $y = -1$. Label this image *B*.

d What are the coordinates of the vertices of image *B*?

D

6 **a** Copy the diagram on *x*- and *y*-axes labelled −5 to 5.

b Rotate the shape 90° clockwise about the origin.

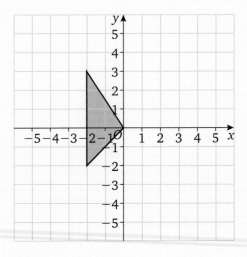

C

7 Describe the translation that maps shape *A* onto shape *B*.

Use vectors to give your answer.

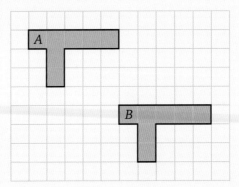

8 What is the equation of the line of reflectional symmetry in this diagram?

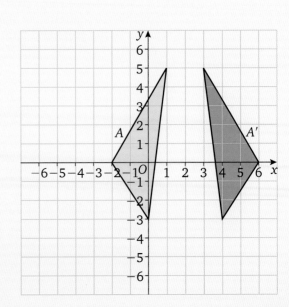

9

a Copy the diagram.

b Write down the coordinates of the vertices of the triangle A.

c Reflect the triangle in the line $x = -y$. Label the image B.

d Write down the coordinates of the vertices of triangle B.

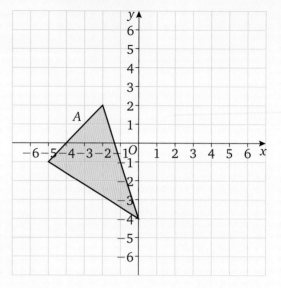

C

Practice questions

1 Triangles A, B and C are shown on the grid.

a Describe fully the single transformation that maps triangle A onto triangle B. *(3 marks)*

b Write down the vector which describes the translation of triangle A onto triangle C. *(1 mark)*

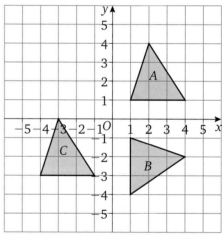

AQA 2009

19 Measures

Did you know?

Going metric

We didn't always pay for things using pounds and pence. Before 1971 we used pounds, shillings and pence.

We didn't always measure lengths using metres. Before 1965 we used 'imperial units'. We measured lengths using yards, feet and inches. Some people still do!

We still use some very old measures. For example, the length of a cricket pitch is 22 yards.

You should already know:

✔ how to multiply and divide by 10, 100 and 1000.

 **Learn...** **19.1 Measurements and reading scales**

Measurements

Whenever you measure something you only get an approximate answer.

If you measure the length of the school hall you will probably give your answer to the nearest metre.

If you wanted to find a more accurate answer you might measure to the nearest centimetre.

When you measure something, you have to make these decisions.

- Decide on the most appropriate **units** to use.
- Decide what to use to make the measurement.
- Read the measurement and decide how to record it.

Units of **length** are:

kilometres (km), metres (m), centimetres (cm) and millimetres (mm).

Units of **mass** are:

tonnes (t), kilograms (kg), grams (g) and milligrams (mg).

Units of **capacity** are:

litres (l) and millilitres (ml).

Units of **time** are:

hours (h), minutes (min) and seconds (s).

> **Study tip**
>
> **All** metric units are linked by multiples of 10, but units of time are not.
>
> 60 seconds = 1 minute
>
> 60 minutes = 1 hour.

Example: Which of the units kilometres (km), metres (m), centimetres (cm) and millimetres (mm) would be used to measure:

    a   the distance from York to London

    b   the length of a pen

    c   the length of a cricket pitch

    d   the diameter of a pen?

Solution: **a**   Kilometres. As it is a long way from York to London you would use large units.

    b   Centimetres. As the length of a pen is much less than a metre, it would be sensible to use centimetres. Millimetres could be used, but most pens would be more than 100 millimetres long.

    c   Metres. The length of a cricket pitch is between 1 m and 1 km, so it is best to use metres.

    d   Millimetres. The width of most pens is between 1 mm and 1 cm, so millimetres are the best units to use.

Reading scales

When you measure anything you need to read from a scale. Only the main numbers are written on a scale. The gap between these numbers is divided up so that you can read between the main numbers.

Example: **a**   How much water is in the measuring cylinder?

b What weight do the weighing scales show?

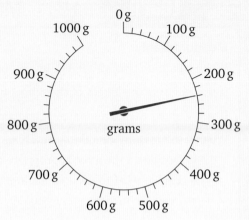

c What is the length of the nail?

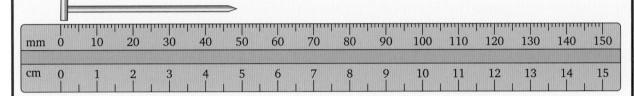

Solution:

a There are 5 divisions between 50 ml and 100 ml. That is 5 divisions for 50 ml. Each division is 50 ml ÷ 5 = 10 ml. The level of the water is one division above 50 ml. The measuring jug contains 60 ml of water.

b There are 5 divisions between 200 g and 300 g. That is 5 divisions for 100 g. Each division is 100 g ÷ 5 = 20 g. The pointer is at 2 divisions more than 200 g.

200 g + 40 g = 240 g. The scales show 240 g.

c The ruler is marked in millimetres (mm) and centimetres (cm). We can give the length of the nail in different ways.

To the nearest centimetre:
The nail is between 4 cm and 5 cm long.
The point of the nail is nearer 5 cm than 4 cm.
The nail is 5 cm to the nearest centimetre.

To the nearest millimetre:
The nail is between 48 mm and 49 mm.
It is nearer to 49 mm.
The nail is 49 mm to the nearest mm.

Using centimetres and millimetres:
1 cm is 10 mm and 1 mm is 0.1 cm.
4 cm is 40 mm and 9 mm is 0.9 cm.
49 mm can be written as 4 cm and 9 mm, or 4.9 cm.

19.1 Measurements and reading scales

Practise...

G F E D C

G

1 Measure each of the following lines to the nearest centimetre.

a ——————————————————

b ————————————————

c ——————————

d ——————————————

2   The diagram shows a pen and a ruler.

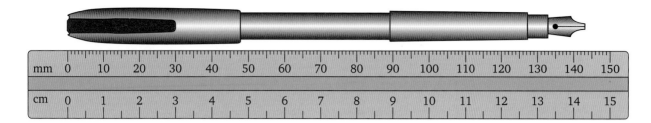

   a   What is the length of the pen to the nearest centimetre?

   b   What is the length of the pen to the nearest millimetre?

3   **kilometres, metres, centimetres, millimetres**

Which of these units would be most appropriate for measuring each of the following?

   a   The height of Blackpool tower

   b   The thickness of a paperback book

   c   The length of a football pitch

   d   The thickness of a matchstick

   e   The distance from Leeds to Manchester

   f   The height of a chair seat above the ground

   g   The thickness of a coin

   h   The height of a building

   i   The distance from New York to London

   j   The height of a tree

4   **tonnes, kilograms, grams, milligrams**

Which of these units would be most appropriate for measuring each of the following?

   a   The weight of a car

   b   The weight of a bag of sugar

   c   The weight of an adult

   d   The weight of a sugar lump

   e   The weight of the amount of butter in a cake

   f   The weight of a bag of sweets

   g   The weight of a feather

5   **litres, millilitres**

Which of these units would be the most appropriate for measuring the capacity of each of the following?

   a   A cup

   b   A reservoir

   c   A bath

   d   A bucket

   e   A car's petrol tank

   f   A teaspoon

G

G

6 Jim is baking a cake. He weighs butter, flour and sugar.

How much of each does he use?

a Butter

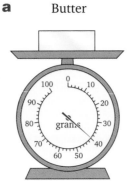

b Flour

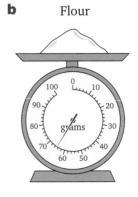

c Sugar

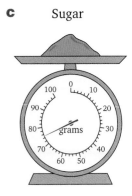

7 Gina is riding her bike. The speedometers show her speed in km/h.

What speeds do they show?

Study tip

Remember to work out how much each division of the scale is worth.

8 These thermometers show the temperature in different rooms in a house.

Write down the temperature in each room.

a

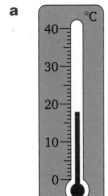

Kitchen

b

Bathroom

c

Bedroom

d

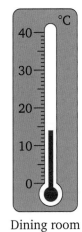

Dining room

9 **a** Estimate the length and width of this textbook.

b Check your estimates by measuring.

10 **a** Estimate the length and width of your classroom.

b Check your answers by measuring. (Agree with your teacher when would be a convenient time to measure the classroom.)

G
F

11   How many millilitres of milk are in this jug?

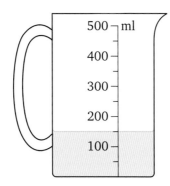

Learn... 19.2 Conversion between metric units

To convert from one metric unit to another, multiply or divide by a **conversion factor**.

To convert from a large unit to a smaller unit, multiply by the conversion factor as there will be more of the smaller units.

To convert from a small unit to a larger unit, divide by the conversion factor as there will be fewer of the larger units.

You are expected to know the following conversions between metric units.

Distance

1 kilometre = 1000 metres	(1 km = 1000 m)
1 metre = 1000 millimetres	(1 m = 1000 mm)
1 metre = 100 centimetres	(1 m = 100 cm)
1 centimetre = 10 millimetres	(1 cm = 10 mm)

Mass

1 tonne = 1000 kilograms	(1 t = 1000 kg)
1 kilogram = 1000 grams	(1 kg = 1000 g)
1 gram = 1000 milligrams	(1 g = 1000 mg)

> **Study tip**
>
> You are expected to know the metric equivalents as they are listed here.

Capacity

1 litre = 1000 millilitres	(1 l = 1000 ml)
1 litre = 100 centilitres	(1 l = 100 cl)
1 centilitre = 10 millilitres	(1 cl = 10 ml)
1 litre = 1000 cubic centimetres	(1 l = 1000 cm^3)

The metric system is based on 1000s.

'kilo' means 1000, so 1 'kilo'metre means 1000 metres.

'milli' means $\frac{1}{1000}$, so 1 'milli'metre means $\frac{1}{1000}$ of a metre.

'centi' means $\frac{1}{100}$ so 1 'centi'metre means $\frac{1}{100}$ of a metre.

Example: Convert the following lengths to metres.

    a   14 km

    b   23.5 cm

    c   45 mm

Solution: **a**   There are 1000 metres in every 1 kilometre, so the conversion factor is 1000.

To change 14 kilometres to metres you multiply by 1000. (This is because you are converting from large units to small units so there will be more of them.)

Using the fact that 1 kilometre = 1000 metres

$$14 \text{ kilometres} = 14 \times 1000 \text{ metres}$$
$$= 14\,000 \text{ m}$$

   b   1 metre is made up of 100 centimetres, so the conversion factor is 100.

To change 23.5 cm to metres you divide by 100. (This is because you are converting from small units to large units so there will be fewer of them).

23.5 cm = 23.5 ÷ 100 = 0.235 m

   c   There are 1000 millimetres in every metre, so the conversion factor is 1000.

To change 45 mm to metres you divide by 1000. (This is because you are converting from small units to large units so there will be fewer of them).

45 mm = 45 ÷ 1000 = 0.045 m

or using the fact that 1 metre = 1000 millimetres

$$1000 \text{ millimetres} = 1 \text{ metre}$$
$$1 \text{ millimetre} = \frac{1}{1000} \text{ metre} = 0.001 \text{ metres}$$
$$45 \text{ millimetre} = 45 \times 0.001 \text{ metres}$$
$$= 0.045 \text{ m}$$

> **Study tip**
>
> Remember to give the correct units with your answer.

Example: Gerald's car has a mass of 1.4 tonnes. Convert this to kilograms.

Solution: There are 1000 kilograms in 1 tonne, so the conversion factor is 1000.

To convert from 1.4 tonnes to kilograms you multiply by 1000 (you are converting from large units to small units so there will be more of them).

$$1.4 \text{ tonnes} = 1.4 \times 1000 \text{ kg}$$
$$= 1400 \text{ kg}$$

Practise...

19.2 Conversion between metric units

1   Measure and write down the lengths of these lines in millimetres.

    a ——————————————

    b ——————

    c ————————————————

    d ————

    e ——

2   What is the length of each line in Question 1 in centimetres?

G

3 Jemima measured the distance from her house to school as 3 kilometres.
What is this distance in metres?

4 Gill measured the length of her classroom as 4.5 metres.
What is this in centimetres?

5 Harold walked 1250 metres across the school playing field.
How far did Harold walk in kilometres?

6 Convert the following to kilograms.

a	1.2 tonnes	**c**	0.9 tonnes	**e**	2500 g
b	3.1 tonnes	**d**	2000 g	**f**	250 g

7 Samantha buys a bottle of juice containing 70 centilitres.

a How many millilitres does the bottle contain?

b How many litres does the bottle contain?

8 Copy and complete the following, filling in the missing units.

a	2 km = 2000 …	**f**	30 cl = 300 …
b	20 cm = 200 …	**g**	1.5 kg = 1500 …
c	30 mm = 3 …	**h**	6.2 m = 6200 …
d	400 m = 0.4 …	**i**	6.2 m = 620 …
e	3 t = 3000 …	**j**	1500 ml = 1.5 …

9 Jeremy buys a bag of flour weighing 2.5 kg. He bakes 10 cakes, each of which uses 65 g of flour.
How much flour does he have left?

10 Tom walks 950 metres to school every morning. He walks the same distance home every afternoon.
How many kilometres does Tom walk in one week?

11 Fay has a recipe for fruit punch using 1.5 litres of orange juice, 2 litres of apple juice, 1 litre of water and 2.5 litres of lemonade. She makes some fruit punch using this recipe, but only needs half the quantity.

a How much does she need of each ingredient? (Give your answers in millilitres.)

b She shares the punch equally with six of her friends.
How many 250 ml glasses will they each have?

12 Jan bought a 2 m roll of wrapping paper for presents. She used 45 cm for James's present, and 97 cm for Carlos's present. She needs 65 cm to wrap Ian's present.
Does she have enough paper or will she need another roll? Show your working.

13 **a** Janet has four pieces of wood. They are 2 cm, 3 cm, 6 cm and 12 cm long.

  i Show how these can be used to measure lengths of 1 cm, 4 cm, and 7 cm.

  ii What other lengths can be measured with these four pieces of wood?

  b You have five pieces of wood.
  They can be any length you want.

  What lengths would you choose in order to measure the largest possible number of lengths?

> **Hint**
> Work systematically to find all the possibilities.

Learn... 19.3 Conversion between metric and imperial units

To convert between metric and imperial units, you multiply or divide by a conversion factor.

You need to know, and be able to use, the following conversion factors.

5 miles ≈ 8 kilometres

4.5 litres ≈ 1 gallon

2.2 pounds ≈ 1 kilogram

1 inch ≈ 2.5 centimetres

> **Hint**
>
> The symbol ≈ means approximately equals. So that a distance of 5 miles is approximately equal to 8 kilometres.

> **Study tip**
>
> These are the only equivalents you need to know. Learn them, as they may not be given in the exam. Other conversions may be given.

The conversion factors give you information about which is the smaller unit if you are not sure. For example, 2.2 pounds ≈ 1 kilogram, so pounds must be smaller than kilograms.

For conversions between miles and kilometres, 5 miles ≈ 8 km

This can be difficult to use in practice.

You can use the conversion factor for 1 km: $\frac{5}{8}$ miles ≈ 1 km

so 0.625 miles ≈ 1 km

or 1 mile ≈ $\frac{8}{5}$ km

so 1 mile ≈ 1.6 km

> **Study tip**
>
> 0.63 miles ≈ 1 km is used in exam papers.

All of these give exactly the same answers, but some may be easier to use than others at times.

> **Study tip**
>
> Use 'multipliers' in ratio to convert. Remember there are **more** kilometres than miles for the same distance. For example:
>
> 30 miles = 30 × $\frac{8}{5}$ km = 48 km (greater answer)
>
> 120 km = 120 × $\frac{5}{8}$ miles = 75 miles (fewer miles)

Example: Convert 42 miles to kilometres.

Solution: 1.6 km ≈ 1 mile, so the conversion factor is 1.6

You are converting from large units to smaller units. (You know this because 1 mile is more than 1 km). So you multiply by 1.6 (as you are converting from a larger unit to a smaller unit, there will be more of them).

42 miles ≈ 42 × 1.6 kilometres

≈ 67.2 kilometres

≈ 67 kilometres (nearest km)

Example: Convert 50 litres to gallons.

Solution: 4.5 litres ≈ 1 gallon, so the conversion factor is 4.5

Litres are smaller than gallons. (You can tell this because 1 gallon is more than 1 litre; in fact it is about 4.5 litres.) So you divide by 4.5 (as you are converting from a smaller unit to a larger unit, there will be fewer of them).

50 litres ≈ 50 ÷ 4.5 gallons

50 litres ≈ 11.1 gallons

or using the fact that 4.5 litres ≈ 1 gallon

Therefore 1 litre ≈ $\frac{1}{4.5}$ gallons

50 litres ≈ 50 × $\frac{1}{4.5}$ gallons

50 litres ≈ 50 ÷ 4.5 ≈ 11.1̇ gallons

50 litres ≈ 11 gallons

19.3 Conversion betwen metric and imperial units

Practise...

G F E D C

F

E

1 Convert 3 gallons to litres.

2 Convert 3 pounds to kilograms.

3 Alan measures a rod in a science lesson. It measures 6 inches.
What is this in centimetres?

4 A recipe for jam uses 10 pounds of sugar.
Approximately how many kilograms is this?

5 Chicken is priced at £8.50 per kilogram.
Approximately how much is this per pound?

6 Petrol is advertised at £1.12 per litre.
Approximately how much is this per gallon?

7 Carol weighs 126 pounds. Jane weighs 132 pounds.
Approximately how many kilograms heavier is Jane than Carol?

8 Karen cycles 20 miles around a forest trail.
Approximately how many kilometres is this?

9 Rebecca drives 42 km to work.
How many miles is this? Give your answer to the nearest mile.

10 The speed limit on motorways in the UK is 70 mph. The speed limit on motorways in France is 120 km/h. Jack says that you can drive faster on French motorways. Jill says that UK motorways have a faster speed limit.
Who is correct? Show your working.

11 Bill enters a 10 km race. He says it is the same distance as the 6 mile training runs he has been doing. Is Bill correct? Show your working.

12 Iqbal says that 40 miles is the same as 25 km.
a What mistake has Iqbal made?
b What is 40 miles in kilometres?
c What is 25 kilometres in miles?

13 Janet, Liz and Peter are doing a sponsored walk.
The walk is 24 km.
Janet will raise £400 if she completes the walk.
Peter will get £30 for **each mile** he walks.
They are hoping to raise £1000 for charity. They all complete the walk.
How much does Liz need to raise for each mile she walks?

14 Fran buys milk at her corner shop. She pays 96p for a container which holds 2 pints. The mini-market next door sells milk in containers which hold 1 litre for 85p. There are 8 pints in 1 gallon.
Which shop sells milk at the cheaper price? You must show your working.

Learn... 19.4 Compound measures

Compound measures combine two different units. For example,

$$\text{speed} = \frac{\text{distance}}{\text{time}} \qquad \text{fuel consumption} = \frac{\text{number of miles travelled}}{\text{number of gallons used}}$$

Be careful with the units. They give you clues about what to divide by.

Speed is measured in kilometres per hour (km/h).

This tells you the formula:

$$\text{speed} = \frac{\text{distance (km)}}{\text{time (hours)}}$$

Fuel consumption is measured in miles per gallon or kilometres per litre.

Example: Jamie is a runner in a club. He runs 200 metres in 32 seconds. Find his average speed in:

    a   metres per second

    b   kilometres per hour.

> **Hint**
>
> metres per second
> = metres/second
> = metres ÷ seconds

Solution: **a**   Using the formula above:

$$\text{average speed} = \frac{\text{distance}}{\text{time}} = \frac{200}{32} \text{ m/s} = 6.25 \text{ m/s}$$

    b   6.25 m/s means 6.25 metres every second.

    In 60 seconds he runs $6.25 \times 60 = 375$ metres

    In 60 minutes he runs $375 \times 60 = 22\,500$ metres

    $22\,500$ metres $= 22\,500 \div 1000 = 22.5$ km

    Jamie runs at a speed of 22.5 km/h.

Example: Work out the average speed in mph of:

    a   a train that takes $1\frac{1}{2}$ hours to travel 102 miles

    b   a plane that travels 1450 miles in 2 hours 45 minutes.

> **Hint**
>
> mph = miles per hour
> = miles/hour
> = miles ÷ hours

Solution: **a**   Using the formula above:

$$\text{average speed} = \frac{\text{distance}}{\text{time}} = \frac{102}{1.5} = 68 \text{ mph}$$

    b   Using the formula, $\text{average speed} = \dfrac{\text{distance}}{\text{time}}$

$$\text{Average speed} = \frac{1450}{2.75} = 527 \text{ mph}$$

> **Study tip**
>
> Change the time to hours, using decimals, when the time is in hours and minutes and the answer is in mph.

Practise... 19.4 Compound measures   G F E D C

D

1   Work out the average speed for each of the following.
State the units of your answers.

    a   A car travels 200 metres in 8 seconds.

    b   A man takes 28 seconds to run 200 metres.

    c   A train takes 2 hours to travel 230 miles.

2   Express each of these times as decimal fractions of an hour.

   a   30 minutes

   b   15 minutes

   c   4 hours 45 minutes

3   Write each of these times as hours and minutes.

   a   2.5 hours

   b   3.25 hours

   c   1.75 hours

4   Find the speed in mph of:

   a   a car that travels 85 miles in 1 hour 15 minutes

   b   a lorry that travels 75 miles in 1 hour 30 minutes.

> **Study tip**
>
> Remember to divide by time in hours when you find a speed in miles per hour (mph) or kilometres per hour.

5   A snail crawls at 5 cm per minute.

   a   How far does it crawl in 1 hour?

   b   How long does it take to crawl 1 metre?

6   Work out the time taken for each of these journeys.
Give your answer in hours and minutes.

   a   A car travels 40 km at 50 km per hour.

   b   A bus travels 20 km at 30 km per hour.

   c   A cyclist travels 45 km at 25 km per hour.

7   Work out the distance travelled for each of these journeys.

   a   A person walks at 4 km per hour for 75 minutes.

   b   A train travels at 110 km per hour for 90 minutes.

   c   A lorry travels for 45 minutes at 50 km per hour.

8   Jan drives 255 miles in her car and uses 6 gallons of fuel.

   a   What is her fuel consumption in miles per gallon?

   b   How many gallons of fuel would Jan use for a similar journey of 400 miles?

   c   The fuel tank in Jan's car holds 15 gallons of fuel when it is full.

       Is it possible for Jan to travel 600 miles on one full tank of fuel?

9   John runs at 9 km per hour for 40 minutes. He then walks 2.5 km in 30 minutes.
What is John's average speed in km per hour over the whole journey?

10   Sam drives 265 miles from Kendal to Bristol.

His average fuel consumption for this journey is 50 miles per gallon (mpg).

His fuel tank holds 15 gallons of fuel when full.

He then drives 221 miles from Bristol to Norwich with an average fuel consumption of 48 mpg.

Lastly, he drives 278 miles from Norwich back to Kendal, with an average consumption of 47 mpg.

Is it possible for Sam to complete this journey on one tank of petrol?

Learn... 19.5 Accuracy in measurements

When you measure in centimetres and millimetres, any length between 6.5 cm and 7.5 cm will round to 7 cm.

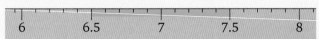

Study tip

6.5 cm to 7.5 cm means any value in the range 6.5 up to but not including 7.5

On this scale any measurement in the shaded area rounds to 7 cm.

The shaded area is from 6.5 cm up to 7.5 cm.

Notice: 'to the nearest cm' means the actual distance could be any value from half a centimetre below to half a centimetre above.

Example: Zac measures the length of a shelf. He says it is 43 cm to the nearest centimetre. What are the smallest and the largest possible lengths of the shelf?

Solution: Zac's measurement rounds to 43 cm, so the actual length must be in the shaded area on the scale.

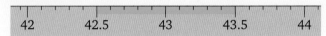

The shaded area is from 42.5 cm up to 43.5 cm .

The smallest length is 42.5 cm.

The largest length is 43.5 cm.

Practise... 19.5 Accuracy in measurements

1 Round each of the following to the nearest whole number.

    a   12.9 cm   **c**   49.9 miles   **e**   43.56 kg

    b   81.2 m   **d**   6.5 g   **f**   47.4999 litres

2 Each of these lengths rounds to 15 cm, to the nearest centimetre.

    14.6 cm, 15.4 cm, 14.91 cm, 15.49 cm

    a   Write down some other lengths that also round to 15 cm to the nearest cm.

    b   What is the minimum value of a measurement which has been rounded to 15 cm?

    c   What is the maximum value of a measurement which has been rounded to 15 cm?

3 George measured the length of a post for a washing line in his garden. He found it was 3 metres to the nearest metre.

    What are the smallest and largest possible lengths of the post?

4 Faye measured some of the crayons in her pencil case. She found they were all 8 cm to the nearest cm.

    Does this mean they were all the same length? Give a reason for your answer.

5 Mike measured the distance from his home in Windermere to his school in Kendal. He found it was 18 km to the nearest kilometre.

    a   What is the smallest distance that Mike's measurement could be?

    b   What is the largest distance that Mike's measurement could be?

6 The weight of a letter is 43 g to the nearest gram.

What are the smallest and largest values for the weight of the letter?

7 A bridge has a sign stating the maximum weight allowed on it is 2 tonnes.

A van driver knows his van weighs 2 tonnes to the nearest tonne.

Can the van driver be sure that it is safe for him to drive over the bridge?
Give a reason for your answer.

8 The contents of a packet of crisps weigh 33 g to the nearest gram.

Which of the following could be the weight of the crisps?

a 33.2 g   **c** 33.49 g   **e** 32.5 g

b 33.6 g   **d** 33.94 g   **f** 32.29 g

9 Rachel weighs the books in her school bag.
All her textbooks together weigh 3 kg to the nearest kilogram.
All her exercise books together weigh 1 kg to the nearest kilogram.
There are no other books in her bag.
What is the maximum weight of the books in her bag?

10 Mark buys some food from the grocer's shop. He buys 1 kg of carrots, 5 kg of potatoes, both weighed to the nearest kilogram.
What is the minimum possible weight of his shopping?

11 George, Mildred and Henrietta all get into a lift.
George weighs 95 kg, Mildred weighs 83 kg and Henrietta weighs 71 kg.
The lift states: Maximum weight 250 kg.
Is it safe for George, Mildred and Henrietta to use the lift?
Does it make a difference if the weights have been rounded? Give a reason for your answer.

19 Assess ⓚ

1 Measure the following lines. Record your measurement to the nearest centimetre.

a ————————————

b —————————

c ——————————————

d —————————————

2 What are the most appropriate units for measuring each of the following?

a The mass of a car

b The height of a house

c Your mass

d The mass of a bag of sweets

e The capacity of a teaspoon

G

3   What number does each arrow point to?

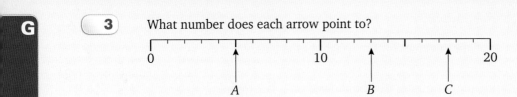

4   A bottle contains 2 litres of water.

How many millilitres is this?

5   Sam trains at the athletic track. He completes 5 laps of a 400 metre track.

How far does Sam run? Give your answer in kilometres.

F

6   Jack buys a 4 kg bag of potatoes from his local shop.

What is the mass of the potatoes in pounds?

7   James buys a 4 pint bottle of milk.

How many litres of milk are in the bottle?

E

8   Frank is driving his car in France. The speed limit is 110 km per hour.

What is this in miles per hour?

D

9   A van travels 230 miles in 7 hours.

What is the average speed of the van?

C

10   A car takes 45 minutes to travel 17 miles.

What is the average speed of the car?

11   The temperature in a classroom is 18°C to the nearest degree.

What are the highest and lowest temperatures that would round to 18°C?

Practice questions (k)

1   Dipak travels a distance of 30 miles.
Wendy travels a distance of 40 kilometres.

Who travels further?
You **must** show your working.

(3 marks)

AQA 2008

20 Coordinates and graphs

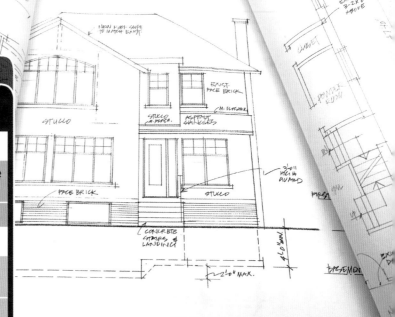

Examiners would normally expect students who get these grades to be able to:

G

use coordinates in the first quadrant, such as plotting the point (2, 1)

recognise the net of a simple solid

F

use coordinates in all four quadrants, such as (2, −1), (−2, −3) and (−2, 1)

use simple real-life graphs, such as read values from conversion graphs

draw the net of a simple shape, such as a matchbox tray

E

draw lines such as $x = 3$, and $y = x$

interpret horizontal lines on a distance–time graph

use real-life graphs to find values, such as find distances from distance–time graphs

draw a simple shape, such as a cuboid, on isometric paper

D

make simple interpretations of real-life graphs

draw the front elevation, side elevation and plan of a solid on squared paper

C

carry out further interpretation of real-life graphs, for example find the average speed in km/h from a distance–time graph over time in minutes.

Did you know?

Draw the right house, build the house right

Plans and elevations are very important to people who design and build houses.

When a house is built for someone, an architect will draw out accurate plans to ensure they get the house they want, and so they can see what it will look like when it is finished.

The builder uses the plans to build the house. Following the plans carefully will ensure that the walls, doors, and windows are in the correct place.

Key terms

coordinates
origin
axis
vertex
edge
face
plan
elevation
net

You should already know:

✔ negative numbers and the number line

✔ the meaning of the words vertex, vertices, axis, axes, horizontal and vertical

✔ names of common quadrilaterals and their properties

✔ how to substitute into a formula

✔ 3-D shapes such as cube, cuboid, tetrahedron, pyramid and prisms.

Learn... 20.1 Coordinates and equations of a straight line

Coordinates are used to describe the position of a point relative to a starting point called the **origin** labelled O in the diagram.

The horizontal **axis** is called the x-axis, coloured blue in the diagram.

The vertical axis is called the y-axis, coloured red in the diagram.

The axes divide the graph paper into four quadrants (quarters).

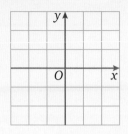

The next diagram shows the first quadrant, where x- and y-values are both positive.

The coordinates of point B are (4, 3). The x-coordinate is always first. They are given in alphabetical order, x before y. The coordinates are always separated by a comma, and have brackets around them to keep them together as a pair.

The coordinates of C and A are (3.5, 2) and (1.5, 1.5). It is acceptable to use either decimals or fractions when the coordinates are not integers.

Take care not to confuse D which is (4, 0) and E which is (0, 4).

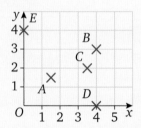

Study tip

Sometimes students forget which axis is x and which is y. To help you remember which is which you need to '**Wise up, X is a cross**' (y's up, x is across).

This diagram shows all four quadrants.
Some points have negative coordinates.

Point A is in the first quadrant (as above) and has coordinates (1, 4).

Point B has coordinates $(-1, 4)$.

Point C is $(-3, -1)$.

Point D is $(1, -3)$.

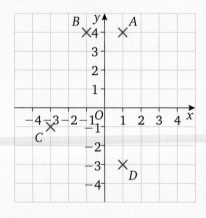

Equations of horizontal and vertical lines

The equation of a straight line is a 'rule' that applies to every point on that line.

The coordinates of A, B and C are (1, 3), (2, 3) and (4, 3) respectively. They all have the y-coordinate = 3.
If you draw a line through them, $y = 3$ for every point on the line.
The equation for this line is $y = 3$.
This line is green on the diagram and is labelled $y = 3$

The coordinates of points C, D and E are (4, 3), (4, 0) and (4, 2).
They all have the x-coordinate = 4.
If you draw a line through them, $x = 4$ for every point on the line.
The equation for this line is $x = 4$.
This line is blue on the diagram and is labelled $x = 4$

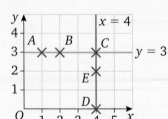

Study tip

Always label the x- and y-axes. When you draw a straight line always remember to label it with its equation.

20.1 Coordinates and equations of a straight line

Practise...

G F E D C

1   Write down the coordinates of each of the points on the grid.

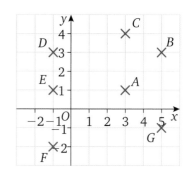

2   Draw a pair of x- and y-axes from -5 to 5 on squared paper.
Plot and label the following points.

$A(2, 3), B(4, 3), C(2, -1), D(-1, 2), E(-2, 2), F(2, -2), G(-2, -2)$

3   The diagram shows three vertices of a rectangle ABCD.
Write down the coordinates of D, the fourth
vertex of the rectangle?

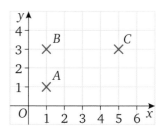

4   The diagram shows part of a pattern made of identical
rectangles.

a   Write down the coordinates of the four vertices
of rectangle 3.

b   Work out the coordinates of the four vertices
of rectangle 4.

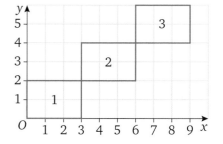

5   **a**   Write down the equations of the lines on the grid.

b   Declan said that line A crosses line D at the point (1, 4).
What mistake has Declan made?

c   Write down the coordinates of the points where:
   i   lines A and B cross
   ii   lines B and C cross
   iii lines A and E cross
   iv   lines B and F cross
   v   lines D and F cross.

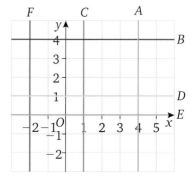

6   **a**   Draw a pair of x- and y-axes from -5 to 5 on squared paper. Draw and label the lines with the
following equations.
   i $y = 3$
   ii $x = 2$
   iii $y = -2$
   iv $x = -1$

b   Write down the coordinates of the points where the lines cross. What do you notice about the
coordinates of the points and the equations of the lines?

E
D

7 The equation $y = x$ tells you that the x- and y-coordinates are equal.
The point (3, 3) is on this line.

a Give two other points that are on the line.

b Draw a pair of x- and y-axes from −5 to 5 on squared paper.
Plot your points, join them and label the line.

c What are the coordinates of the point where the line crosses the x-axis?

8 The equation $y = -x$ tells you that the x- and y-coordinates are the same number, but with different signs. For example $y = -2$ when $x = 2$. So (2, −2) is on the line.

a Write down the coordinates of two other points on this line.

b Draw a pair of x- and y-axes from −5 to 5 on squared paper.
Plot your points, join them and label your line.

c What do you notice about the lines you have drawn in this question and Question 7?

9 The diagram shows three of the vertices of a square.
What are the coordinates of the fourth vertex?

> **Hint**
> You may find it helpful to copy the diagram and draw the square.

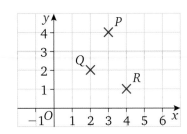

⚠ 10 The diagram shows three of the vertices of a parallelogram.

Write down the coordinates of the fourth vertex.
There is more than one possible place to put the fourth vertex. Find them all.

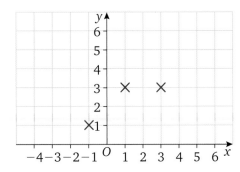

Learn... 20.2 Real-life graphs

Tables and formulae are often used to show connections between data. It is often easier to see at a glance what is going on when you use a graph.

Graphs can be used to represent many different situations.

Conversion graphs can be used to convert from one unit to another. This includes distances such as miles and kilometres, or currency conversions such as pounds (£) and euros (€).

The gradient of a straight line is found using the formula:

$$\text{gradient} = \frac{\text{increase in } y}{\text{increase in } x}$$

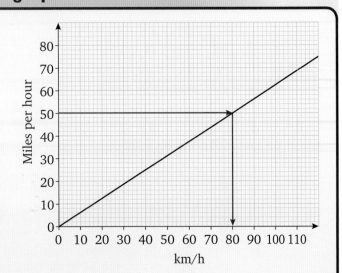

Distance–time graphs can be used to help calculate speeds. The gradient of a distance–time graph tells you the object's speed.

You can use this kind of graph see how far an object travelled in each unit of time.

You need to learn the formula:

$$\text{average speed} = \frac{\text{total distance}}{\text{total time}}$$

Graphs which show costs can be used to compare prices, such as the cost of different contracts for mobile phones. If cost is on the vertical axis and time in minutes on the horizontal axis, the gradient tells you the cost per minute.

Example: An oven is set at a temperature of 200°C. This graph shows the temperature inside the oven over a two-hour period.

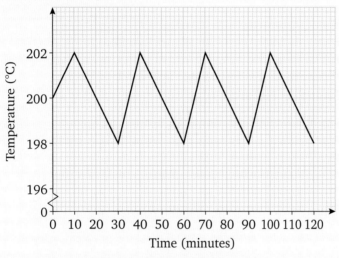

a   Explain what is happening in the graph.

b   What is the temperature in the oven after 45 minutes?

c   Between 30 and 40 minutes the oven is warming up.
What does the gradient of this section tell you?

d   What does the gradient of the line between 70 minutes and 90 minutes tell you?

Solution: **a**   The graph tells you that the oven warms up, then cools down. When the graph goes up, this shows the temperature is rising. When the graph goes down this tells you the oven is cooling down. The temperature goes up more quickly than it cools down. You know this because the graph is steeper when the oven is warming up.

b

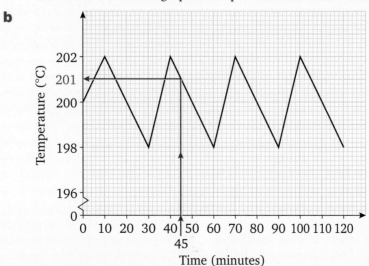

Read up from 45 minutes on the horizontal axis to the graph. From there read across to the vertical axis and write the temperature down. It is 201°C. This is shown with an arrow on the graph.

c Between 30 and 40 minutes the temperature rises from 198°C to 202°C.
The temperature rises 4°C in 10 minutes.

$$\text{The gradient} = \frac{\text{increase in } y}{\text{increase in } x} = \frac{4}{10} = 0.4$$

This tells you the temperature increases at a rate of 0.4°C per minute.
The gradient tells you the rate at which the temperature increases.

d The gradient of the line between 70 and 90 minutes tells you the rate at which the oven cools down.

$$\text{The gradient} = \frac{\text{increase in } y}{\text{increase in } x}$$

The temperature is decreasing, that is a negative increase. The temperature decreases by 4°C in 20 minutes.

$$\text{Gradient} = \frac{-4}{20} = -0.2 \text{ so the temperature is decreasing at 0.2°C per minute.}$$

Example: Benny is doing a science experiment looking at springs. A spring stretches when weights are added to it. The formula for its length is $L = 3M + 12$ where M is the mass in kg and L is the length in cm.

a Copy and complete the table.

M	2	4	6	8	10
L	18			36	

b Draw the graph for the values in the table.

c Benny hangs a weight on the spring. He measures the length of the spring.
It is 35 cm long. Use your graph to find the weight Benny has used.

d Calculate the gradient of this line. What does the gradient represent?

e The line meets the vertical y-axis at 12 cm. What does this tell you about the spring?

Solution: **a** Use the formula $L = 3M + 12$

For a 4 kg mass: $L = 3 \times 4 + 12 = 12 + 12 = 24$

For a 6 kg mass: $L = 3 \times 6 + 12 = 18 + 12 = 30$

For a 10 kg mass: $L = 3 \times 10 + 12 = 30 + 12 = 42$

M	2	4	6	8	10
L	18	24	30	36	42

b Plot the points carefully.

c Read across from 35 cm on the vertical axis to the graph.
From the graph read down to the horizontal axis. Write down the value of 7.6 kg.
The red arrows on the graph show this.

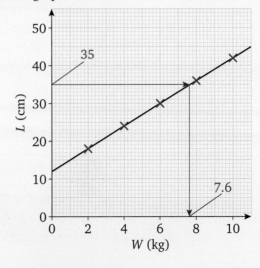

d Using the formula, gradient $= \dfrac{\text{increase in } y}{\text{increase in } x}$

$$= \dfrac{(42 - 18)}{(10 - 2)}$$

$$= \dfrac{24}{8}$$

Gradient $= 3$

The gradient is **length** divided by **mass**. It shows the length the spring stretches for every kg added.

e The line meets the vertical axis at 12 cm. This tells you the length of the spring when there is no mass on it, when it is not stretched.

Practise... 20.2 Real-life graphs

1 Janet is organising a birthday party at a leisure centre for her son. The cost is £50 to book the room plus £5.50 per child for food.

a Copy and complete this table for the total cost of a party at the leisure centre.

Children	10	20	30	40
Cost (£)	105			

b Draw a pair of axes with the cost in pounds (£) on the *y*-axis and the number of children on the *x*-axis. The *y*-axis should go from 0 to 300. The *x*-axis should go from 0 to 40. Plot the points from the table completed in part **a**.

c Use your graph to find the cost when the number of children is:

i 15

ii 22

iii 31

d Janet has £200 to spend on a party. What is the maximum number of children her son can invite?

2 Water comes out of a tap at a rate of 125 ml every second.

a Copy and complete the table for the amount of water coming out of the tap.

Time (seconds)	0	1	2	3	4	5
Water (ml)	0	125				

b Draw a graph to show this information.

c Use your graph to find how much water comes out of the tap in 3.2 seconds.

d How long does it take to get 200 ml of water out of the tap?

e A kettle holds 1.7 litres of water when full. 1.7 litres = 1700 ml How long will it take to fill the kettle using this tap?

D

3 This graph shows the amount of petrol used by a car.

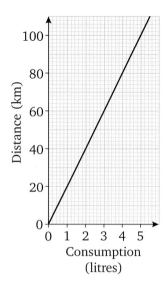

a How much petrol is used when the car travels:

 i 60 km

 ii 35 km?

b How many km are travelled when the amount of petrol the car uses is:

 i 4 litres

 ii 2.5 litres?

c Calculate the gradient of the line. What does this tell you about the car?

4 Ace Energy supply electricity. They have a standing charge of £8.50 each quarter (this means a customer has to pay £8.50 every 3 months no matter how much electricity they use). They then charge 10.5p per unit of electricity used.

a Copy and complete the table for the cost of electricity from Ace Energy.

Units used	0	500	1000	1500	2000
Cost (£)	8.50	61			

b Draw a graph showing this information.
Betta-supplies have a standing charge of £11.50. They then charge 10p for each unit of electricity used.

c Add a line to your graph showing the cost of electricity from Beta Supplies.

d Which of these electricity suppliers would you advise a new customer to use? Give a reason for your answer.

D
C

5 Budget Pens supply pens to schools. Their prices are shown in the graph. Large orders get a discount.

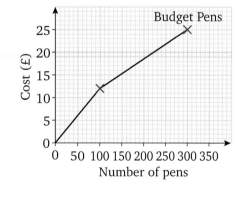

a What is the total cost of 80 pens from Budget Pens?

b A school buys 80 pens, what is the cost of each pen?

c What is the cost of 250 pens from Budget Pens?

d How many pens does a school have to buy from Budget Pens to receive a discount?

Cheapo Pens are a rival company who also supply pens to schools. They charge 9p for each pen, no matter how big the order.

e Copy and complete the table for the cost of pens from Cheapo Pens.

Number of pens	100	200	300
Cost (£)	9		

f Copy the graph and add a line to show the cost of Cheapo Pens.

g A school wants to order 150 pens. Which company is cheaper and by how much?

h When do Budget Pens and Cheapo Pens charge the same for the same number of pens? How many pens is this and what is the cost?

i A school sells pens to students for 10p each. They use Budget Pens as a supplier. How many pens do they need to sell before they start making a profit?

j A second school buys 300 pens from Budget Pens. How much do they need to sell each pen for so they don't make a loss? Give your answer to the nearest 1p.

6   Tom went for a walk. His walk is represented on this graph.

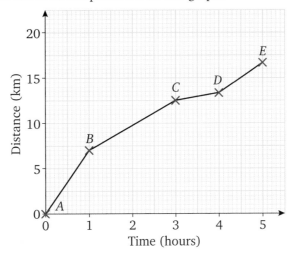

a   In which section of his walk was Tom walking:

   i   fastest

   ii   slowest?

b   What was his average speed in section *BC*?

c   What was his average speed for the whole walk?

 7   A small exercise club uses cross trainers, treadmills and exercise bikes. On average a cross trainer burns off 9 calories per minute, and a treadmill 7 calories per minute.

John trains for 30 minutes. The graph shows the calories he burns off. He starts on an exercise bike.

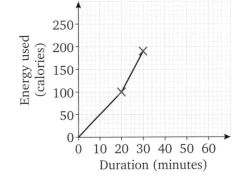

a   How many calories does the exercise bike burn off per minute?

b   What exercise equipment does John use after he has used the exercise bike?

c   Mary uses the cross trainer for 10 minutes then spends 20 minutes on the treadmill. Draw a similar graph for the calories that Mary burns off.

d   Design an exercise programme for Jenny. She wants to burn off over 300 calories, and wants to use all three exercise machines.

Learn...   **20.3 Drawing 2-D representations of 3-D objects**

Definitions

This diagram shows a cube.

Vertex is the correct name for a corner of the cube. The plural of vertex is **vertices**. A cube has 8 vertices. You can only see 7 in the diagram, there is also one at the back that cannot be seen.

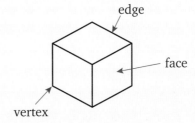

An **edge** joins two vertices. The edges are shown by the lines in the diagram. A cube has 12 edges.

A **face** is the flat part of the cube. A cube has 6 faces. There are three that can be seen in the diagram plus two at the back and one underneath.

Drawing shapes

There are two ways to represent cubes and cuboids in 2-D.

Method 1

This uses special paper, either isometric dotty paper (which just has dots and is sometimes called triangular dotty paper) or isometric paper (with lines).

Using dotty paper

The dots are arranged in triangles 1 cm apart. You need to make sure the paper is the correct way round in order for your diagrams to work.

You should be able to draw triangles like these.

If you can only draw triangles like these

then your paper is the wrong way around.

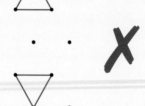

To draw a cube it is easiest to start with the top. Join the dots to make a rhombus. Then draw in the vertical edges. Finally complete the edges on the base of the cube.

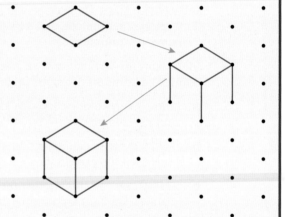

To draw shapes made of cuboids, start with the cube at the front, then work your way back. Remember you cannot see the front face of any cubes that are behind the cube at the front.

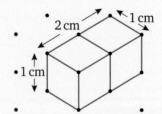

Using isometric paper

This is just like the dotty paper, but the dots have all been joined up. Like dotty paper you need to make sure that it is the correct way round. You need to be able to draw the triangles the same way as for dotty paper. Another way to do this is to make sure there are vertical lines on the page.

These are correct.

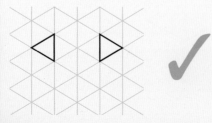

These are not correct.

   **X**      **X**

Method 2

This method involves a sketch without dotty or isometric paper.

Start with a square (this is the front).

Then draw three parallel lines going backwards like this.

Then join the ends of these lines.

Any edges you cannot see need to be shown with dashed lines.

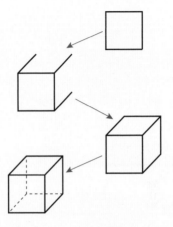

Example: Draw a representation of the following shape on isometric paper.

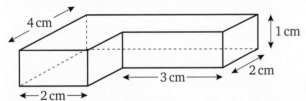

Solution: Make sure your paper is the correct way round. Then start by drawing the top of the shape.

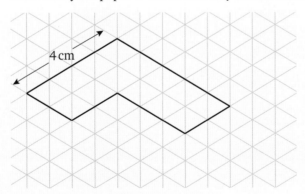

Then start adding the remaining faces.

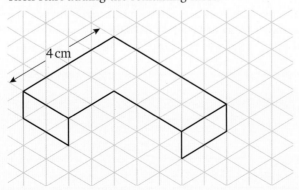

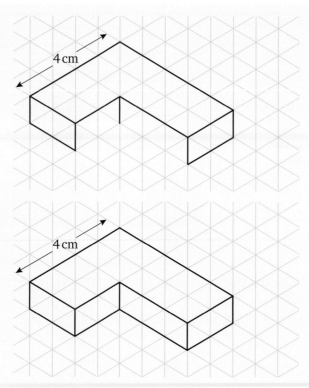

Label your final diagram.

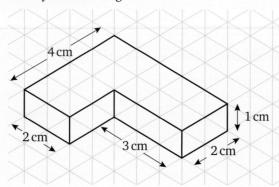

Example: On plain paper, draw a sketch of the cuboid 2 cm by 2 cm by 1 cm, shown here.

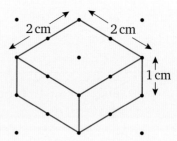

Solution: Start with the front face.

Then add the edges joining the front face to the face at the back.

Join these edges to make the outline of the back that is visible.

Join the vertices to show the edges which are not visible. Remember to use dashed lines for these.

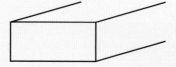 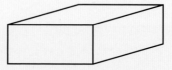 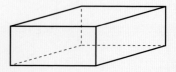

20.3 Drawing 2-D representations of 3-D objects

Practise...

1 This object is made from four Multilink cubes. If you have 3-D Multilink cubes you can make the object for yourself.

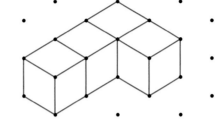

a Use isometric paper to draw this object. Make sure you have the paper the right way round.

b Make as many different shapes as you can using four Multilink cubes. Draw each object on isometric paper.

2 On plain paper, draw and label a sketch of a cuboid 3 cm by 3 cm by 2 cm.

3 On plain paper, draw and label a sketch of a cuboid 2 cm by 3 cm by 4 cm.

4 These are drawings of some 3-D shapes. Which drawings are different views of the same shapes? Use Multilink cubes to help you.

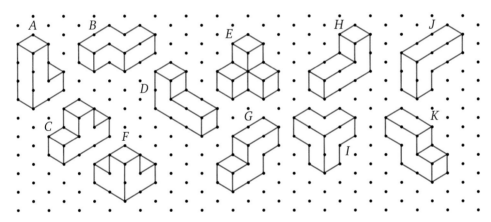

5 Hector has 24 cubes and each is a 1 cm cube. Draw and label a sketch of a cuboid box which will just hold these 24 cubes.

6 **a** Use Multilink cubes to make the shapes shown. Six of the shapes use four cubes and one uses just three cubes. (It may help you to make them using different colours.)

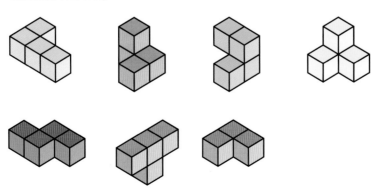

b Draw each shape on isometric paper.

c Using your Multilink cubes, fit the shapes together to make a cube. This is called the Soma cube and was invented by a Danish mathematician, Piet Hein.

E

7 **a** Use Multilink cubes to make the following shapes.
(It may help you to make them using different colours.)

  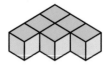

  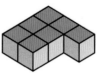

b Draw each shape on isometric dotty paper.

c Fit the shapes together to make a cube. This cube is called the Diabolical cube and was 'invented' by Professor Louis Hoffman. It was included in his book *Puzzles Old and New* in 1893.

 8 **a** Make these two shapes from Multilink cubes. (It may help you to make them using different colours.)

b Each of these drawings is an outline of a solid made from these two shapes.

Copy the outlines onto isometric dotty paper. Draw in the missing lines. Shade in the two shapes to show how they fit together to make the solid.

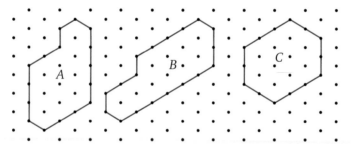

 9 **a** Using five Multilink cubes make as many different shapes as you can.

b Draw each of them on isometric dotty paper.

c How can you tell you have found them all?

d Repeat parts **a** and **b** with six Multilink cubes.

Hint

You will find it easier to answer this if you work systematically.

Learn... 20.4 Plans and elevations

3-D objects may be viewed from different directions.

The view from above is called the **plan** view.

The view from the front is called the front **elevation**.

The view from the side is called the side elevation.

Sometimes the front elevation will look the same as the side elevation.

Lines which cannot be seen are drawn using dashed lines.

Example: Henri has made a model with five Multilink cubes.
Draw a plan view and front and side elevations of
Henri's model.

Solution: This diagram shows where the views are from.

Plan

Side

Front

The plan view is from
above:

All that can be seen from
above are four squares.

The front elevation looks
like this:

The side elevation looks
like this:

The side elevation could have
been drawn from the 'other'
side. If it had been, the side
view would have been the
same as the front elevation.

Example: Jez makes this model using five Multilink cubes.
Draw the plan view and the front and side elevations
of Jez's model.

Solution: From above only three cubes
can be seen. The plan view
looks like this, the two dashed
lines show where the gap is
underneath.

The front elevation
looks like this:

The side elevation looks like
this; the dashed line shows
the top of the gap
underneath.

Practise...   20.4 Plans and elevations

D

1 Each of the following shapes is made using Multilink cubes.

For each shape draw the plan view and the elevations from the directions labelled F (front) and S (side).

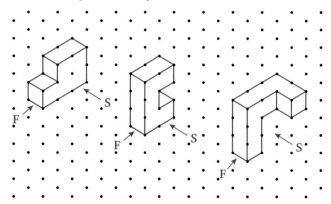

2 Here are the plan and elevations for an object made from Multilink cubes.

Draw the object using isometric dotty paper.

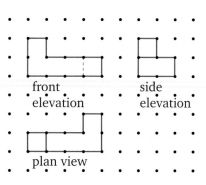

front elevation   side elevation

plan view

3 Four mugs of coffee are arranged on a table as shown. John sees the mugs as shown in the diagram.

a Sketch the mugs as Jane sees them.

c Sketch the view that Charlie sees.

b Sketch the view that Chim sees.

d Sketch the plan view looking down from Jane's side.

4 This is a picture of a garden shed.

Draw a front elevation for this shed.

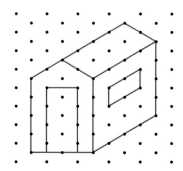

5 The following sketches show some pieces of furniture from a doll's house.

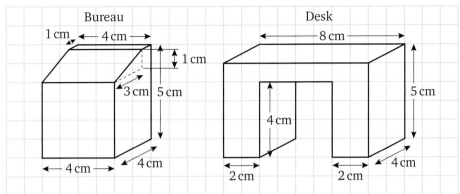

Bureau   Desk

a Ian drew these plan views of the furniture. What mistakes has Ian made?

Bureau   Desk

4 cm   4 cm

4 cm   8 cm

b Draw the plan views accurately and label the dimensions of the desk and bureau.

6 Alan, Bridgette, Charlotte and Dan are doing some work on plans and elevations in a mathematics lesson.

They have arranged two books on the table. They are sitting around the table as shown in the diagram.

a They each draw the front elevation that they see.
Which of the following does each draw?

i   ii   iii   iv

b They rearrange the books as shown.

Draw the front elevation that each person sees.
Label them clearly.

Learn... 20.5 Nets

A **net** is a flat shape that can be made into a 3-D shape when you fold it up.

Example: Draw the net of an open cube.

Solution:

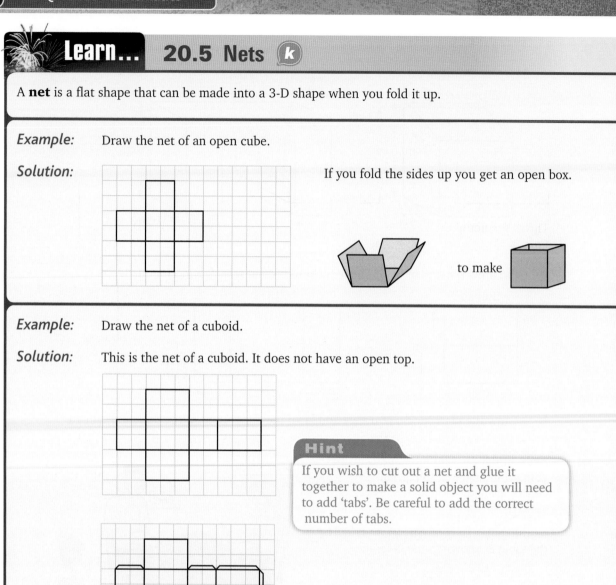

If you fold the sides up you get an open box.

to make

Example: Draw the net of a cuboid.

Solution: This is the net of a cuboid. It does not have an open top.

> **Hint**
>
> If you wish to cut out a net and glue it together to make a solid object you will need to add 'tabs'. Be careful to add the correct number of tabs.

Practise... 20.5 Nets

G F E D C

G

1 Which of the following are nets of a cube?

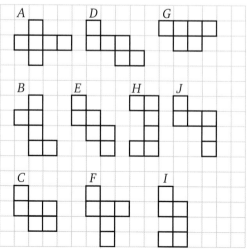

2 The following diagrams show two views of the delivery box for a computer.

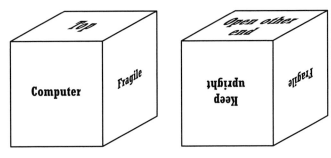

This is the net of the box.
Copy and complete the labelling of the box.

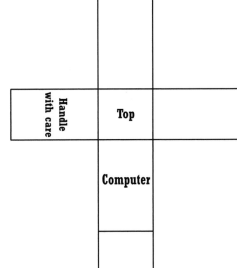

F

3 This is the sketch of a solid.

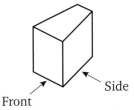

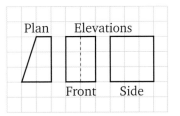

E

a Use squared paper to draw an accurate net of the solid.

b Add tabs to your net, cut it out and glue it together to make a model of the solid.

4 A tetrahedron has four faces, each of which is an equilateral triangle.

a Use triangular dotty paper, or isometric paper, to draw the net of a tetrahedron. Each of the four equilateral triangles should have sides 4 cm long.

b Add tabs and cut out your net and stick it together to make a tetrahedron.

5 The diagram shows a triangular prism.

Three of the faces are squares and two are equilateral triangles.
Which of the following could be nets of the triangular prism?

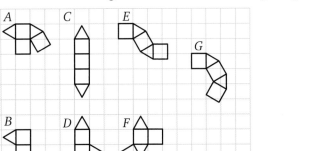

E

6 The diagram shows a square-based pyramid.

It has a square base, and four identical isosceles triangles as faces.

Max drew this net for the square-based pyramid.

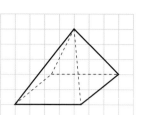

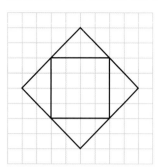

a What is wrong with this net?

b Draw a net that does make a square-based pyramid.

**E
D**

7 Mike uses card to make a gift box for his mother's birthday present as shown.

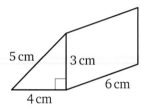

a Draw an accurate net of the gift box on squared paper.

b What is the area of the card Mike uses?

c What is the volume of the gift box when it is made?

⚠ 8 This is a regular octahedron. It has eight identical faces, each of which is an equilateral triangle.

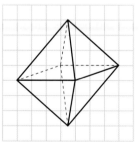

Draw the net of an octahedron on dotty paper.
Add tabs and make the octahedron to check it works.

⚠ 9 Which of the following nets could be a net of this cube?

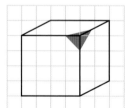

A 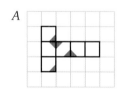   *C* 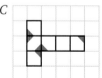   *E*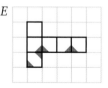

B   *D*   *F*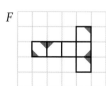

10 James has bought his mother a present for Mother's Day. It is in a cylindrical pack as shown.

James wants to make a gift box in the shape of a pyramid that is large enough to contain the cylinder.

Design a gift box for James. Draw the net and make the gift box.

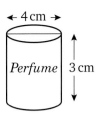

← 4 cm →

Perfume   3 cm

11 **a** Draw the net of a cube with an open top. It is an example of a polyomino.

b Because it is made from five squares it is called a pentomino. Find all the different pentominoes. Which ones are the net of an open box?

c A hexomino is made of six squares. Find all the possible hexominoes. How can you be sure that you have found them all? Which ones are the net of a cube?

20 Assess ⓚ

1 This is a map of Pirate Island.

Write down the coordinates of:

a Sharp Point

b Pirate Falls

c High Mountain

d both ends of the Ancient Wall

e Smugglers' Cave.

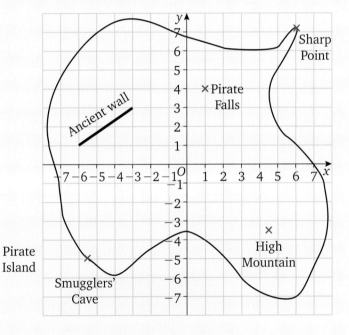

Pirate Island

Ancient wall

Sharp Point

✕ Pirate Falls

✕ High Mountain

✕ Smugglers' Cave

G
F

2 The diagram shows a cuboid.

Draw the net of this cuboid accurately on squared paper.

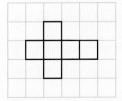

5 cm

3 cm

2 cm

F

3 This is the net of a cube.

A dice has the numbers 1 to 6 on its faces. The numbers on faces opposite each other add up to 7. So 1 is opposite 6.

Copy this net and put the numbers 1 to 6 on it.

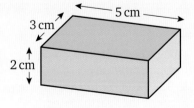

F **4** This is the net of a 3-D shape. It is made from three identical rectangles and two equilateral triangles.

What is the name of the shape it makes?

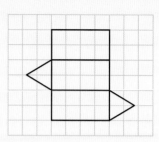

E **5** Draw a sketch of a cuboid which is 4 cm long, 3 cm high and 3 cm wide.

F **6** A car salesman is paid a monthly salary plus a bonus for each car he sells.
E His pay is shown in the graph.

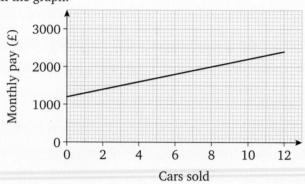

a What is his basic monthly salary?

b How much does he receive if he sells:

   i 6 cars   **ii** 5 cars?

c How much does he get paid for each car he sells?

d How many cars does he need to sell if his income is to be £2800 in one month?

e Calculate how much he will earn if he sells 22 cars in one month.

E **7** **a** Write down the equations of the lines A, B and C.

b Draw a pair of x- and y-axes from -5 to 5 on squared paper.
Draw and label lines with the following equations:

   i $x = -2$

   ii $y = -2$

> **Study tip**
>
> Always label the x- and y-axes. When you draw a line on the grid remember to label it with its equation.

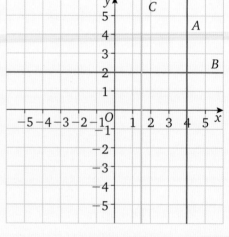

8 This diagram shows three points, A, B and C.
Each point is the vertex of a parallelogram.
Write down the coordinates of the three possible positions of the fourth vertex.

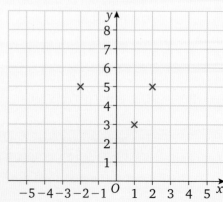

9 Linda arranges two books as shown.

a Draw four diagrams showing the views that Linda, Laura, Lynne and Lucy see.

b Draw a plan view of the arrangement.

Practice questions

1 The graph shows Adil's bicycle journey.

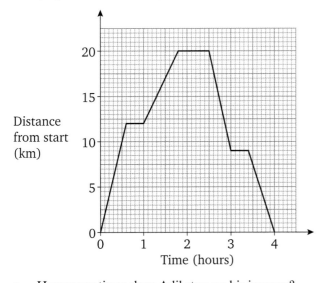

a How many times does Adil stop on his journey? *(1 mark)*

b How many times is Adil exactly 10 km from the start of his journey? *(1 mark)*

c What is the total distance that Adil travels on his journey? *(1 mark)*

d Calculate Adil's average speed during the first 30 minutes of his journey.
Give your answer in kilometres per hour. *(2 marks)*

AQA 2007

Glossary

acute angle – an angle between 0° and 90°

alternate angles – angles formed by parallel lines and a transversal that are on opposite sides of the transversal.

amount – the principal + the interest (this is the total you will have in the bank, or the total you will owe the bank, at the end of the period of time).

angle of rotation – the angle by which an object is rotated.

anticlockwise – the opposite direction to which the hands of a clock travel.

arc – a section of the circumference of a circle.

area – this is the amount of space that a shape covers.

ascending – the terms are increasing.

average – the name given to a single value that represents a set of data.

axis (pl. axes) – the lines used to locate a point in the coordinates system; in two dimensions, the x-axis is horizontal and the y-axis is vertical. This system of Cartesian coordinates was devised by the French mathematician and philosopher René Descartes.

balance – how much money you have in your bank account.

base – the lowest part of a 2-D or 3-D object (that is, the side that it stands on).

bearing – an angle that denotes a direction.

BIDMAS – gives the order in which to carry out operations: brackets, indices, multiplication and division, then addition and subtraction.

bisect – to divide into two equal parts.

brackets – these show that the terms inside should be treated alike, for example $2(3x + 5) = 2 \times 3x + 2 \times 5 = 6x + 10$

capacity – the amount of liquid a hollow container can hold, commonly measured in litres.

centre of rotation – the fixed point around which an object is rotated.

chord – a straight line that joins any two points on the circumference, but does not pass through the centre.

circle – a 2-D shape made up of points that are all the same distance from a fixed point.

circumference – the distance all the way around a circle (that is, the perimeter of a circle).

class interval – the range of values within a group (class) of grouped data.

clockwise – the direction in which the hands of a clock travel.

closed questions – questions that control the responses allowed by using option boxes.

coefficient – the number (with its sign) in front of the letter representing the unknown. For example, in $4p - 5$, 4 is the coefficient of p. In $2 - 3p^2$, -3 is the coefficient of p^2.

common factor – factors that two or more numbers have in common.
For example, the factors of 10 are **1**, 2, **5**, 10
the factors of 15 are **1**, 3, **5**, 15
the common factors of 10 and 15 are 1 and 5.

compound measure – a measure formed from two or more measures. For example, speed $= \dfrac{\text{distance}}{\text{time}}$.

congruent – exactly the same size and shape; the shape might be rotated or flipped over.

continuous data – quantitative data that are measured but must be rounded to be recorded, such as heights, weights, times.

controlled experiment – data collection by a planned investigation of some type such as checking heart rates of runners.

conversion factor – the number by which you multiply or divide to change measurements from one unit to another.

coordinates – a system used to identify a point; an x-coordinate and a y-coordinate give the horizontal and vertical positions.

corresponding angles – angles in similar positions between parallel lines and a transversal.

credit – when you buy goods on 'credit' you do not pay all the cost at once. Instead you make a number of payments at regular intervals, often once a month. NB when your bank account is 'in credit' this means you have some money in it.

cube number – a cube number is the outcome when a number is multiplied by itself and then multiplied by itself again.
125 is a cube number because $5 \times 5 \times 5 = 125$
-5 cubed is $-5 \times -5 \times -5 = -125$

cube root – the cube root of a number such as 125 is the number whose outcome is 125 when multiplied by itself and then multiplied by itself again. The cube root of 125 is 5, as $5 \times 5 \times 5 = 125$

data collection sheet – prepared tables to record responses to questionnaires or outcomes for an observation such as noting car colours.

data logging – data collection by automatic machine such as in a shop entrance.

decagon – a polygon with ten sides.

decimal – a number in which a decimal point separates the whole number part from the decimal part, for example, 17.46

decimal place – the digits to the right of a decimal point in a number.

denominator – the bottom number of a fraction, indicating how many fractional parts the unit has been split into. For example, in the fraction $\frac{4}{7}$ the denominator is 7 (indicating that the unit has been split into 7 parts).

deposit – an amount of money you pay towards the cost of an item; the rest of the cost is paid later.

depreciation – a reduction in value (of used cars, for example).

descending – the terms are decreasing.

diagonal – a line joining two vertices (that are not next to each other).

diameter – the distance from one side of a circle to the other, through the centre. The diameter is double the radius.

difference – difference – the result of subtracting numbers. For example, the difference between 8 and 2 is 6.

digit – any of the numerals from 0 to 9.

directed number – a number with a direction (expressed by using a positive or negative sign) as well as a size; examples: +3, −0.3

discount – a reduction in the price; sometimes this is for paying in cash or paying early.

discrete data – quantitative data taking exact values such as frequencies, shoe size, dice scores.

edge – a line that joins two vertices of a solid. On a cube, such as a dice, an edge is the straight 'line' which is between each pair of faces.

elevation – this is the view of an object when viewed from the front or side; sometimes called front elevation (view of the front), or side elevation (view of a side).

equilateral triangle – a triangle that has all three sides equal in length.

equivalent fractions – two or more fractions that have the same value. Equivalent fractions can be made by multiplying or dividing the numerator and denominator of any fraction by the same number.

expanding – removing brackets to create an equivalent expression (expanding is the opposite of factorising).

expression – a mathematical statement written in symbols, for example, $3x + 1$ or $x^2 + 2x$

exterior angle – the angle between one side of a polygon and the extension of the adjacent side.

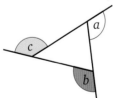

a, b and c are exterior angles

face – one of the flat surfaces of a solid. For example, a cube (such as a dice) has six flat faces.

factor – a whole number which divides exactly into another number with no remainder. For example, the factors of 18 are 1, 2, 3, 6, 9, 18.

factorise – to take common factors out of an equation or expression, often by the inclusion of brackets.

frequency table – a table showing total number (frequency) against data values; like a tally chart but with a number instead of tallies.

gradient – a measure of how steep a line is.

$$\text{Gradient} = \frac{\text{change in vertical distance}}{\text{change in horizontal distance}}$$

grouped data – data that are separated into data classes.

hexagon – a polygon with six sides.

highest common factor (HCF) – the highest factor that two or more numbers have in common.

For example, the factors of 12 are **1**, **2**, 3, **4**, 6, 12
the factors of 20 are **1**, **2**, **4**, 5, 10, 20
the common factors are 1, 2, 4
the highest common factor is 4.

horizontal axis – the x-axis goes across the page – the *horizontal* axis.

hypothesis – an idea that is put forward for investigation; for example, 'More girls are left handed than right handed'. Data would be collected and analysed in order to investigate whether the hypothesis might be true or not.

image – a shape after it undergoes a transformation, for example, reflection, rotation, translation or enlargement.

improper fraction – or top-heavy fraction – a fraction in which the numerator is bigger than the denominator, for example, $\frac{13}{5}$ which is equal to the mixed number $2\frac{3}{5}$

index – the index (or power or exponent) tells you how many times the base number is to be multiplied by itself.

Index (or power or exponent)

5^3

Base

5^3 tells you that 5 (the base number) is to be multiplied by itself 3 times (the index or power or exponent). So $5^3 = 5 \times 5 \times 5$

indices – the plural of index – see **index**.

integer – any positive or negative whole number or zero, for example −2, −1, 0, 1, 2, ...

interest – the money paid to you by a bank or building society when you save your money with them. NB it is also the money you pay for borrowing money from a bank.

interior angle – an angle inside a polygon.

a, b, c, d and e are interior angles

inverse operation – the opposite operation. For example, subtraction is the inverse of addition. Division is the inverse of multiplication.

isosceles triangle – a triangle that has two sides equal in length.

least common multiple (LCM) – the least (or lowest) multiple that two or more numbers have in common. For example, the multiples of 4 are 4, 8, **12**, 16, 20, **24**, 28, 32, **36**, ...
the multiples of 6 are 6, **12**, 18, **24**, 30, **36**, ...
the common multiples are 12, 24, 36
the least common multiple is 12.

like terms – $2x$ and $5x$ are like terms. xy and yx are like terms.

line of symmetry – a shape has reflection symmetry about a line through its centre if reflecting it in that line gives an identical-looking shape.

line of symmetry

line segment – a portion of a straight line, defined by the end points.

linear equation – an equation which can be represented by a straight line graph; the equation will not contain powers of x, such as x^2 or x^3.

linear sequence – in a linear sequence, the differences are all the same.

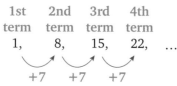

This is a linear sequence.

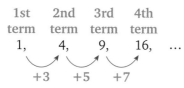

This is not a linear sequence.

lowest common denominator – the lowest denominator that two or more fractions have in common. This is the least common multiple of the denominators of the fractions. For example, the fractions $\frac{2}{3}$, $\frac{1}{2}$ and $\frac{3}{4}$ have the lowest common denominator 12 because this is the least common multiple of 3, 2 and 4.

mass – the weight of an object, measured in tonnes (t), kilograms (kg), grams (g) and milligrams (mg).

mean – the total of all the values divided by the number of values (also called the arithmetic mean).

$$\text{Mean} = \frac{\text{the total of (frequencies} \times \text{values)}}{\text{the total of frequencies}} = \frac{\Sigma fx}{\Sigma f}$$

median – the middle value when the data are listed in order.

midpoint – the point in the middle of a given line, or line segment.

mirror line – the line of symmetry; the line in which an image is reflected.

mixed number – a fraction that has both a whole number and a fraction part. Examples: $1\frac{4}{7}$, $3\frac{1}{2}$, $5\frac{3}{4}$

modal class or modal group – the class or group within a frequency table that occurs most often.

mode – the value or item that occurs most often.

multiple – the multiples of a number are the products in its multiplication table. For example, the multiples of 7 are 7, 14, 21, 28, 35 …

multiplier – a quantity or number by which a given number (or unknown) is to be multiplied.

multiply out – to expand brackets.

negative number – a number less than zero, expressed with a negative sign, for example, −5.3, −400

net – a net shows the faces and edges of an object. When the net is folded up it makes a 3-D object. For example, the net of a cube when folded up makes a cube.

nonagon – a polygon with nine sides.

'nth' term – this phrase is often used to describe a 'general' term in a sequence. The nth term is sometimes called the position-to-term rule.

numerator – the top number of a fraction, indicating how many parts there are in the fraction. For example, in the fraction $\frac{4}{7}$ the numerator is 4.

object – a shape before it undergoes a transformation, for example, translation or enlargement.

observation – data collection by watching something happen.

observation sheet – prepared tables to record responses to questionnaires or outcomes for an observation such as noting car colours.

obtuse angle – an angle between 90° and 180°

octagon – a polygon with eight sides.

open questions – allow for any response to be made by using an answer space.

operation – a rule for combining two numbers or variables, such as add, subtract, multiply or divide.

order of rotation – the number of ways a shape would fit on top of itself as it is rotated through 360° (shapes that are not symmetrical have rotation symmetry of order 1 because a rotation of 360° always produces an identical-looking shape).

origin – this is the starting point from which all measurements are taken.

parallel – two lines that stay the same perpendicular distance apart.

pentagon – a polygon with five sides.

percentage – the number of parts per hundred, for example, 15% means '15 out of a hundred' or $\frac{15}{100}$.

perimeter – this is the distance all the way around a shape.

perpendicular – at right angles to; two lines at right angles to each other are perpendicular lines.

perpendicular height – the height of a shape that is 90° to the base.

pilot survey – a small scale survey carried out before the main survey.

place value – the value that a digit has depending on its position in a number. For example, in the number 25 674 the value of the digit 7 is 70 and the value of the digit 5 is 5000.

plan – this is the view when an object is seen from above; sometimes called the plan view.

polygon – a closed two-dimensional shape made from straight lines.

population – every possible item that could occur in a given situation.

positive number – a number greater than zero, sometimes expressed with a positive sign, for example, +18.3, 0.36

power – see **index**.

primary data – data you have collected yourself, usually for a specific purpose.

prime number – a natural number with exactly two factors.

The first seven prime numbers are:

2	3	5	7	11	13	17
Factors	Factors	Factors	Factors	Factors	Factors	Factors
1 & 2	1 & 3	1 & 5	1 & 7	1 & 11	1 & 13	1 & 17

1 is not a prime number because it has only one factor.
2 is the only even prime number.

principal – the initial amount of money put into the bank (or borrowed from the bank).

product – the result of multiplying numbers. For example, the product of 8 and 2 is 16.

proportion – if a class has 10 boys and 15 girls, the proportion of boys in the class is $\frac{10}{25}$ (which simplifies to $\frac{2}{5}$). The proportion of girls in the class is $\frac{15}{25}$ (which simplifies to $\frac{3}{5}$). A ratio compares one part with another; a proportion compares one part with the whole.

quadrant – the axes divide the page into four *quadrants*.

quadrilateral – a polygon with four sides.

qualitative data – data that cannot be measured using numbers, e.g. hair colour, sports, breeds of sheep.

quantitative data – data that can be measured or counted such as heights, ages, times, frequencies.

questionnaire – data collection by a series of questions requiring responses.

quotient – the result of dividing numbers. For example, when 8 is divided by 2, the quotient is 4.

radius (pl. radii) – this is the distance from the centre of a circle to a point on the circumference.

range – the difference between the highest value and the lowest value in a distribution (a measure of spread, not a measure of average).

rate – the percentage at which interest is added.

ratio – a means of comparing numbers or quantities; a ratio shows how much bigger one number or quantity is than another; if two numbers or quantities are in the ratio 1 : 2, the second is always twice as big as the first; if two numbers or quantities are in the ratio 2 : 5, for every 2 parts of the first there are 5 parts of the second.

raw data – data before they have been sorted in any way.

reciprocal – the reciprocal of a number is 1 divided by that number. Any number multiplied by its reciprocal equals 1. For example, the reciprocal of 6 is $\frac{1}{6}$ because $6 \times \frac{1}{6} = 1$ and $1 \div 6 = \frac{1}{6}$

recurring decimal – a decimal whose digits after the point eventually form a repeating pattern. A dot over the digits indicates the repeating sequence, for example, $\frac{2}{7} = 0.\dot{2}8571\dot{4}$

reflection – a transformation involving a mirror line (or line of symmetry), in which the line from the shape to its image is perpendicular to the mirror line. To describe a reflection fully, you must describe the position or give the equation of its mirror line, for example, the triangle A is reflected in the mirror line $y = 1$ to give the image B.

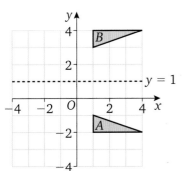

reflex angle – an angle between 180° and 360°

regular – a shape that has all sides of equal length is regular.

right angle – an angle of exactly 90°. It is always represented on a diagram by a small square.

right-angled triangle – a triangle with one right angle.

rotation – a transformation in which the shape is turned about a fixed point called the centre of rotation. To describe a rotation fully, you must give the centre, angle and direction (a positive angle is anticlockwise and a negative angle is clockwise). For example, the triangle A is rotated about the origin through 90° anticlockwise to give the image C.

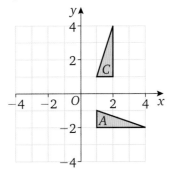

round – give an approximate value of a number; numbers can be rounded to the nearest 1000, nearest 100, nearest 10, nearest integer, significant figures, decimal places, etc.

sample – a small part of a population from which information is taken.

sample size – the number of people or items in the sample.

scalene triangle – a triangle with three sides of different lengths.

secondary data – data that others have collected; anything from newspapers, the internet and similar sources.

sector – this is the area between two radii and an arc.

segment – the area enclosed by a chord and an arc.

sequence – a sequence is a list of numbers or diagrams which are connected in some way.

significant figures – the digits in a number. The closer a digit is to the beginning of a number, the more important or significant it is; for example, in the number 23.657, 2 is the most significant figure.

simplify – to make simpler by collecting like terms.

solution – the value of the unknown quantity. For example, if the equation is $3y = 6$, the solution is $y = 2$

speed – speed is the gradient of a line on a distance–time graph. It is found using the same method as in Chapter 10. For distance–time graphs this is:

$$\text{Speed} = \frac{\text{distance travelled}}{\text{time taken}}$$

square number – a square number is the outcome when a number is multiplied by itself.
16 is a square number because $4 \times 4 = 16$
-4 squared is $-4 \times -4 = 16$ also.

square root – the square root of a number such as 16 is the number whose outcome is 16 when multiplied by itself. The square root of 16 is 4, as $4 \times 4 = 16$.
Also, the square root of 16 is -4, as $-4 \times -4 = 16$

straight angle – an angle of 180°

substitution – in order to use a formula to work out the value of one of the variables, you replace the letters with numbers. This is called substitution.

sum – the result of adding numbers. For example, the sum of 8 and 2 is 10.

survey – general name for data collection using interviews or questionnaires.

tally chart – a method of organising raw data into a table using a five bar gate method of tallying.

tangent – a straight line outside a circle that touches the circle at only one point.

term – a number, variable or the product of a number and a variable(s), such as 3, x or $3x$

term-to-term rule – the rule which tells you how to move from one term to another.

$$\begin{array}{cccc} \text{1st} & \text{2nd} & \text{3rd} & \text{4th} \\ \text{term} & \text{term} & \text{term} & \text{term} \\ 5, & 16, & 27, & 38, \quad \dots \end{array}$$
$$+11 \quad +11 \quad +11$$

The rule to find the next number in the sequence is $+11$. The rule is called the term-to-term rule.

translation – a transformation where every point moves the same distance in the same direction so that the object and the image are congruent.

transversal – a line that crosses two or more parallel lines.

triangle – a polygon with three sides.

two-way table – a table showing information about two sets of data at the same time.

unit – a standard used in measuring. When a measurement is made units need to be chosen. Different units are appropriate for measuring items of differing size.

unitary method – a way of calculating quantities that are in proportion, for example, if 6 items cost £30 and you want to know the cost of 10 items, you can first find the cost of one item by dividing by 6, then find the cost of 10 by multiplying by 10.

unitary ratio – this is a ratio in the form $1 : n$ or $n : 1$. This form of ratio is helpful for comparison as it shows clearly how much of one quantity there is for one unit of the other.

unknown – the letter in an equation representing a quantity that is 'unknown'.

unlike terms – $2x$ and $5y$ are unlike terms. x and x^2 are unlike terms.

Value Added Tax (VAT) – this tax is added on to the price of some goods or services.

variable – a symbol representing a quantity that can take different values, such as x, y or z.

vector – a quantity with direction and magnitude (size). In this diagram, the arrow represents the direction and the length of the line represents the magnitude.

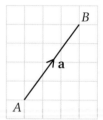

In print, this vector can be written as AB or a. In handwriting, this vector is usually written as $\overrightarrow{AB}$ or $\underline{a}$. The vector can also be described as a column vector:

where $\begin{pmatrix} x \\ y \end{pmatrix}$ $\leftarrow x$ is the horizontal displacement
$\leftarrow y$ is the vertical displacement

vertex (pl. vertices) – the point where two or more edges meet.

vertical axis – in two dimensions, the y-axis is the vertical axis.

vertically opposite angles – the opposite angles formed when two lines cross.

Index

Key terms are given in **bold** and can be found in the glossary.